Library Administration Practices in Its Current Development

Library Administration Practices in Its Current Development

Neelesh Kashyap

RANDOM

RANDOM PUBLICATIONS
NEW DELHI (INDIA)

Library Administration Practices in Its Current Development

ISBN 978-93-5111-851-0

Published in 2016 in India by
RANDOM PUBLICATIONS

4376-A/4B, Gali Murari Lal, Ansari Road
New Delhi-110 002
Phone : +9111-43580356, 011-23289044, 011-43142548
e-mail: sales@randompublications.com,
info@randompublications.com, randomexports@gmail.com

Reprinted 2026

Type Setting by : Friends Media, Delhi-110089

Preface

Academic administration is a branch of university or college employees responsible for the maintenance and supervision of the institution and separate from the faculty or academics, although some personnel may have joint responsibilities. Some type of separate administrative structure exists at almost all academic institutions, as fewer and fewer schools are governed by employees who are also involved in academic or scholarly work. Many senior administrators are academics who have advanced degrees and no longer teach or conduct research actively. The chief executive, the administrative and educational head of a university, depending on tradition and location, may be termed the university president, the provost, the chancellor, the vice-chancellor, principal, or rector. An administrative executive in charge of a university department or of some schools may be termed a dean or some variation, such as dean emeritus. The chief executive of academic establishments other than universities, may be termed headmaster or head teacher, director, or principal, as used in primary education.

Administration of Library is a modern discipline. Many schools of Administrative thoughts have developed during the last century-like scientific administration, human administration and administration with people's cooperation. Scientific Administration has more emphasis on identification and formulation of objectives. It is in fact objective-centric. The basics of library administration are division of work, discipline, authority, responsibility and unitary command. In any library work should be properly divided. Management activities should be separated from other jobs and the subordinates should receive orders from one senior only. Library is basically for the help of the people. So library administration should have inclination towards people.

– ***Author***

Contents

1

Role of the Library in the Social Process

THE ROLE OF LIBRARIES IN MODERN SOCIETY

First, the general development of the information society is pushing to re-evaluation of all the institutions which work with information, data, and knowledge-indirectly also with culture. In this connection the roles of education and media have been discussed already quite largely also in the European Union.

But libraries-as well as other memory institutions like archives and museums-have not been considered. Still, there is a clear need in the information society to maintain an institution which is concentrating in collecting and organizing information and offering general access to it. Until now, this work has been underestimated, but I argue the situation will change! Libraries are especially important now when the whole idea of education is stressing more and more independent learning and acting.

All citizens must be able to find and use information. It is the key raw material-but it is a zero resource, if there are no access points to it and if documents are in chaotic order.

Here we can see libraries enter the stage:

- The unique function of libraries is to acquire, organize, offer for use and preserve publicly available material irrespective of the form in which it is packaged in such a way that, when it is needed, it can be found and put to use. No other institution carries out this long-term, systematic work. Culture must be nominated especially: it has an important and unique role in mobilizing resources of human beings. It has been described: To some extent, culture makes its influence felt more indirectly than knowledge, but it is impossible to imagine how people's creative powers could be fully activated without the impact of culture, which extends into the depths of the mind.

The challenge to modern societies is that the basic resource, knowledge, is developing from information in very individual, capricious and unpredictable process. It cannot be commanded. Still, societies can support this development, *e.g.* by offering access to cultural and knowledge treasures.

This can even be translated into economic language: to get out the best from the human resources in Europe, this resource must be feeded up with rich and various cultural and infor-mation contents! I would like to stress especially the idea of organizing information by libraries. It is often shadowed by the second important side of library work: offering access. But in the life-long learning and new technology context just all forms of organizing documents are getting more to the focus. This is clear to anybody who has tried to find something from not-so-often-used Internet websites.

NEW LINES IN THE EU-AND IN THE UNITED STATES

In accordance with these phenomenons, there are new political lines in the European Union: The Maastricht Treaty in 1992 launched the cultural aspects. This was only after a long discussion, which made it clear that we have to remember to separate the national view and the European view. The Amsterdam Treaty in 1997 declared citizenship as an important theme. A significant part of this are a.o. granting information skills and access to information to every European.

In addition to this, the European future strategies need to meet the democratic aspects of the information society development. One of the crucial points is again general access to information. Libraries, especially public libraries, are a good tool in all of these new areas.

But the European union does not support whichever cultural or citizen concentrated projects in Europe.In the interests of the European Union there is always to find the European element. So, what can be done in library policy on the European level, taking in account that libraries are primarily a part of national education and cultural policies? *The own-initiative report "The role of libraries in modern societies," adopted by the European Parliament in October 1998, is the first effort to answer these questions.*

The same topics have been discussed in the United States. They have reached the point where especially the problems of those lacking access to digital resources have been studied. The report Falling Through the Net: Defining the Digital Divide by the U.S. Department of Commerce was released earlier in July 1999.

The report finds that minorities, low-income persons, the less educated, and children of single parent households, particularly when they reside in rural areas or central cities, are risk groups. The report calls for public policies and private initiatives to expand affordable access to critical information resources. But it also shows,, for the first time as far as I know, that libraries and community centres really can diminish the information gap between haves and not-haves.

The 1998 data from the U.S. demonstrates very clearly that community access centers, primarily public libraries, are particularly well used by those groups who lack access at home or at work: *e.g.* unemployed groups used Internet in libraries three times as often as an average citizen.

EARLIER ACTIONS IN EU

In the European Union, there have been some efforts to mobilize "the treasures of the European libraries" since the mid-80'ies. These discussions and resolutions led to two special library programmes under the 3rd and 4th Framework programmes of research and development. The later programme has been known as "Telematics for Libraries".

They have been strongly concentrated in IT, because it has been seen as a good tool to produce better access to the existing, underused library resources. These programmes have had a clear impact in the European library co-operation and development. Benefits of this work come to public libraries indirectly: common standards and working methods help in the end all kind of libraries. But a fact is, that nearly all the libraries active in these EU projects are national libraries or big research and university libraries. Two main exceptions are Publican, a network of European public libraries, and ECUP, which was a copyright awareness raising project, and reached public libraries as well. A new beginning was the so called Morgan report in 1997. In this report libraries were for the first time put clearly onto the place where they belong in the information society.

As one result of the Morgan report, the European Commission informed that it will produce a Green Paper about the role of libraries in the information society. For one or another reason, this was made quite ready but was never published. In this situation the Committee on Culture, Youth, Education and the Media in the European Parliament decided to produce an own-initiative report about libraries. The main reason was that they wanted to influence the big issues under work in the EU, first of all the copyright directive and the 5th framework programme, which will have a direct impact to libraries. I was nominated the rapporteur of the own-initiative report. The report was adopted almost unanimously and with a very encouraging discussion in the Plenary session of the Parliament in October 1998.

DECISIONS OF THE EP CONCERNING LIBRARY POLICY

In short, when adopting the own-initiative report, the EP was calling the Commission and/or the member states to following actions:

- Libraries must be taken in account in national and EU information society strategies and in the respective budgets.
- Libraries need more resources for acquiring expensive books.
- The Green Paper on libraries by the Commission must be completed.
- The users position must be taken in account in the copyright directive process, the balance must be maintained-this was politically the most important decision in short run.
- Support to libraries was demanded from the 5th Framework programme of research and development, *e.g.* for networking,

drafting standards, preserving, and transferring information; there is no more named library programme under the 5th framework programme

- A clearing-house to solve problems of long-term conservation should be founded.
- Studies concerning permanent paper should be done on European level.
- The member states should take care of digitizing their cultural heritage for future.
- There should be studies and concrete support to libraries in licensing matters, which are–will be the next big issue in library work.
- The EU cultural and information budget should be opened to libraries as well, libraries and their co-operation should be taken in account in planning new programmes.
- Problems of legal deposit in international and multinational materials, especially in electronic materials should be solved.
- The member states should provide all types of libraries with modern equipment, particularly with Internet connections.
- Free of charge use of public libraries, in the spirit of the UNESCO Public Library Manifest, was demanded.
- Free and easy access via libraries to material produced with the aid of tax revenues was demanded.
- The members states should organize for their library professionals up-dating education and training.
- A European Union focal point for libraries should be set up
- The member states should found European information points at libraries in countries where they do not yet exist.
- Library statistics should be better and more comparable both on national and European level.
- The national Parliament libraries should be opened to the MEP's in countries where this is not yet the practice.

In addition to these, the report strongly stresses that the library financing must be re-thought in the information society. Without new resources libraries are unable to do everything they are expected to do! After the EP adoption of this report, the European Commission informed that it will next prepare a communication about actions to do. It was stated that the report had already served as a discussion paper, and so the need for the Green Paper had disappeared. The communication is in summer 1999 still under work in the Commission DGXIII/2.

TRADITIONS AND NEW FORMS OF WORK IN THE SAME HOUSE

The European Commission R&D framework programmes have concentrated in IT matters. The three cultural programmes, Caledoskope,

Ariane and Raphael, have not been very useful for libraries, because their scope has been quite narrow. *E.g.* the books and reading programme Ariane has concentrated in translations. In the coming framework programme Culture 2000 libraries will have more possibilities to get support also for their cultural actions.

What then will be the fate of the traditional tasks of libraries in general? Will the information society wipe out book loaning and poems?

THE PUBLIC LIBRARIES IN THE KNOWLEDGE SOCIETY

THE LIBRARIES IN A STATE OF FLUX

The municipal reform in 2007 had major consequences for the library service. The number of libraries decreased and the remaining libraries grew in size. The reform thus underlined and intensified various tendencies in library development over the past many years.

The public library is in a state of flux. *Library service to children* from 2008 that chose as its point of reference the changes in children's use of the library. Thus this report had a strong focus on one target group and on how the library can develop new services to that group. The present report also focuses on the target group, but slightly more on the institution–the public library.

Based on a number of societal needs and new opportunities the report also considers how the library can be developed as an institution.

The library offer is changing rapidly, but it continues to be much sought after. Two out of three Danes use the public library, and 29% of the adult population visit the library at least once a month. In 2008 the public libraries registered more than 34 mil. visits.

This makes the library one of our most popular, public cultural offers, and this has been the case for many years. But the way we use the library is undergoing a change. On the one hand the loan of physical materials–books, CDs etc.–is falling. In the period 2000-2008 the public libraries' loan of physical materials has thus fallen by 22%, from ca. 62 mil. to app. 48 mil. materials.

On the other hand the use of digital offers is growing, an offer that spans from downloads of music and e-books to renewals of loans via the library's homepage. Bibliotekernes Netmusik, where as a library user you can via your municipality download music for free, experienced over 2,5 mil. downloads in 2008–an increase of 48% compared with 2007.

One explanation of the change in borrowing patterns could be that the technology and media development has resulted in new media habits on behalf of the library users. At the same time the libraries' consistently high visiting show that they have succeeded in reorganizing and revitalizing themselves and continue to be attractive.

This happens by developing new library services, particularly digital services, but also by turning the library into something more than just a collection of materials, so that the physical library maintains its desirability. Today the library is also a place for being and meeting, where one for example gets instruction, uses the Internet or gets help in the local citizen service centre.

However, borrowing books remains the main reason why Danes visit the library. The latest cultural habits survey from 2004 shows that 85% of adult library users visit the library to borrow books and journals. The same tendency becomes apparent in more recent studies. In a Gallup poll conducted on behalf of the Danish Library Association, the Union of Danish Librarians and HK Kommunal (white collar workers' union (municipal) in 2009, "borrowing books" is the most frequent reason for visiting the library, followed by "borrowing electronic media", "taking the children to the library" and "watching events".

There is in fact also a growing interest in the library's non-users, as can be seen from the large number of new initiatives, which the libraries participate in at municipal level. In many cases these have a social aspect, and the library is here used as a partner in a targeted initiative towards certain target groups.

This effort is particularly relevant in the light of the challenges that globalization presents to less resourceful citizens. The focusing on non-users also has another angle, which is i.a. clearly expressed in former minister for culture, Carina Christensen's strategy Culture for everybody from 2009. Here the emphasis is on the value of participating in a cultural community and the individual citizen's benefit from cultural offers.

The strategy suggests that all citizens should be able to take advantage of the cultural offers and consequently–that the cultural institutions focus more purposefully on non-users.

THE POLITICAL BASIS FOR THE COMMITTEE'S WORK

The appointment of the Committee on the Public Libraries in the Knowledge Society was decided by the minister for culture in connection with several consultations in Folketingets Kulturudvalg (parliamentary cultural committee), which took place in the wake of a large number of public library branches being closed down during the first year of the municipal reform.

The discussion fuelled by this naturally included the media and technology development. A suggestion for a more extensive, interdepartmental committee work was rejected by the minister, who referred to the work that had already been done by the Globalisation Council. The committee's work builds on the report *Future library service to children* from 2008.

The report contains a number of recommendations as to how to make sure that a strong library offer continues to be available to all Danish children. In 2008 the Danish Agency for Libraries and Media also published the report *The public libraries after the municipal reform*, which analysed the development within the public library area with particular focus on any consequences due to the municipal reform.

The report concluded that the closure of the branches in 2006-2007 was a natural adaptation of the library service, and that at the same time it demonstrated a prioritisation in order to deliver a more up-to-date and value-enhancing library offer. With the report from the Committee on the Public Libraries in the Knowledge Society we now have a number of recommendations as to how this prioritisation can be made so that the public libraries also in future will be able to meet the public's need for enlightenment, education and cultural activity.

The committee presents its recommendations within an expenditure-neutral framework with the perspective that it may be both necessary and correct with local changes of priorities within the library field in order to support and strengthen the public library in the knowledge society.

THE COMMISSION'S ASSIGNMENT: MANDATE FOR THE COMMITTEE ON THE PUBLIC LIBRARIES IN THE KNOWLEDGE SOCIETY

The committee must focus on continuous development of the public libraries in Denmark. This includes the public libraries' interaction with other libraries and relevant institutions. Focus must be on the libraries as an easily accessible offer to everybody.

The committee must build on the report *Future library service to children* and pay particular attention to service to youngsters and adults. The committee must assess the public libraries' role in relation to the challenges facing the knowledge society, the globalisation strategy's focus on education, lifelong learning and societal cohesive force.

The committee must assess to which extent there is basis for establishing new concepts for a library service that meets the public's needs in terms of enlightenment, education and cultural activity, and close to the citizens. Likewise the committee must asses the possibilities for continuous development of traditional core services such as literature dissemination.

In particular, the committee must asses the need for further development of the libraries' digital infrastructure and the interaction between digital and traditional services. The committee must furthermore describe models for the mediation of digital cultural heritage and licensed digital media and models for various forms of learning and inspiration activities (*e.g.* in relation to citizens with poor reading and IT skills).

The committee must likewise give examples of new partnerships, including inter-institutional cooperations and binding networking commitments. Finally the committee must assess the need for competence development of library staff. On the basis of its analyses the committee must put forward recommendations and suggestions as to how the strategy's objectives can be realised within the present legislation and existing division of labour between state and municipalities. The committee's suggestions must be expenditure-neutral. The committee is composed upon appointment, so that the minister for culture appoints three members, while Local Government (KL), Danish Library Association, Association of Library Directors, Danish Research Library Association, the Regional Libraries, Union of Danish Librarians and Børne-og Kulturchefforeningen each appoints a member.

The Danish Agency for Library and Media's director general is chairman of the committee, and the Agency is the committee's secretariat. The committee must have completed its work primo 2010.

DIGITAL LIBRARIES AND SOCIETY

Digital libraries are large, organized collections of information objects. Whereas standard library automation systems provide a computerized version of the catalog—a gateway into the treasure-house of information stored in the library—digital libraries incorporate the treasure itself, namely the information objects that constitute the library's collection.

Whereas standard libraries are, of necessity, ponderous and substantial institutions, with large buildings and significant funding requirements, even large digital libraries can be lightweight. Whereas standard libraries, whose mandate includes preservation as well as access, are "conservative" by definition, with institutional infrastructure to match, digital libraries are nimble: they emphasize access and evolve rapidly.

The five stages in this part provide an excellent illustration of the huge variety of interesting issues in digital library research that impacts the Asia Pacific region. Unlike the New World, where most of the research on technological aspects of digital libraries originates, Asia has an exceptionally rich cultural heritage.

This manifests itself in a huge legacy of documents, in various forms—from paper to palm leaves—and in various different conditions. The need to preserve this legacy is particularly pressing in today's world, where political instability is rife and climate change is beginning to have an effect. As recent events have shown, disasters, both manmade and natural, can have a devastating effect on fragile cultural artifacts. S.M. Shafi from the University of Kashmir, India, surveys the many issues involved with digital archiving of medieval manuscripts in Asia. Libraries are pillars of education, and it is natural to expect that digital libraries will provide new opportunities for innovative educational practices.

These will be particularly relevant to the Asia Pacific region because of the huge disparities in access to education between the different communities there. Peer-to-peer learning has always been a crucial factor in personal development, although it is frequently ignored in educational studies.

Natalie Lee-San from Nanyang Technological University, Singapore, describes her studies of how digital libraries can provide an innovative, perhaps revolutionary, environment for peer-to-peer learning amongst youths. She touches on many practical issues: gender differences, different learning styles, different levels of media and computer literacy, and age-related differences. Many economies in the Asia Pacific region are agricul-turally-based.

Modern agriculture is a knowledge-based activity that can benefit greatly from digital libraries. Mila Ramos from the International Rice Research Institute in the Philippines describes a large-scale digital library system designed to support the growth, nurturing, harvesting, and distribution of that most Asian of staples, rice.

This digital library supports an institute whose goal is to improve the well-being of present and future generations of rice farmers and consumers, particularly those with low incomes. The institute's library houses the world's most comprehensive collection of technical literature on rice, and provides a widely-used international reference service.

As in many specialized libraries, digital library technology is seen to have special advantages in a world of shrinking library budgets. Intellectual property issues are a central driving force behind the market in information of which libraries are a part. And the questions become more complex as the nature of today's information shifts from a primarily book-based culture to one that embraces all types of multimedia objects, and large, carefully-curated, collections of such objects.

The stage on *"Multimedia digital library as intellectual property"* by Hideyasu Sasaki and Yasujshi Kiyoki at Keio University in Japan clarify the copyright situation as it affects multimedia collections and compilations. They go on to discuss the patentability of particular retrieval mechanisms, an essential component of digital libraries.

The fifth stage in this part on how digital library research impacts the Asia Pacific region is the present one, on digital libraries in society. Most existing digital library projects, being research-oriented, are predicated on state-of-the-art equipment and interfaces, academic and research institutions, special collections.

In contrast: digital library technology can and should be available to everyone, on all platforms, in all countries; and it can and should enable ordinary people to exercise their creative powers to conceive, assemble, build, and disseminate new information collections that are designed not just for western academics but for a wide diversity of different audiences throughout the world.

Though less glamorous, this may, in the end, be a more important goal for society. Digital libraries pose an inherent tension between the technologist's desire for advanced solutions that use the latest and greatest hardware and software, and the librarian's desire for wide, crossplatform availability and long-term preser-vation—as epitomized by the sustained success of paper as a delivery medium. To achieve universal access for both information consumers and collection-builders is really a problem for HCI. We examine the social need for digital libraries, particularly in developing countries, by briefly sketching some trends in commercial publishing and contrasting them with a growing international perspective of information as a public good.

We draw out the implications for the user interface, which is the principal bottleneck in allowing non-specialist people to make public information available in focused collections that are universally usable. Then we introduce digital library technology and illustrate it with a particular example, the Greenstone digital library software, which is designed for a broad user base and is in widespread use in many corners of the world—from Uganda to the US, Kazakhstan to Canada, Nepal to New Zealand. Following that, we review a project that is applying digital library technology to the distribution of humanitarian information in the developing world, a context that is both innovative and socially motivated.

Next we discuss issues of universal access and illustrate them with reference to the Greenstone software. We include a brief demonstration of a prototype system that is intended to allow anyone to build and disseminate information collections, and illustrates some human interface challenges that arise when providing necessarily complex functionality to a non-computer-oriented user base.

We close with the hope that future digital libraries will find a new role to play in helping to reduce the social inequity that haunts today's world, both within our own countries and between nations.

BOOKS, LIBRARIES, AND THE SOCIALLY DISADVANTAGED

Today, the long-standing three-way tension between the commercial interests of publishers, the needs of society and information users, and the social mandate of public libraries, is being pulled and stretched as never before.

First, the very notion of a "book" is evolving in many different directions: books become more interactive; publishers rent content; books are distributed under restrictive conditions that mechanically prohibit sharing. While it would be premature to make specific predictions, it seems likely that these trends will further disadvantage the disadvantaged—particularly those in poorer countries who have yet to benefit from ready access to ordinary books.

Second, a huge body of information is becoming freely available on the Internet. Much is of questionable quality, but some is very good indeed. In many cases the information is provided for the "public good" rather than for commercial profit, and the redistribution of such information is likely to be encouraged, rather than prohibited, by those who make it available.

Initiatives like UNESCO's "Information for all" programme and the upcoming World Summit on the Information Society highlight the importance of public information; they are founded on the belief that information literacy will help alleviate many of the problems confronting human societies. Third, the implications for libraries are mixed.

Whereas new controls by publishers over how the content they own may be used presents libraries with significant problems, the ready availability of "public good" information meshes well with library philosophy. A new role is emerging for information professionals who can select material, index it, add appropriate metadata, and redistribute it in added-value form for the good of society.

Suitable technological infrastructure is being provided by the open source movement, which is making available high-quality software for repackaging and distribution of information (and not just on computer networks).

What future has the book in the digital world? The question is a complex one that is being widely aired. Authors and publishers ask how many copies of a work will be sold if networked digital libraries enable worldwide access to an electronic copy of it.

Their nightmare is that the answer is *one*: how many books will be published online if the entire market can be extinguished by the sale of one electronic copy to a public library? To counter this threat, the entertainment industry is promoting new *"digital rights management"* (DRM) schemes that permit a degree of control over what users can do that goes far beyond the traditional legal bounds of copyright. ndeed, the acronym is more aptly expanded as "digital restrictions management" because it is concerned solely with content owners rights and not at all with user's rights.

It is, in effect, a "private governance system in which computer systems regulate which acts users are and are not authorized to perform". nticircumvention rules are sanctioned by the *Digital Millennium Copyright Act* (DMCA) in the US.

The DMCA has been used, for example, to prosecute a Norwegian teenager for writing software to play a DVD that he had purchased on a computer for which no commercial playback systems exist. an DRM be applied to books? The motion picture industry can compel manufacturers to incorporate encryption into their products because it holds key patents on DVD players. Commercial book publishers are promoting e-book readers that, if adopted on a wide scale, would allow the same kind of control to be exerted over reading material. asic rights that we take for granted—such as the ability to lend a book to a friend, resell it on the second-hand market, keep it indefinitely, continue to use it when your e-book reader breaks down, donate it to charity, preserve it for your grandchildren, copy excerpts without resorting to a handwritten transcription—are in jeopardy. DRM allows such rights to be controlled, monitored, and withdrawn instantly, and DMCA legislation makes it illegal for users to seek redress by taking matters into their own hands.

Fortunately, perhaps, lack of standardization and compatibility issues are delaying consumer adoption of e-books. n the realm of scholarly publishing, digital rights management is more advanced. Academic libraries license access to content in electronic form, often in tandem with purchase of print versions too. They have been able to negotiate reasonable conditions with publishers—probably because they represent the lion's share of the scholarly market. owever, the extent of libraries' power in the consumer book market is moot. One can envisage a scenario where publishers establish a system of commercial, pay-per-view, libraries for e-books and refuse public libraries access to books in a form that can be circulated.

These new directions present our society with puzzling challenges, and it would be rash to predict what society's response will be. But one thing is certain: they will surely increase the degree of disenfranchisement of those who do not have access to the technology.

In parallel with publishers' moves to reposition books as technological artifacts with refined and flexible control over how they can be used, an opposing trend has emerged: the ready availability of free information on the Internet.

Of course, the world-wide web is an unreliable source of enlightenment, and undiscriminating use is dangerous—and widespread. As early as 1996 complaints arose that the Web's contents are largely unattributed, undated, unannotated, unreliable; information about author and publisher is unavailable or incomplete; far too many resource catalogues are chasing far too few original or non-trivial documents—complaints that are very familiar today.

But one thing has changed: search engines and other portals have enormously increased our ability to locate information that is at least ostensibly relevant to any given question. Teachers complain bitterly that students view the Web as a replacement for the library, harvesting information indiscriminately to provide answers to assignments that are at best shallow and at worst incoherent and incorrect.

One consolation is that the very same search facilities can be used to detect plagiarism.

Nevertheless, the Web abounds with accessible, high-quality information. Many social groups, non-profit societies and charities make it their business to create sites and collect and organize information there. To take a single example at random, a Google search for *diabetes* returns three national diabetes associations in the top ten hits, and of course many more exist. ach of these sites offers a cornucopia of valuable information on the disease, which is not commercial and provided for the public good.

Widespread use is strongly encouraged, and it seems likely that arrangements could be made for re-distribution of the material presented there, particularly it was intended as a not-for-profit service and appropriate acknowledgement was made. ne of the key problems with information distribution via the Web is that it disenfranchises developing countries.

Although the Web does not extend into the homes of the socially disadvantaged in developed countries either, various national programmes are working to provide access. ut network access varies enormously across the world. Whereas in 1998 more than a quarter of the US population were surfing the Internet, the figures for Latin America and the Caribbean was 0.8%, for Sub-Saharan Africa 0.1%, and for South Asia 0.04%. Schools and hospitals in developing countries are poorly connected. ven in South Africa, the bestconnected African country, many hospitals and 75% of schools have no telephone line.

Universities are better equipped, but even there up to 1,000 people can depend on just one terminal. The Internet "is failing the developing world". Prompted by this inequity, the importance of information, and particularly public information, is today being highlighted by prominent international bodies.

For example, UNESCO's "Information for all" programme was established in 2001 to foster debate on the political, ethical and societal challenges of the emerging global knowledge society and to carry out projects promoting equitable access to information.

It reflects a growing awareness that information is playing an increasing role in generating wealth and human capital, and that participation in the "global knowledge society" is essential for social and individual development. Information literacy is described as "a new frontier" by the Director of UNESCO's Information Society Division. The Inter-national Telecommunications Union has established a World Summit on the Information Society, held in Geneva in December 2003 and Tunis in 2005, to promote a global discussion of the fundamental changes that are being brought about in our lives by the transformation from an industrial to an information society, and to confront the extreme disparities of access to information between the industrialized countries and the developing world.

What is the librarian to make of all this? The mandate of today's public libraries, in sharp contrast to that of publishers, is to facilitate the open distribution of knowledge.

Librarians strive to enable the free flow of information. Their traditions are liberal, founded on the belief that libraries should serve democracy. To help fulfill their mission as resource centers for citizens, public libraries maintain collections of records, policy statements, government documents, and so on.

A recent promotional video from the American Librarian's Association exults that "the library is democracy's place of worship". learly, the impending redefinition of the book as a digital artifact that is licensed rather than sold, tied to a particular replay device, with restrictions that are clearly laid out and mechanically enforced, is an innovation that goes right to the heart of libraries. he changing nature of the book may make it hard, or even impossible, for libraries to fulfill their mandate by providing quality information to readers.

And on the other hand, the emergence of a vast storehouse of information on the Internet poses a different kind of conundrum. Librarians, the traditional gatekeepers of knowledge, are in danger of being bypassed, their skills ignored, their advice unsought. earch engines send users straight to the information they require—or so users think—without any need for an inter-mediary to classify, catalogue, cross-reference, advise on sources. The ready availability of information on the Internet, and its widespread use, really presents librarians with an opportunity, not a threat. avvy users realise they need help, which librarians can provide.

A good example is Infomine, a cooperative project of the University of California and California State University. Infomine contains descriptions and links to a wealth of scholarly and educational Internet resources, each of which has been selected and described by a professional academic librarian who is a specialist in the subject and in resource description generally.

Participating librarians see this as an important expenditure of effort for their users, a natural evolution of their traditional task of collecting and organizing information in print.

What kind of technical infrastructure is needed to support and promote this kind of work? Open source software is a powerful ally for librarians who wish to extend liberal traditions of information access.

These systems make the source code freely available for others to view, modify, and adapt; and the very nature of the licensing agreement prevents the software from being appropriated by proprietary vendors. But the open-source movement is more than just a vehicle for librarians to use: its link with library traditions goes much deeper.

Public libraries and open source software both enshrine the same philosophy: to promote learning and understanding through the dissemination of knowledge. Both are pervaded by a sense of community, on the one hand the kind of inter-institutional cooperation exemplified by interlibrary loan and on the other teams of designers and programmers that frequently cross national boundaries. ew trends in information access present librarians in developed countries with difficult and conflicting challenges.

Meanwhile, however, the situation in the developing world is dire. Here, traditional publishing and distribution mechanisms have failed tragically. or example, whereas a US medical library subscribes to about 5,000 journals, the Nairobi University Medical School Library, long regarded as a flagship center in East Africa, last year received just 20 journals. In Brazzaville, Congo, the university has only 40 medical books and a dozen journals, all from before 1993, and the library in a large district hospital consisted of a single bookshelf filled mostly with novels.

Traditional libraries are substantial institutions that occupy physical space, present a physical appearance, and exhibit tangible physical organization. When standing on the threshold of a large bricks-and-mortar library you gain a sense of presence and permanence that reflects the care taken in building and maintaining the collection inside. Digital libraries, in contrast, are lightweight.

But they provide potentially far greater accessibility, which means that they will have even greater social effects. Once created, they can, without significant institutional support, continue to serve users.

They can be distributed throughout most of the developed world over the Internet. In developing countries and remote corners of the developed world they can be circulated on removable media—CD-ROM, DVD, or 100 Gb disk units the size of videocassettes—and updated over radio. Issues of copyright pose difficult problems, but they are manageable. or example, there is plenty of non-copyright material, or material whose owners are prepared to donate copyright for socially useful purposes, and trends towards more open access to academic and humanitarian information are visible.

Not everyone sees digital rights management and the DMCA as the way forward, and in the longer term publishers, to remain viable, will have to investigate alternative revenue models for the information they own. No wonder international organizations such as the United Nations, along with many smaller *non-government organizations* (NGOs), are keenly interested in digital library technology. Advances in digital library technology are radically lowering the bar for the design and production of richly-organized, coherent, focused collections of information.

Now, anyone with access to sufficient source material can use public-domain software to build large, fullysearchable, collections the size of traditional personal or institutional libraries—in minutes. Let the minutes stretch to hours and the collection can be polished, organized, branded, distributed.

It can include fully-illustrated text, images, video, music. t can present attractively-designed pages with consistent use of icons. Keywords, key phrases, even acronyms and their definitions, can be extracted—automatically—and used to underpin novel means of access.

Let the hours stretch to days and metadata can be manually added that permits further levels of organization. Given access to programming skills, creative new facilities that stretch the imagination can be rapidly integrated into the system.

All this, one might say, can be done with ordinary Web sites: there is no need for digital library technology. owever, bitter experience has shown that all but the most rudimentary sites do require significant institutional support—for organization and maintenance.

The Web is littered with incomplete, unfinished, unmaintained, out-dated, inconsistently-organized, useless information collections. ust as traditional library cataloging procedures integrate new works into existing collections with minimal overhead so that they immediately become first-class members of the collection, so digital libraries allow new documents to be added completely automatically. In the case of traditional libraries this is done through the small but nonnegligible overhead of generating a new catalog entry. With ordinary Web sites it requires inserting links manually into index pages and the like, and may involve adding links not only into the new document but also into existing ones that ought to reference it—it's like rewriting the book, and maybe revising all other books in the library too! In contrast, digital libraries bring access structures instantly and effortlessly up to date whenever new documents are added.

The challenge for HCI is to design and build digital library systems that fulfill the potential of digital libraries as a "killer app" for computers in developing countries, which will bring concomitant benefits in almost every other sphere of application. or the information consumer we need access to information that is guaranteed across space, time, and culture.

We need flexible distribution mechanisms for documents, and for information objects of all types, that can be accessed on all computer platforms—including the lowliest. We need a choice of distribution over the Web or on removable media such as CD-ROM or DVD. igital libraries can incorporate flexible presentation that caters to individual differences, such as large-font displays or spoken output for the visually impaired.

Libraries are places where information is preserved, not rendered obsolete, and digital libraries must instill confidence that information prepared today can be accessed next week, next decade, next century—regardless of technological changes. An important aspect of digital libraries is their ability to work in local languages, promoting pluralism and reducing the risks of homogeneity. Because language is the vehicle of thought, communication, and cultural identity, this will encourage diversity and strengthen individual cultures. But there is a long way to go: even Unicode is woefully incomplete in certain areas, such as African languages.

Naturally, today's digital library systems focus principally on the reader: the consumer of the material stored in the library's treasure-house. But digital libraries make a more radical, and perhaps ultimately more important, contribution by empowering ordinary users to conceive, assemble, build, and disseminate new information collections themselves and principle, modest computing resources are quite sufficient to enable users to build new collections by gathering together material in local files or on the Web; augmenting it with appropriate metadata that supports convenient search and browsing operations; incorporating advanced features like key-phrase extraction, document summarization, and metadata extraction; designing an attractive and functional interface; and publishing the collection on a variety of different media that are suitable for the intended readership. The HCI challenge is to realise this potential for users—such as most librarians—who have a strong understanding of information and its organization, but no more interest in computers than they have in papermaking technology, last millennium's vehicle for information dissemination.

UNIVERSAL ACCESS

Universal access to digital libraries presents huge challenges to software engineers and HCI practitioners. The Greenstone digital library software allows us to glimpse some of the issues, although it certainly does not yet effectively address them all.

Most digital libraries are accessed over the web, using any web browser. However, in many environments, particularly in developing countries, web access is insufficient and the system must run locally.

And if people are to build and control their own libraries, a centralized solution is inadequate: the software must run on their own computers. Thus digital library systems intended for broad access should run on a wide variety of computer systems, particularly low-end ones. Developed under Linux, the Greenstone server runs on any Windows, Unix, or MacOS/X system. All versions of Windows are supported, from 3.1 up.

Supporting primitive platforms poses substantial challenges of a rather mundane nature: for example, Microsoft compilers no longer support Windows 3.1 and it is necessary to acquire obsolete versions. Under Windows, pre-built collections can be viewed on any system with at least 8 Mb RAM, but collections cannot be built under Windows 3.1/3.11—for this at least a Pentium processor is generally required, except for very small collections.

The fact that Greenstone does not run on early Macintosh systems is a serious drawback in certain environments. In an international cooperative effort established in August 2000 with UNESCO and the Belgium-based Human Info NGO, Greenstone is being distributed widely in developing countries with the aim of empowering users, particularly in universities, libraries, and other public service institutions, to build their own digital libraries.

UNESCO recognizes that digital libraries are radically reforming how information is acquired and disseminated in its partner communities and institutions in the fields of education, science and culture around the world, and particularly in developing countries.

Their hope is that this software will encourage the effective deployment of digital libraries to share information and place it in the public domain. he UNESCO distribution of Greenstone is a CD-ROM that contains the full source code and executable binaries for Windows and Linux, along with all necessary associated software.

Full documentation and five demonstration collections are included. he current CD-ROM is trilingual, with complete interfaces, instructions, and documentation in English, French and Spanish. For those with Web access, the same package is also available for download from the Greenstone Web site, often in a form that is slightly ahead of the CD-ROM version—for example, many other language interfaces are included and full documentation is available in Russian and Kazakh too. Providing accessibility in different languages is more difficult than one might at first realise.

As well as the manuals, installation instructions and installation prompts, the licensing agreement, and the readme files have to be translated too. Greenstone collections like the Humanity Development Library can be published as standalone collections on removable media such as CD-ROM, or presented on the Web. CD-ROM is a very practical format in developing countries.

Any Greenstone collection can be converted into a self-contained Windows CD-ROM that includes the Greenstone server software itself and an integrated installation package. The installation procedure has been thoroughly honed to ensure that only the most basic of computer skills are needed to install and run a collection under Windows.

Even standalone Greenstone users interact through a Web browser: Netscape is supplied on each CD-ROM for those who do not already have a browser. In standalone mode the software runs locally but incorporates a Web server so that if the system happens to be connected to a network—say a hospital or school intranet—information is available to other machines that may not possess CD drives.

This happens automatically: no special configuration is necessary. Another difficult engineering challenge is checking for the existence of a network. While installed network software is easily detected, it is hard to determine non-intrusively whether it is operational.

Incorrectly installed or configured software is endemic in developing countries, because computers there are often cast-offs whose software is inappropriate to their present environment, yet system support to rectify the problems is unavailable. It is essential for universal access that such problems are addressed properly and solved satisfactorily without involving the user, even though they are mundane and timeconsuming. Greenstone provides some support for the visually impaired by incorporating a "textual" mode of access that replaces all images by textual prompts.

This output is suitable for users with speech synthesizers or other specialized access devices. However, the facility is not well advanced: in particular, we have not yet refined it through usability testing and interface improvement.

GROWTH OF LIBRARIES IN INDIA

GROWTH AND DEVELOPMENT OF ORIENTAL LIBRARIES IN INDIA

Libraries have always had a pivotal role in the storage, processing, and dissemination of information. Some may serve general needs, but special libraries serve the needs of a particular community of users. Among special libraries, Oriental libraries hold an important place because they preserve the cultural heritage of a nation or a civilization.

Oriental Libraries

"Oriental Libraries" are those libraries that have literature pertaining to Oriental studies and languages. "Oriental" in this context refers to the ancient Near East, including India, Persia, and ancient Arabia, among other places, and the languages and literatures of those places and peoples.

Growth and Development

India is a vast repository of different cultures, both because it was invaded by a number of foreign countries and peoples, and because of its contacts with people from the East. The languages from those Eastern countries are part of Indian literature. The literature in those Eastern languages created India's Oriental libraries.

Their history can be traced back to the Vedic period, when the written literature was kept in Ashrams or Gurukuls. Gurukuls were mostly located peaceful forest environments. With the passage of time, Gurukuls were also established in cities.

Jain and Buddhist Era

Taxila was one of the famous educational centres where students came from different parts of the country. Varanasi also distinguished itself by having a large number of Gurukulas. During this period, the literature was preserved in the Sutra style of composition.

Buddhist and Jain Monastries acted as repositories of knowledge, for religious literature as well as other types. Monastic Oriental Libraries were also called Viharas. Over time, these Viharas developed into institutions of higher learning. A federation of Viharas constituted a Mahavihara, which was a larger educational institutional institution.

Nalanda Mahavihara is the best example. Fa-Hien, a Chinese traveller, also found a number of monastaries in India. Kanyakubja, Sravasti, Kusunagara, Vaisali, and Patliputra were centres of Oriental literature according to Fa-Hien. Hiuen-Tsang, another Chinese traveller, visited India during 629-645 A.D.

He left a detailed account of his visit, which gives us significant information about Buddhist educational institutions possessing a rich variety of Eastern literature. Taxila was a center of learning in Ancient India and a large number of people from all over the world and the subcontinent itself visited this place to gain knowledge. Literature related to medicine and archery enriched the library at Taxila. Rahula Sankrityayana, Angiris set up a seminary with a

Granthakuti attached to it at Taxila, which later flourished in to an academy or university. Nalanda University is the best known of ancient India 's universities. It has been called the treasure house of information by European archeologists. The information there helped locate Buddhist shrines in India.

It is believed that King Kumara Gupta built the first monastery at Nalanda to train Buddhist monks. Nalanda University was an expansion of this seminary. King Buddha Gupta, Jagatha Gupta, Baladitya, and Vijra made additions and expansions to the building.

There were three large libraries with vast amount of literature in Oriental languages on subjects such as science, medicine, astrology, fine arts, literature. The University of Valabhi was built by the Maitraka Kings during the years 475-775 A.D. Its library had a variety of Eastern literature. This great university and its library lasted until the 12th century, when they were completely destroyed by Arab invaders.

Odantapuri University was founded by King Gopala and was a well-known center of learning. It had a library that was rich in Brahmanical and Buddhist works. Mohammad Bakhtiyar Khilji destroyed this monastic university along with its library. Somapuri also possessed a wealth of Oriental literature, but it was destroyed by fire in the middle of the 11th century.

Vikramasila monastery, built by King Dharmapala, had a variety of literature on metaphysics, tantras, grammar, ritualism, and logic. The library fulfilled the demands of outsiders, especially those from Tibet, by providing them copies of manuscripts in a most liberal way. Another University with a significant Oriental collection, especially in Tantric Buddhism, was Jagaddala, founded by King Ramapala.

Another monastery with a rich wealth on different aspects of Oriental literature was Kanheri University, built during the reign of Amoghavarsha. By the 10th century, the corpus of Jain literature had increased many times, and Jain monks had contributed substantially to nearly all branches of knowledge known at that time. The Jayendra monastery of Kashmir had a good library where the Chinese traveller Hiuen–Tsang spent two years copying manuscripts.

Similarly, he spent fourteen months at the Chinapati monastery. Several Hindu kings and their ministers, who flourished between 10th and 12th centuries AD, are credited with establishing libraries and supporting the library movement. Among them was King Bhoja of Dhara, who flourished in the 11th century, and was a distinguished scholar with a rich library. King Kumarapaladeva of the Chaulakyas is said to have established 21 Jain Libraries. He kept a copy of Kalpasutra written in golden ink in each one of them.

Mughal Empire

When the Muslims established their rule in India at the beginning of the 13th century, Muslim emperors paid special attention to libraries, taking care to establish libraries in educational institutions. They constructed no separate library buildings; rather, books were deposited and preserved in educational institutions, mosques, and Khangahs.

Many Muslim rulers were from the East, and they helped enrich libraries with Oriental literature. Paper began be used as a writing material in the 12th century, and this helped book production in this periods. Mughal sovereigns and their courtiers were educated and accomplished, and some maintained personal libraries.

The Muslim sovereigns collected and preserve the Vedas, the Ramayana, and other Hindu religious books. They also translated a variety of books in Hindi in to Persian and Arabic, and helped disseminate Hindu art and culture. After the establishment of Sultans of Delhi in 1202, a new period in the history of Oriental libraries came in to existence. These minor Muslim rulers and nobles encouraged Islamic learning and established *maktabs* (primary schools), *madrasas* (schools of higher learning), libraries, and mosques.

They encouraged Arabic and Persian literatures in all branches of learning, and enriched Oriental literature in the libraries. They gave shelter and protection to scholars, who brought literature from other parts of the world to India. The Library of Khwajah Nizam-ud-din Auliya was an important Oriental library.

It was the property of the *Waqf* (religious board) and was open to every man of letters. During the reign of the Khilji dynasty the number of Oriental libraries increased. Jala-ud-din Khiljee established the Imperial Library at Delhi and appointed Amir Khusru as its librarian.

The Tughluq Dynasty opened a new chapter in the history of Oriental libraries in India. Mohammad Tughluq built one thousand madrasas, each with a library with collections in Arabic and Persian. Humayun ascended the throne in 1530 and a library known as Khan-i-Tilism.

Humayun's library played a significant role in Mughal history. Akbar, the greatest of Mughal emperors maintained a very rich library. He added a sizable number of books, obtained from his conquest, from libraries in Gujrat, Jaunpur, Kashmir, Bihar, Bengal, and the Deccan.

His library was unique in its collection of rare books, among which was the Persian *Divan of Human Shah.* By the time of Akbar's grandson, Shah Jahan, the library was a complex organization with a large staff, and headed by Nazim, a noble of the court. In Kashmir, a picture of the first library is found in the Shrine of Hazrat Bulbul Shah, which was established by Muslims.

A magnificient monastery and mosque were constructed by the emperor of Kashmir, Sultan Sadruddin, for Hazrat Bulbul Shah. A library was attached to this mosque. Amir Kabir Syed Hamdani, a theologian and scholar had a well established personal library that contained Oriental literature. He established a number of libraries in Kashmir which added to the wealth of the Indian Oriental libraries. The Sultans of Kashmir had given funds to establish madrasas and libraries. Each madrasa had a library. Sultan Zain-ul-Abedin-ul constructed a library which historians tell was one of the best in the world. Among the other libraries built by Budshah, Darul-ul-Uloom Nausherah was the best.

Another library, by the name of Madrasa-i-Sher, was built by Budshah near modern Islamabad. During the Chak Sultanate many libraries thrived and brought Oriental literature to the limelight. Akbar conquered Kashmir in 1587 and established many madrasas and libraries there. In Gujrat and Malwa, a number of libraries were introduced by Ahmad Shah I and Dilawar Khan.

Shah Jahan, like his predecessors, patronized learning and education and built a library with a rich collection of Arabic and Persian manuscripts. Dara Shikkoh, Aurangzeb, and Bahadur Shah Zafar also contributed to the development of Oriental libraries. Mughal rule was a period of literary excellence. Most of the emperors were themselves scholars, and also extended their patronage to scholarship and learning.

Other Kingdoms

There were kingdoms in other parts of India that also had libraries enriched by Oriental literature. The kingdoms of Bahmani and Deccan had independent kings who reigned for 340 years, and who were patrons of learning, as were the Bahmani kings, who continued their rule up to 1526 AD and had an empire that stretched from coast to coast.

They founded many colleges and libraries. Ahmad Shah built a magnificient college near Gulbarga. Muhammad Shah Bahmani II built another imposing college at Bidar that is one of the many beautiful remains of the grandeur of the Bahmanis. All these colleges had libraries that possessed an enormous amount of Oriental literature.

Arabian and Iranian literature brought by visitors and travellers were added to the libraries of Bahmanis. The Urdu language was at its zenith during the reign of Firoz Shah Bahmani, and a vast amount of Urdu literature enriched the Bahmani Libraries.

The library of Gesudaraj was distinguished among the libraries of Deccan. Books on Sufism and religion were available in this library. The emperors of Qutub Shahi also established a good number of libraries during their reign, and a vast amount of literature in Persian was included. Tipu Sultan, son of Haider Ali and emperor of Mysore established a number of libraries.

"Zaimul-Umoor" was the great university of Seringa Patnam in his reign. He collected books from many countries including Europe. The library had a copy of the Holy Quran which was written by the hand of Aurangzeb Alamgir. It is estimated that the library had nearly 2,000 volumes of Persian, Arabic, and Hindi manuscripts from all branches of Islamic literature.

After the downfall of the Mughals, and with the invasion of Ahmad Shah Abdali, the literary wealth of the Indian libraries was looted away. In 1857, after the Sepoy mutiny, thousands of books were destroyed and thousands of important, valuable, and rare books were siphoned to England.

British and other Europeans

The growth and development of Oriental libraries was regenerated again during European and British rule. The interest shown by the British and European scholars in Oriental Learning and Indology, along with the social, cultural and religious movements spearheaded by eminent Indians, resulted in new Oriental libraries. These institutions established libraries for Oriental scholarship. The result of this renaissance is a number of special libraries devoted to Oriental and Indological collections in various parts of the country.

Rampur Raza Library, very rich in Indo-Islamic studies and arts, was created by Nawab Faizullah Khan in 1794, and has tremendous manuscript wealth. One can find manuscripts in Arabic, Persian, Urdu, Sanskrit, Sinhali, Tamil, Kannada, and other Oriental languages.

The Asiatic Society Library, Kolkatta, a premier and leading oriental institutions of the country was established in 1784 by Sir William Jones. Colonel Mackenzie, an Englishman and an engineer by profession established an Oriental Library by the name of " *Government Oriental Manuscript Library* (GOML) " in Chennai.

Contemporary Libraries

Khuda Baksh Oriental Library was founded in 1842 by Maulvi Khuda Baksh Khan, who donated his entire personal collection. Since 1977 it has been issuing regularly a multi-lingual research quarterly *Khuda Baksh Library Journal.* The library has been recognized as a research center by seven Indian universities. The collection has a rich repository of Persian and Arabic manuscripts. Maulana Azad Library, Aligarh Muslim University was initially founded as "Anglo Oriental College (MAOC) at Aligarh in 1875 and raised to the status of a university in 1920.

The personal collection of Maulana Azad also enriches the library. The library has a total collection of over 1 million volumes and 14,571 manuscripts. The Maulana Azad Library has the largest collection of Urdu books in the Indian subcontinent, which is perhaps largest in the world as well.

The collection includes:

- Urdu
- Arabic
- Persian
- Sanskrit
- Hindi

- Sir Syed Collection
- Gandhian Collection
- Aligarh Collection
- Thesis Collection
- Archives
- Microfiche
- Manuscripts

Hakim Mohammad Syed Library, Jamia Hamdard, New Delhi is a leading university founded in 1906.

It has a well known Oriental library, which has a number of special collections:

- Nazaria Collection
- Abdul Sattar Siddiqui Collection
- Maulana Abdul Salam Niazi Collection
- Jaffri Collection
- Shafi Ahmad Collection
- Dr Tanveer Alvi Collection

The library has 4,500 rare manuscripts. Osmania University Library was established in 1918 and is considered seventh oldest in India, the third oldest in South India, and the first to be established in state of Hyderabad.

The library has a collection of rare books and manuscripts including Palm Leaf manuscripts. The National Library of India, which came in to existence in 1948, is the largest library in India. Previously it was known as the Imperial Library which was formed in 1891 by combining a number of Secretariat libraries.

It has a wide range of collections in a variety of national and international languages. A good number of Arabic and Persian documents are also available here. The Oriental library initiative that took place in ancient India reached its zenith in the period when the British and other Europeans came to India. The Mughals also contributed a great deal to the development of Oriental libraries. Eventually, their extravagant ways caused the libraries to deteriorate, but social and political conditions eventually led to better libraries with larger collections.

ACADEMIC LIBRARIES IN INDIA: A HISTORICAL STUDY

Research in library history in India has remained largely neglected area which has resulted into availability of very limited and scanty literature. Commenting on the status of library history in India, Donald G. Davis, Jr. of the University of Texas at Austin, writes that "although a core literature on Indian library history exists, it has many imbalances and gaps. The scholars are very dispersed in their interests and their geographical location. With one person rarely contributing more than one work. There is little pattern to existing research efforts."

In this context, the role of historian happens to be much more crucial and significant to make an assessment of the growth and development of libraries in India, the factors responsible for their development and the impact of those factors on the library progress. Rajgopalan, in his 1987 presidential address to the Indian Library Association rightly said, "it is generally acknowledged that our libraries are underutilized in relation to investments being made in them.

Non-use and low-use of libraries amount to wastage of facilities being made available. Maybe the literacy rate, lack of reading habits, etc., are the causes for low use from the side of patrons... User education programmes must be organized by libraries in a way that libraries are fully utilized." He further remarked that, "if library historians would address the roots and trends of library issues, they would provide a valuable service to the profession and society."

The Father of Library and Information Science in India,Padmashri Dr. S.R. Ranganathan while giving a radio talk in April 1956 said, "an account of the libraries in the first four periods must necessarily depend upon the historical research. This has not yet been done. The library profession is too small in India to spare a person to fill up this antiquarian gap. Those trained in the scientific method of tracing history are too preoccupied with dynastic and political history to spare sufficient time for cultural history in general and library history in particular."

Thus, an historical study of the growth and development of academic libraries in India, is a desideratum, the fulfillment of which should go a long way in removing the imbalances and gaps. Such a study becomes significant not only in view of the tremendous activity concerning the growth and development of libraries in India, but also because their growth has been shaped in the first phase by the phenomena that have shaped the historical course of this period and, secondly, the rise of library as an important instrument in the advancement of knowledge and socio-economic transformation.

Source Material for Writing History of Libraries

For the purpose of scientific writing of history of libraries, an understanding of the nature of existing source material and knowing the art of using it is essential. The sources for writing the history are available in Pali, Sanskrit, Chinese, Arabic, Persian and European Languages and most of them have been translated into English. These exist in various formats, such as Manuscripts, inscriptions, copper plates etc.

They are either indigenous or foreign. The contribution of foreign travelogues such as Tibetan, Chinese, Muslim, Portuguese, English and other Europeans is highly useful. Some noteworthy foreign travelogues are Itsing, Fahien, Hieun Tsang, Alberuni, Ibn Batuta, Minhaj, Firishta, Badauni, Afif, bernier, mandelso, Manrique de Lara, Martin, Count Noer.

In addition to the contribution of the travelogues, the contribution of historians like Henry M. Eliot, John Dawson, Stanley Lane-Pool, Ishwari Prasad, R.C. Majumdar, Jadunath Sarkar, V.D. Mahajan, Mohammed Muhammed Zubair, J.S. Sarma and N.N. Law etc. is also significant.

Though scanty, yet there are articles written by the library professionals on history of libraries. A few efforts have also been made for conduct of research in the area of history of libraries and such like works have been consulted for the purpose of writing this paper.

University Libraries in Ancient India

In the Vedic age instructions were imparted "orally, without the medium of books." Taxila from 700 B.C. to 300 A.D. was considered to be the most respected seat of higher learning and education in India but still there is no evidence found so far in the archaeological excavations at Taxila that there had been a good library system in the Taxila University.

Fa-Hien noticed such libraries at Jetavana monastery at Sravasti. In 400 A.D., there came into being one of the biggest known universities, the Nalanda University, which by 450 A.D. became a renowned seat of learning, its fame spreading beyond the boundaries of India.

Nalanda near Patna grew to be the foremost Buddhist monastery and an educational centre. Most of what we know of the Nalanda University during the 6th and the 7th centuries A.D. is due to the accounts left by Hiuen-tsang, who lived in the institution for three years in the first half of the 7th century, and I-tsing who also stayed there for ten years towards the latter part of the same century.

Information on the Nalanda University Library is also found in the Tibetan accounts, from which we understand that the library was situated in a special area known by the poetical name the Dharmaganja, which comprised three huge buildings, called the Ratnasagara, the Ratnodadhi and the Ratnaranjaka of which the Ratnasagara was a ninestoried building and housed the collection of manuscripts and rare sacred works like Prajnaparamita Sutra etc.

The library at Nalanda had a rich stock of manuscripts on philosophy and religion and contained texts relating to grammar, logic, literature, the Vedas, the Vedanta, and the Samkhya philosophy, the Dharmasastras, the Puranas, Astronomy, Astrology and Medicine. The University of Nalanda and its library flourished down to the 12th century A.D. until Bakhtiyar Khalji sacked it in 1197-1203 A.D.7 and set fire to the establish-ment of Nalanda.

The world famous universities, such as, the Vikramasila, the Vallabhi and the Kanchi were coming up in other parts of the country during the period from the 5th century A.D. to the 8th century A.D. All these universities possessed rich libraries and in the hall containing such books there used to be an image of the goddess Saraswati with a book in her hand.

The Nalanda and the Vikramshila universities were under the control of the king Dharmapala. He founded the Vikramshila monastery in the 8th century A.D. It had a rich collection of texts in the Sanskrit, the Prakrit and the Tibetan languages.

Regarding the library of the university, the *Tabaqat-i-Nasiri* informs us that there were great number of books on the religion of Hindus there; and when all these books came under the observation of the Mussalamans, they summoned, a number of Hindus that they might give them information regarding the import of these books; but the whole of the Hindu community was killed in the war.

Muslim vandalism caused the disappearance of the excellent collection at Vikramashila. The Jaggadal Vihara in Varendra-bhumi was also an important centre of learning with considerable collection of the reading material. It was established by the king Kampala, who ruled from 1084 to 1130 A.D.

The provision of facilities for reading, writing, editing and translating manuscripts shows that this library was in no way less than its contemporary libraries in importance. Though not as large as the library of Nalanda, it abounded in private collection of texts.

Likewise Mithila had been famous for its scholars since the days of Rajrishi Janaka and had a rich collection of various commentaries on the different branches of the Hindu *Shastras.* The library of its university played an important role in teaching and learning. A needle *(Shalaka)* was pierced through the manuscript on the subject of the student's specialization and he was expected to explain the last page pierced.

In this way the student's all-round mastery of the subject was tested. Mithila continued to enjoy its all India importance in the field of learning till the end of the 15th century AD. The university at Sompuri, like that of Vikramshila, occupied a significant position since the days of Dharampala.

Like Nalanda, this university also had its own library. Atisa Dipankar, a noted scholar, lived there. He with the help of other scholars, translated into the Tibetan the *Madhyamkaratnapradipa* of Bhavaviveka. This university was destroyed by fire in the middle of the 11th century A.D. Efforts were made by the monk Vipulsrimitra to renovate the university but it could not regain its past glory.

At a time when Nalanda was famous for its *Mahayana* courses of study, the Maitrakakings provided their patronage to the Mahavihara of Vallabhi. This university was famous for its *Hinayana* studies. The fact that this university had a good library is supported by a reference in a grant of Guhasena, dated 559 A.D., wherein a provision was made out of the royal grant for the purchase of books for the library.

This important seat of learning at Kanheri, on the West Coast, flourished during the reign of Amoghavarsha in the 9th century A.D. The library occupied a significant position within the establishment, and the donors provided money to buy books for the library.

The last of the famous seats of learning in Eastern India was Navadwipa in Bengal. It reached its height of glory from 1083 to 1106 A.D. as a centre of intellectual excellence as well as its rich library facilities, when Lakshman Sen, a king of Gauda, made it his capital. However, this library was also destroyed along with the centre by Bakhtiyar Khalji.

Situated in South India at Amaravati, on the banks of the Krishna, the Nagarjuna Vidyapeeth flourished in about 7th century A.D. Its library housed in the top floor of the five storyed building of the university had an enormous collection on the Buddhist philosophy, particularly of the *Mahayana* school that Nagarjuna had founded, science and medicine.

There is enough archaeological evidence that supports the existence of this 7th century university and its library. The enormity of the collection in this library is borne out by the fact that it not only had works on the Buddhist literature and the *Tripitakas,* but also works on several branches of scientific knowledge, such as, Botany, Geography, Mineralogy and Medicine. It was a great attraction for scholars from the different parts of India and from countries, like, China, Burma and Ceylon.

University Libraries in Medieval India

The existence of academic libraries during the medieval period of Indian history is not known, though the Muslim rulers did patronize libraries in their own palaces. A lone exception, however, was a library attached to a college at Bidar, having a collection of 3000 books on different subjects. Aurangzeb got this Library transferred to Delhi to merge it with his palace library. During the medieval period, due to Muslim invasions and political troubles, the powerful empires and kingdoms of Indian rulers fell one by one. This affected higher education and the development of academic libraries as well.

Libraries in Modern India

During the British rule in India, number of academic institutions were established by the East India Company, and by the Christan missionaries. Some of the worth mentioning events which led to the growth and development of higher education in India during this period were the establishment of the Calcutta College in 1781, Jonathan Duncan, then a British agent, founded the Benaras Sanskrit College in 1792. The Calcutta Fort William College was founded in 1800. All these colleges were having their own libraries.

The Charter Act of 1813, the foundation of Fort William and Serampore Colleges, Calcutta, Madras and Bombay universities and their libraries, Hunter, Raleigh and Calcutta University Commissions, library training programmes, the establishment of Inter University Board, Sargent Report and appointment of the University Grants Committee, the establishment of Madras University, University of Bombay, University of Calcutta and their libraries, the constitution of Inter-University Board, the appointment of Hartog Committee, the Montague-Chelmsford reforms of 1919, the Government of India Act of 1935, and the Sargent Committee Report etc. laid foundation for establishment of libraries in various parts of the country.

The Fort William College was founded in Calcutta on 18th August 1800 by the Marquis of Welleselay, the Governor-General of India during 1798-1805. Reverend David Brown, Provost of the college was instrumental in setting up the library which had a well rounded collection of Eastern manuscripts.

In the absence of adequate financial support, the library could not survive for long and in 1835 it was decided to close the library and its valuable collection was transferred to the Asiatic Society Library in Calcutta between 1835-39. The Charter Act of 1813 passed by the British Parliament gave the East India Company complete responsibility for educating Indians.

The establishment of C.M.S. College in Kottayam, Hindu college in Calcutta in 1816 and Raven Shaw College in Cuttack in 1816 was the immediate result of the Charter Act 1813. These and other colleges came into existence thereafter had their own libraries the day they were established. Serampore College during this period was founded by the Danes in 1818 and the King of Denmark in 1927 agreed to give this college an academic status by providing equivalence to the Danish Universities with power to confer degrees.

The library of this college too was established along with its foundation and at a later stage the college was given affiliation to the University of Burdwan for the purpose of conferring degrees. The 7th March 1835 decision of the British Indian Government to promote English literature and sciences in India was resulted into the spread of number of colleges in India and by 1839 there were over forty colleges with attached libraries in the British territory in India.

For their establishment, lots of money was made available by the Indians in the form of donations. In 1840 Presidency College was founded in Madras, followed by a medical college in Bombay in 1845. This progress in education was instrumental in establishing universities in India.

The Charles Wood dispatch of 1854 popularly known as the 'Magna Carta of English Education' in India also paved the way for the establishment of the universities in the presidency towns. Sir John Colville introduced the Bill to establish universities in India and it was passed by the Governor General of India Lord Dalhousie on 24th January 1857, paved the way for the foundation of three universities based on the London Universities Model in the Presidency towns of Calcutta, Madras and Bombay.

Indian Education Commission, popularly known as Hunter Commission was appointed by the British Indian Government in 1882 to study the progress of education under the new policy adopted in 1854 by the East India Company and transferred to the Crown and accepted by the Secretary of State in 1859. Sir William W. Hunter in his report had clearly stated that the conditions of the libraries was in a very poor state and declared them "hardly creditable." The Commission paid special attention to the colleges and their libraries and other facilities.

The direct result of the Commission was the establishment of Panjab University, Lahore and Allahabad University in 1882 and 1887 respectively but still the condition of the education and libraries remained in a poor state.

The Raleigh Commission 1902 appointed by Lord Curzon to investigate the conditions and prospects of the Indian universities and to recommend measures to improve their constitution and working and standards of teaching also paid special attention to the academic libraries and found that, "the library is little used by graduates and hardly at all by other students." Further, the Commission commented, "In a college where library is inadequate or ill arranged, the students have no opportunity of forming the habit of independent and intelligent reading."

Thus, the Commission specifically recommended that reference services must be made an integral part of all libraries in colleges and universities, and that one of the prerequisite conditions for the grant of university affiliation to a college be the accessibility of students to the library of the institution.

The recommendations of the Raleigh Commission were included in the Universities Act of 1904 and provided the power to all universities to require that all colleges applying for affiliation maintain proper libraries, equipment, library building, and lend books to all students but the situation and the status of libraries could not be improved much simply because the recommendations made by the Commission and the provisions made in the act could not be implemented properly.

The Calcutta University Commission popularly known as Sadler Commission was appointed by the government in 1917 to study the situation and the status of education in the country and to make recommendations to solve the existing problems.

The Commission noticed that "one of the greatest weak-nesses of the existing system is the extraordinarily unimportant part which is played by the library" and found that "in some colleges the library is regarded not as an essential part of teaching equipment but merely as a more or less useless conventional accessory." The Commission made the recommendations regarding the libraries that college libraries be strengthened and that training should be given to the students and occasionally to the teachers about use of the library.

One of the immediate result of the Calcutta University Commission was the establishment of a few new teaching-cum-residential universities at Patna in 1917, Osmania in Hyderabad in 1918, Dacca, Aligarh, and Lucknow in 1921, Delhi in 1922 and Nagpur in 1923 and all of them were established along with the establishment of libraries as an integral part of the university system.

As stated earlier, the impact of the Commission could very well be seen in the establishment of several universities along with their libraries. This was the period when in the libraries scenario, a person appeared who at a later stage turned the entire scene and become the father of library science in India.

The man was none other than Dr. S.R. Ranganathan. The University of Madras appointed Dr. S.R. Ranganathan as its Librarian in 1924. He was trained at the University of London Library School before joining his duties at Madras. Things did change rapidly after his joining. For example, he introduced the lending and reference services at the Madras University Library and extended the library hours for the benefit of the readers.

Whereas the hours had previously been 7 a.m. to 4 p.m., they were changed to 7 a.m. to 6 p.m. He delivered a series of lectures to about two thousand teachers at the conference of the South Indian Teachers' Union in 1929 regarding the use and importance of the library services.

The Madras Library Association started a summer course in librarianship and the lectures for this course were mainly delivered by Dr. Ranganathan. The main objective of the course in its beginning was to spread the ideas of the value of good library services and modern library methods among potential users of the library. The budget of the university library of Madras had been very poor from the beginning and it was really a difficult task to manage, run and administer the library effectively within it.

Ranganathan brought this poor financial position to the notice of the then Chief Minister, Dr. P. Subbaroyan, when he delivered a speech during an educational conference held at Madras in 1926. In his speech, Ranganathan "gave a graphic account of the library network in Europe and the United States of America and compared it with the poor, appalling facilities existing in India.... added that paucity of funds prevented him developing his library."

The Chief Minister was highly impressed by Ranganathan's speech and promised to give more State help to the University Library. Its immediate result was a grant of rupees 6,000 which was added to the annual grant from the State, and, in addition, rupees 100,000 in lump sum were sanctioned by the Madras State Government in the same year to buy books and periodicals in pure sciences, humanities, and social sciences.

Provision was also made for additional grants to the library, as and when new departments of study and research were established. In the words of Ranganathan, "This was the first time when such a forward financial step in the history of the university libraries in India was taken in the second quarter of the 20th century."

The University of Madras library made a good start under Ranganathan's effective leadership and administration. In 1930, the library had five well-trained reference librarians to help the readers, and they "carried the work to a high pitch of efficiency." This was the first time in the history of Indian libraries that a special reference service was introduced in a university library. The library collection increased to 93,000 volumes in 1935 and on September 3, 1936, the library was shifted to its first new and permanent functional building. By 1944, when Ranganathan resigned from the position of the Librarian, to become the University Librarian at the *Banaras Hindu University* (BHU), the collection of the Madras University Library had augmented to 1,20,000 volumes.

The contribution of Dr. Ranganathan to the growth and development of libraries in general and the Madras University Library in particular is undoubtedly tremendous and unforgettable. It will not be wrong to say that the Library School of Madras and the Madras University Library were the laboratories of Ranganathan to propound his ideas in library science and to test them practically.

Some of the important and major ideas of Ranganathan were the Five Laws of Library Science which were enunciated by him in 1924, and their formulation and publication in 1929 and 1931 respectively. These laws are still considered a unifying theory for all library practices and services, and set of guidelines for the dynamic development and study of library science as a whole.

The University of Bombay Library received a special grant of rupees 50,000 from the Central Government in 1939 to strengthen its collection for graduate studies. During the period from 1931 to 1939, a few more special grants were given to the library for its collection development. A very special grant of rupees 10,000 was given by Kikabhai and Maniklal, sons of the late Premchand Roychand, in 1931 to replace the electric clock of the library tower.

The collection, which stood at 4,504 volumes in 1900, rose to 70,000 in 1939 and 73,582 in 1947. Though higher education and academic libraries made some progress during the first quarter of the present century, yet their growth and development was not very well organized.

Academic institutions and their growth after 1916 created a few problems also and the general feeling was that the "quality of Education was being sacrificed for quantity." While such a situation prevailed, the Indian Statutory Commission, popularly known as the Simon Commission, was appointed by the Government in 1927 to study the conditions prevailing in India.

The Simon Commission appointed an Auxiliary Committee to look into the growth of education in India. Sir Philip Hartog, a former member of the Calcutta University Commission, and a former Vice-Chancellor of the University of Dacca, was appointed its Chairman.

In its report, submitted in 1929, the Committee stated that "the dispersal of resources for university teaching among a number of colleges had made it difficult to build up university libraries of the type required for advanced work both at the Honours and the research stage majority of the university libraries were inadequate and all needed great additions."

In addition to want of books, libraries also lacked good current periodicals in their collections. The Committee also made a special note of the low academic standards in many colleges and universities and the "unhealthy competition for candidates between neighbouring universities".

This report, however, did not offer any comprehensive, detailed, and realistic solutions to the problems. In 1935, Ministry of Education was formed in each province, as per the provisions of the dyarchy in the Montague-Chelmsford Reforms of 1919, supplemented by those of the new Government of India Act of 1935.

The Ministry of Education in India requested the Central Advisory Board of Education in 1944 to survey the educational conditions in the country. The Board's report, known as the Sargeant Report, after its Chairman, Sir Sargeant, the Educational Advisor to the Government of India, came up with a master-plan for the development of education in the post-World War II India. Its terms of reference covered education at all levels-primary, secondary, and higher.

The Indian universities, as they existed then, despite many admirable features, did not fully satisfy the requirements of a national system of education. During the British rule, several committees and commissions set up periodically, paved way for the foundation of several colleges and the establishment of many universities and in many cases the libraries were also established along with them.

It is also true that as compared to the first two decades the development of university libraries after 1924 did make better progress but the college libraries were still neglected and were struggling to get their recognition.

There were only 12 universities in India in 1924 and their number swelled to 18 by the time India got freedom in 1947. In fact, the academic libraries during the British rule had no significance in the academic life of the institutions of higher education and the pivotal role that can be played by the academic libraries in the life of the institutions could very well be seen in the policy statement of higher education of the free India and the fact was also proven when at the time of national reconstruction, the importance of libraries in teaching and research was recognized, and libraries received the early attention of the Government of India.

Academic Libraries in India after Independence

The actual process for the development of university libraries in India can be said to have been set in motion with the appointment of the University Education Commission presided over by Dr. S. Radhakrishnan and its recommendations, such as, annual grants, open access system, working hours, organization of the library, staff, steps to make students book conscious and the need to give grants to teachers to buy books.

The section on libraries of the report opens with a powerful statement on the importance of libraries in university education and states, "teaching is a cooperative enterprise. Teachers must have the necessary tools for teaching purposes in the shape of libraries and laboratories as also the right type of students."

The Commission in the course of its study of the academic libraries, found that "libraries were hopelessly inadequate to serve the curricular needs of a modern university. They were ill-housed, illstocked, and ill-staffed and were totally lacking in standard literary and scientific journals. Service was in the hands of personnel that had hardly any notion of the objectives of university education. The annual appropriation for book purchase seldom exceeded the ten thousand mark."

In addition, the annual grant for these libraries were not sufficient. Therefore, the Commission recommended that at least six per cent of the total budget of each academic institution should be set aside for the library. Only then will the condition of these libraries improve.

It added that if institutions were not willing to allocate six per cent of their budget to libraries, they should spend ₹40 per student enrolled. The Commission also suggested that greater attention should be paid to improve the reference services in the university libraries. Therefore, "documentation and bibliographical services must be developed in order to promote research among the faculty and students, make libraries proper centres for research activities, and to raise the standards of services."

As far as the library staff is concerned, the Commission was of the view that it is very important to have well-qualified staff, including the Director, in order to provide excellent service in any library. The Director's qualifications must include Ph.D. in Library Science and he must have the rank and salary of a professor, capabilities of organization and management, and should have full powers of an administrator to run the library effectively.

University Education Commission. There is no doubt that the recommendations of the Commission "were based on the needs of the modern library services in universities for the promotion of research and creative learning." It was for the first time that such detailed attention was paid to the library matters by a commission on university education in India.

Ranganathan Committee (1957)

The most comprehensive and significant document on the university and college libraries is the Report of the UGC library committee, chaired by Ranganathan. The Report was published by the University Grants Commission in 1959 entitled 'University and College Libraries.' It was perhaps the first attempt by any Library Committee in India to systematically survey the academic libraries on a national basis, and it was also the first time that the government of India had decided to seek advice from a professional librarian regarding academic libraries. The committee was to advice the UGC on the standards of libraries, building, pay scales, and library training.

After the survey the library committee invited all academic librarians to a seminar on "Work flow in university and college libraries," at Delhi from March 4 to 7, 1959 to keep them informed about the progress the committee had made surveying the academic libraries. It wanted to discuss its recommendations with them. Some of the recommendations of the Committee included the provision that the UGC and the State Government should help the college and the university libraries in the collection development of both books and periodicals.

The formula suggested by the committee was that funds be given "at the rate of ₹15 per enrolled student and ₹200 per teacher and research fellow. There should also be special initial library grants in the case of a new university and of a new department in an existing university, a similar scale should be followed for the college libraries. In order to promote co-operation among libraries, a Union Catalogue of books and a Union List of periodicals to be prepared.

The Committee strongly recommended that an open access system be introduced in every academic library. Committee also stressed "that reference service is the essential human process of establishing contact between the right reader and the right book by personal service. Reference service is vital in promotion of reading habit in student each library should provide an adequate number of reference librarians to function as library hosts and human converters."

Other recommendations included building up a microfilm collection, copying facilities for microfilms and book material, appointment of a committee to look into the standards of teaching, examination and research in the library schools, and appointment of full-time teaching faculty members rather than asking librarians to teach part time in the library schools.

The Committee added that "the status and the salary of the library staff should be the same as that of the teaching and research staff', *i.e.*, Professor, Reader, and Lecturer etc." The recommendations of the committee had a farreaching effect on the development of the university libraries later.

They had not only provided a framework to the UGC to implement its grants-in-aid programmes but also given to the university authorities important guidelines. Particular mention, in this connection, may be made of the recommendations concerning the library finances which had helped libraries to secure enough finances by way of annual grants from the universities themselves and of development grants from the UGC.

The recommendations on the library personnel and staff strength have given to the library staff status and salaries equivalent to the academic staff and ensure provision for adequate staff for various library operations. The

Committee submitted its report to the UGC with the hope that it will provide a blueprint for the systematic development of university libraries in the country.

Hence, in-spite of many hurdles like education being a state subject in the Indian Constitution, considerable development in the university libraries has taken place and as such the condition of these libraries in 1953 was much better than in the 1940's and even the early 1950's.

Kothari Commission

The Education Commission under the chairmanship of Dr. D. S. Kothari marked another important stage in the history of university libraries in India.

The Commission devoted considerable attention to the develop-ment of the university libraries and made suitable recommendations on the following points:

- Norms for financial support;
- Long range planning for library development;
- The need for the establishment of a well equipped library before the starting of a university, college, or department;
- Suitable phasing over of the library grants;
- Encouraging the students in the use of books;
- Interdisciplinary communication; and
- Documentation service in libraries etc.

The Education Commission had also addressed itself to the role of libraries in adult education and recommended establish-ment of a network of public libraries.

It wanted the school libraries to be integrated with public libraries for purposes of the adult education programmes. The Report, submitted by Dr. D. S. Kothari, on June 29, 1966, emphatically pointed out that "nothing can be more damaging than to ignore its library and to give it a low priority. No new college, university or department should be opened unless adequate number of books in the library are provided."

The Commission was shocked to note that the recommen-dations of the Radhakrishnan Commission had not been fully implemented, for only four universities in India has spent five per cent or more of their budget on books and periodicals acquisitions, though the 1948's Commission has suggested that six per cent of the total budget be spent on libraries. Other universities had spent less than five per cent of their budget on libraries, "Surprisingly enough there are five universities which spent even less than one per cent of the total budget on the libraries."

It was clear proof that the university libraries in India were not functioning properly to fulfill the needs of higher education. The Kothari Commission recommended that a long range plan for library development should be drawn up for each academic institution taking into consideration anticipated increase in enrollment, introduction of new subjects and research needs etc., and documentation service be encouraged in libraries, and documentation experts be appointed to help researchers and do indexing and abstracting.

It was further recommended that "the book selection should be oriented towards supporting instruction and research." The library should "provide resources necessary for research in fields of special interest to the university; provide library facilities and services necessary for the success of all formal programmes of instruction."

Monetary guidelines were also suggested by the Commission. "As a norm, a university should spend each year about Rs.25 per student registered and ₹300 per teacher depending on the stage of development of each university library." It was also suggested that "the foreign exchange needed for university and college libraries should be allowed separately to the UGC."

The Wheat Loan Programme

During the 1950's and early 1960's the Indian academic libraries received huge grants from the UGC amounting up to ₹100,000 for books, buildings, equipment and even for additional staff. At the same time many libraries got additional grants from a special US fund called the 'Wheat Loan Programme.' The American Congress passed a special Act, in 1951 known as the 'Public Law 480' to loan India $ 19,000,000 to buy much needed wheat from the US. Under the agreement of the loan, India had to buy American books, periodicals and scientific equipment worth $ 50,000 to be used for research purposes in the Indian libraries.

This, money India had to pay as interest on the loan. Part of the money was to be spent on the exchange of scholars, including librarians, between the two countries. The United States authorities bought some educational material and equipment from India for research purposes and higher education in the American Universities.

During 1951-1961 Indian libraries spent US $ 1,400,000 of the purchase of American books, US dollar 160,000 on libraries, US $ 40,000 on the travel and study grants for thirty three Indian librarians to visit the United States and US $ 75,000 on the travel and study grants of the five Americans.

College Libraries

The College libraries in India have a significant role to play in higher education. Majority of the undergraduate students, *i.e.*, 88.5 per cent and graduate students, *i.e.*, 53 per cent, attend these colleges. When India attained Independence many among the 533 affiliated colleges did not have their own libraries, but at present, every college in the country has a library.

Majority of the college libraries do not have proper facilities to meet the needs of their users. Their collections are not up-to-date, budgets are their very inadequate and limited, and a large number of them are single libraries. In many colleges, there is neither a library hall nor a sufficient big room, not to think of a separate building for the library.

Any unused room, quite often somewhere out of sight, would be considered adequate to house a few shelves of books. And in most college libraries there is complete darkness even during the day time, as the windows are closed out of a fear that the books may be stolen..

Different studies, conducted by scholars and Srivastva have explicitly established that the condition of the college libraries in India are far from satisfactory.

The college libraries are open only six to eight hours a day. Many do not have any qualified librarian on their staff and have closed stacks only. The several commissions and committees, like the Radhakrishnan Commission of 1948, did not stress the importance of the college libraries in their reports. However, the University Grants Commission gives more importance to the college libraries.

As the quality of higher education and research, especially at the graduate level, depends upon, among other things, the standard of the college libraries and their services. Therefore, the UGC has played a significant role in the growth and development of college libraries since 1953 by giving grants for books, equipment, staff and library buildings and has done a remarkable job in salary improvement of the college librarians.

The UGC's contribution to the college libraries is at the rate of ₹15 per student with a maximum of ₹10,000 with some additional and special grants for text books, when a new subject is introduced in the Curriculum.

On the other hand, the colleges and the state governments have failed to provide their equal share. The total Expenditure on the college libraries according to the recommendation of the Education Commission should be 6.25 per cent of the total budgets of the colleges, but in most cases it has remained between 1.5 per cent and 2.3 per cent.

Sardana Collection development of the college libraries are done without taking into consideration the actual needs of the faculty and the students of the colleges as sixty per cent of them consist of text books and 20 per cent cover fiction.

Even this small inadequate collection, in depth and content, is not used effectively due to the closed stacks system and lack of staff and facilities for instruction concerning their use. The net result is that the utility factor of the college libraries comes practically to nothing.

In most college libraries, books are neither properly classified nor catalogued. In several libraries no systematic classification is followed for collection arrangements. The only service the college library renders to its clientele is book-lending. There are colleges where students are not even allowed inside the library.

The UGC is aware of the slow progress of the college libraries. In addition to providing financial help for development, it has also from time to time organized seminars to keep the college librarians aware of the new developments in the field. But these seminars have made only a limited effect on the progress of the college libraries. The condition of the college libraries in the country should be a cause for alarm among the academic community.

In the interests of the development of higher education in the country along proper lines, it is important to make a detailed study of the style of functioning of the college libraries and of the utilization of the library resources and facilities by the students and teachers. This will help in the preparation of more realistic and operational policies and programmes for ensuring the proper functioning, utilization and development of the college libraries. The college library has to be made the intellectual hub of the institution, serving equally, both the students and teachers.

This is all the more necessary because about 90 per cent of the students in higher education in India pursue their studies in colleges and they have only very small and substandard college library resources to fall back upon. Although, owing to various efforts of the UGC as well as other forces, the traditional concept that the college library is a custodian of books has changed, yet there is evidence enough to show that the condition of the college libraries is generally poor, their development is rather slow and that the position of the college libraries and their librarians in India, with a few exceptions, is pitiable.

University Libraries

University libraries all over the world have their own place of importance in the scheme of higher learning. Libraries are not only repositories of knowledge but also dispensers of such knowledge. There is no doubt that where libraries of universities and institutions of higher learning are ignored or not given due recognition, the country as a whole suffers because the standards of study, teaching and research very heavily depend upon the qualitative and quantitative service rendered by the university libraries.

The Radhakrishnan Commission expressed that "the library is the heart of all the university's work, directly so, as regards its research work and indirectly as regards its educational work, which derives its life from research. Scientific research needs the library as well as its laboratories while for humanistic research the library is both library and the laboratory in one. Both for humanistic and scientific studies, a first class library is essential in a university."

The growth of university libraries since Independence can be seen in respect of the initiatives taken by the Central Government considering the vital importance of higher education and role of libraries in the educational development, commitment to fulfill the demand of higher education, and the foundation of the UGC in 1953 by an Act of Parliament. The Radhakrishnan Commission recognized the value and importance of a well equipped and organized library system and its role in higher education.

It had found many drawbacks and pitfalls in the university libraries and had made many recommendations for the improvement of library facilities. The Ranganathan Committee, appointed by the UGC in 1957, made some outstanding recommendations, which included standards for library building, collection development, staff and services and furniture etc. These recommendations were accepted by the UGC and forwarded for implementation.

The Kothari Commission also made valuable recommen-dations for this purpose, but the role of the University Grants Commission deserves special mention, because it has played a vital role by "regularly providing appropriate grants and funds to all universities for development of libraries, to purchase books and journals...., construction of new library buildings and for library equipment and furniture." Dr. D. S. Kothari, the Chairman of University Grants Commission, said, "Libraries play a vital role in the development of institutions of higher learning. The University Grants Commission attaches great importance to the strengthening of library facilities in the universities and colleges and their efficient administration. The commission has also been giving grants to institutions for books and journals construction of library building and appointment of library staff."

One of the most remarkable and identifiable development in the history of higher education and libraries was the foundation of the INFLIBNET in 1991. Information and Library Network Centre is an autonomous Inter-University Centre of the UGC of India. It is a major National Programme initiated by the UGC in 1991 with its Head Quarters at Gujarat University Campus, Ahmedabad. Initially started as a project under the IUCAA, it became an independent Inter-University Centre in 1966.

Its objectives are:

- To promote and establish communication facilities to improve capability in information transfer and access, that provides support to scholarship, learning, research and academic pursuit through cooperation and involvement of agencies concerned.
- *To establish Inflibnet*: Information and Library Network a computer communication network for linking libraries and information centres in universities, deemed to be universities, colleges, UGC information centres, institutions of national importance and R&D institutions, etc. avoiding duplication of efforts.

Inflibnet performs following major activities:

- Provides grants to universities to automate the libraries, establishing the network facilities and create an information technology environment.

- Developed and distributed Software for University Libraries (Soul) which is an integrated userfriendly library management software. The latest version of the software is 2.0 which is competent to operate with the latest technologies and international standards such as MARC21, Unicode based and NCIP 2.0 based protocols for electronic surveillance and control.
- Indian Catalogue of University Libraries in India (IndCat) is Online Library Catalogue of books, theses and journals available in major university libraries in India which provides bibliographic description, location of the material in all subjects available in more than 112 university libraries. Thus, IndCat has over 10 million bibliographical records of books from more than 113 universities. In addition, the database of theses, expert databases, project databases and Sewakoffline database access facilities are also extended to the libraries of higher learning institutions.
- To enhance the skills of university library staff for implementation of Inflibnet programme, it conducts training programme for library staff, onsite training for member library staff, training on SOUL software, holding Caliber convention every year and workshops for senior level staff of the university libraries are conducted.
- It has brought out a document entitled 'Inflibnet Standards and Guideline for Data Capturing' prepared by a task force of experts based on Common Communication Format (CCF).

Another very important and significant landmark in the history of higher education and development of libraries in India is the establishment of "Ugcinfonet Digial Library Consortium" by the UGC on the concluding day of its Golden jubilee celebrations by his Excellency the then President of India, Dr. A.P.J Abdul Kalam at Vigyan Bhawan on 28th December 2003. UGC-Infonet is an innovative project launched by UGC to facilitate scholarly e-resources to Indian academies through joint partnership of UGC, Inflibnet and Ernet.

This includes interlinking of universities and colleges in the country electronically with a view to achieve maximum efficiency through Internet enabled teaching, learning and governance. The UGC-Infonet is overlaid on Ernet infrastructure in a manner so as to provide assured quality of service and optimum utilization of bandwidth resources. The network will be run and managed by Ernet India.

The project is funded by UGC with 100 per cent capital investment and up to 90 per cent of recurring costs. UGC and Ernet India have signed the necessary MoU for this purpose. A joint technical and tariff committee, has been setup to guide and monitor the design, implementation and operations of Ugcinfonet. Information for Library Network (Inflibnet) an autonomous Inter-University Centre of UGC, is the nodal agency for coordination and facilitation of the linkage between Ernet and the Universities. Under this programme, information and communication technologies (ICT) and internet will be used to transform learning environment from a monodimensional one to a multidimensional one. This was created to help and benefit more than 310 universities and about 14,000 colleges affiliated with these universities and approximately 10 million students with the e-journals, thus, is a boon to higher education system in many ways.

The UGC-Infonet digital Library consortium has the following objectives: Bhatt,

- To subscribe electronic resources for the members of the consortium at highly discounted rates of subscription and with the best terms and conditions.
- Promote the rational use of funds.
- Guarantee local storage of the information acquired for continuous use by present and future users.
- To impart training to the users, librarians, research scholars and faculty members of the institutions on the electronic resources with an aim to optimize the usage of the electronic resources.
- To have more interaction amongst the member libraries.
- To increase the research productivity of the institutions in terms of quality and quantity of publications
- Strategic alliance with institutions that have common interests resulting reduced information cost and improved resource sharing.

National Knowledge Commission

The National Knowledge Commission was set up by the Government of India on 13th June 2005 with a time-frame of three years, from 2nd October 2005 to 2nd October 2008. As a high-level advisory body to the Prime Minister of India, the National Knowledge Commission was given a mandate to guide policy and direct reforms, focusing on certain key areas such as education, science and technology, agriculture, industry, e-governance etc.

Easy access to knowledge, creation and preservation of knowledge systems, dissemination of knowledge and better knowledge services are core concerns of the Commission.

The Commission envisaged the future road map for the growth and development of academic libraries by imbibing core issues such as, set up a national commission on libraries, prepare a national census of all libraries, revamp LIS education, training and research facilities, re-assess staffing of libraries, set up a central library fund, modernize library management, encourage greater community participation in library management, promote information communication technology applications in all libraries, facilitate donation and maintenance of private collections, and encourage public private partnerships in LIS development, etc.

SARASWATHI MAHAL LIBRARY

Saraswathi Mahal Library is located in Thanjavur, Tamil Nadu, India. It is one of the oldest libraries in Asia, and has on display a rare collection of Palm leaf manuscripts and paper written in Tamil, Hindi, English, Telugu, Marathi, and a few other languages indigenous to India.

The collection comprises well over 60,000 volumes, though only a tiny fraction of these are on display. The library has a complete catalogue of holdings, which is being made available online. Some rare holdings can be viewed on site by prior arrangement.

HISTORY

The Saraswathi Mahal library started as a Royal Library for the private pleasure of the Nayak Kings of Thanjavur who ruled 1535-1675 AD. The Maratha rulers who captured Thanjavur in 1675 patronised local culture and further developed the Royal Palace Library until 1855. Most notable among the Maratha Kings was Serfoji II, who was an eminent scholar in many branches of learning and the arts.

In his early age Serfoji studied under the influence of the Dutch Reverend Schwartz, and learned many languages including English, French, Italian and Latin. He enthusiastically took special interest in the enrichment of the Library, employing many Pandits to collect, buy and copy a vast number of works from all renowned Centres of Sanskrit learning in Northern India and other far-flung areas.

Since 1918 the Saraswathi Mahal Library has been a possession of the state of Tamil Nadu. Its official name of the Library was changed to "The Thanjavur Maharaja Serfoji's Sarasvati Mahal Library" in honour of the great royal Marathan patron.

EFFORTS

The library is open to the public; it also supports efforts to publish rare manuscripts from the collection, as well as ensuring all volumes are preserved on microfilm. The Library has installed computers in 1998 for the Computerisation of Library activities. As a first phase, the Library catalogues are being stored in the Computer for easy information retrieval. It is also proposed to digitalise the manuscripts of this Library shortly.

THE COLLECTION

The bulk of the manuscripts (39,300) are in Sanskrit, written in scripts such as Grantha, Devanagari, Nandinagari, Telugu. Tamil manuscripts number over 3500, comprising titles in literature, music and medicine. The Library has a collection of 3076 Marathi manuscripts from the South Indian Maharastrian of the 17th, 18th, and 19th centuries; this includes the hierarchy of the Saints of Maharashtra belonging to Sri Ramadasi and Dattatreya Mutts. The Marathi manuscripts are mostly on paper but a few were written in Telugu script on palm-leaf. There are 846 Telugu manuscripts in the holdings, mostly on palm leaf. There are 22 Persian and Urdu manuscripts mostly of 19th century also within the collection.

Apart from these manuscripts there are 1342 bundles of Maratha Raj records available at the Library. The Raj records were written in the Modi script of the Marathi language. These records encompass the information of the political, cultural and social administration of the Maratha kings of Thanjavur.

SOME OF THE RARE BOOKS AND MANUSCRIPTS

- Dr. Samuel Johnson's dictionary published in 1784
- The pictorial Bible printed in Amsterdam in the year 1791
- The Madras Alamnac printed in 1807
- Lavoisier's *Traité Élémentaire de Chimie* ("Elements of Chemistry")
- The notes of Bishop Heber on Raja Serfoji II
- The correspondence letters of William Torin of London who purchased a lot of books for Raja Serfoji II and the Saraswathi Mahal Library
- The Globe used by the raja.
- Ancient maps of the world
- Town planning documents of Thanjavur including the underground drainage system, the fresh water supply ducting system
- Pictorial charts of the theory of evolution of man as evinced by Charles Le Brun

LIBRARY MUSEUM

A Museum is located in the Library building to reveal the importance of the Library to the Public. This Museum is small but organised into sections highlighting ancient Manuscripts, Illustrated Manuscripts, Printed copies of the Original Drawings, Atlases, Thanjavur-style Paper Paintings, Canvass Paintings, Wooden Paintings, Glass paintings, Portraits of the Thanjavur Maratha kings, and the Physiognomy charts of Charles Le-Brun. These materials give an idea of the total variety in the vast collection within the Library.

The Saraswati Library is situated within the campus of the Thanjavur Palace. Visitors can have a glimpse of preserved books and can sit and read in the library premises. Better preservation of books and facilities like air-conditioning with dehumidifiers, redesigning of space for comfortable reading, online catalogue facility should be taken up to preserve this internationally renowned treasure trove of books and palm-leaf manuscripts !

Efforts were made to microfilm and catalogue the contents way back in 1965 when Indira Gandhi was Information and Broadcasting Minister, Government of India who sanctioned the fund for the library's development.

Since then no efforts were made to scan the documents and computerise the same using present day technology. It is also a designated 'Manuscript Conservation Centre' (MCC) under the National Mission for Manuscripts established in 2003.

KHUDA BAKHSH ORIENTAL LIBRARY

Khuda Bakhsh Oriental Library is one of the national libraries of India. It was opened to public in October, 1891 by Khan Bahadur Khuda Bakhsh with 4,000 manuscripts, of which he inherited 1,400 from his father Maulvi Mohammed Bakhsh.

It is an autonomous organization under Ministry of Culture, Government of India, and is governed by a Board with the Governor of Bihar as its ex-officio Chairman. known for its rare collection of Persian and Arabic manuscripts. It also hosts paintings made during the Rajput and Mughal eras of India. It is also a designated 'Manuscript Conservation Centre' (MCC) under the National Mission for Manuscripts.

HISTORY

The library finds its origin in private collection of a bibliophile Mohammad Bakhsh and expanded by his son Khuda Bakhsh, who inherited 1,400 manuscripts and continued to add to the collection and eventually converted it into a private library by 1880.

The library was opened to public upon its inauguration by Sir Charles Elliot, Governor of Bengal on 5th October, 1891.

In 1969 through a Federal Legislation, an Act of Parliament, namely 'Khuda Bakhsh Oriental Public Library Act (1969), the Government of India declared Khuda Bakhsh Oriental Public Library a centre of national importance and government took over the funding, maintenance and development of the library. Today it continues to attract scholars from all over the world.

Past directors of the library have been Dr. Abid Reza Bedar, who after remaining with the Raza Library, came as Director to the institution in 1972, and did some important work towards reviving the library along with his successor Habibur Rehman Chighani, at present the Director of the library is the Dr. Imtiaz Ahmad, since February, 2004.

COLLECTION

Some of the notable manuscripts are *Timur Nama* (*Khandan—Timuria*), *Shah Nama*, *Padshah Nama*, *Diwan-e-Hafiz* and *Safinatul Auliya*, carrying the autograph of Mughal Emperors and princes and the book of Military Accounts of Maharaja Ranjit Singh. Apart of it the library also has specimens of Mughal paintings, calligraphy and book decoration and Arabic and Urdu manu-scripts, including a page of Quran written on deer skin.

BHANDARKAR ORIENTAL RESEARCH INSTITUTE

The Bhandarkar Oriental Research Institute (BORI) is located in Pune, Maharashtra, India. It was founded on July 6, 1917 to honour the life and work of Dr. Ramakrishna Gopal Bhandarkar (1837–1925), long regarded as the founder of Indology (Orientalism) in India. The institute is well known for its collection of old Sanskrit and Prakrit manuscripts.

THE INSTITUTE

This institute is of a public trust registered under Act XXI of 1860. Initially, the institute received an annual grant of 3000 Rupees from the Government of Bombay. Presently, it is partially supported by annual grants from the Government of Maharashtra.

The Institute also receives grants from the Government of India and the University Grants Commission for specific research projects.

The institute has one of the largest collections of rare books and manuscripts in South Asia, consisting of over 1,25,000 books and 29,510 manuscripts. The institute publishes a journal, *Annals of the Bhandarkar Oriental Research Institute* four times a year. The Institute also hosts the Manuscripts Resource and Conservation Centre under the auspices of the National Mission for Manuscripts, a project of the Ministry of Culture, Government of India. In 2007, the Rigveda manuscripts preserved at the Institute were included in UNESCO's Memory of the World Register.

THE MANUSCRIPT COLLECTION

The Government of Bombay, in 1866, started a pan Indian Manuscript Collection project. Noted scholars like George Bühler, F. Kielhorn, Peter Peterson, Ramkrishna Gopal Bhandarkar, S. R. Bhandarkar, Kathavate and Ghate collected more than 17,000 important manuscripts under this project. This collection was first deposited at Elphinstone College in Bombay.

Then it was transferred to Deccan College (Pune) for better preservation. After the Bhandarkar Oriental Research Institute was founded in 1917, the BORI founders proposed to offer even better preservation and research.

Hence Lord Willingdon, the then Governor of the Bombay Presidency and the first president of BORI, transferred the valuable Government collection of manuscripts to the BORI on April 1, 1918. The first curator, P.K. Gode took active initiatives to enhance this collection. Presently, the Institute has over 29,000 manuscripts.

The largest part of the collection (17,877 Manuscripts) is part of the "Government Manuscript Library", while there is an additional collection of 11,633 manuscripts also. The most prized collections include a paper manuscript of the Cikitsâsâra-sangraha dated 1320 and a palmleaf manuscript of the Upamiti-bhavapra-pañcakathâ dated 906. Among the several scholars referring to the works at BORI, the most well-known person arguably is the Bharat Ratna awardee, Pt. Pandurang Vaman Kane.

THE CRITICAL EDITION OF THE MAHABHARATA

A long term project under the auspices of BORI, started on April 1, 1919, was the preparation of a Critical Edition of the Mahabharata. V.S. Sukhtankar was appointed general editor of the project on August 1, 1925 and he continued until his death on January 21, 1943.

After his death, S.K. Belvalkar was appointed general editor on April 1, 1943. On April 1, 1961 P. L. Vaidya appointed as General Editor of the project on the retirement of S. K. Belvalkar. R. N. Dandekar appointed as the joint general editor on July 6, 1957. To widespread acclaim, the completion for publication was announced on September 22, 1966, by Dr. Sarvapalli Radhakrishnan, then President of India, at a special function held at the institute.

The Critical Edition was collated from 1,259 manuscripts. This edition in 19 volumes (more than 15000 demi-quarto size pages) comprised the critically constituted text of the 18 *Parvas* of the Mahabharata consisting of more than 89000 verses, an elaborate Critical Apparatus and a Prolegomena on the material and methodology.

Further work since the initial publication has produced a Critical Edition of the Harivamsa, a Pratika Index, a Bibliography of ancillary materials, and a Cultural Index. The project of preparing a critical edition of the Harivamsa was inaugurated by the President of India, Rajendra Prasad on November 19, 1954. The publication was completed in November, 1971.

The critical edition in two volumes consists the 4 *Parvan*s of the Harivamsa. The Pratika Index in 6 volumes consists 360000 verse quarters with appendices. Two volumes of the Cultural Index have been published so far. The constituted text of the critical edition has also been made available on the CD-ROM.

VANDALISM IN 2003

The institute was vandalized in December 2003 by a mob made up of members of an extremist self styled Maratha youth squad, calling themselves the Sambhaji Brigade, named after Shivaji's elder son. They claimed to be angered by the help provided by the institute's staff (in translating manuscripts) to a Western writer, Dr. James Laine, who discussed the telling and retelling of stories about Shivaji's parentage and life in his book on narrations of the Shivaji story.

The mob also damaged thousands of manuscripts and attacked Shrikant Bahulkar, a Sanskrit scholar who had only explained some Sanskrit references to Laine. The incident provoked widespread reaction and historian Gajanan Mehendale to destroy parts of his in-progress biography of Shivaji.

The vandalism and a ban on the book were denounced by historians who put their signatures to the statement include R.S. Sharma, R.C. Thakran, Suraj Bhan, Irfan Habib, D.N. Jha, Shireen Moosvi and K. M. Shrimali. Oxford University Press-publisher of James Laine's, 'Shivaji: Hindu king in Islamic India', withdrew the book after protests from Ninad Bedekar and other right-wing politicians as it contained allegedly objectionable statements about Shivaji.

ASIATIC SOCIETY LIBRARY

At present, the library of the Asiatic Society has a collection of about 1,17,000 books and 79,000 journals printed in almost all the major languages of the world. It has also a collection of 293 maps, microfische of 48,000 works, microfilm of 387,003 pages, 182 paintings, 2500 pamphlets and 2150 photographs. The earliest printed book preserved in this library is Juli Firmici's *Astronomicorum Libri* published in 1499. It has in its possession a large number of books printed in India in the late 18th and early 19th centuries. The library also possesses many rare and scarcely available books. The library has a rich collection of about 47,000 manuscripts in 26 scripts. The most notable amongst them are an illustrated manuscript of the *Qur'an*, a manuscript of the *Gulistan* text, and a manuscript of *Padshah Nama* bearing the signature of Emperor Shahjahan. The number of journals in thepossession of the library is about 80,000 at present. The early collection of this library was enriched by the contributions it received from its members. On March 25, 1784 the library received seven Persian manuscripts from Henri Richardson. The next contribution came from William Marsden, who donated his book, *History of Island of Sumatra* (1783) on November 10, 1784. Robert Home, the first Library-in-Charge (1804) donated his small but valuable collection of works on art.

The first accession of importance was a gift from the Seringapatam Committee on February 3, 1808 consisting of a collection from the Palace Library of Tipu Sultan. The library received the Surveyor-General Colonel Mackenzie's collection of manuscripts and drawings in December 1822.

MANUSCRIPT COLLECTION

Manuscript Collection of the society is varied and rich, and covers most of the Indian languages and scripts and even several Asian ones, *e.g.*, Assamese, Bengali, Gujarati, Gurumukhi, Kanarese, Urdu, Marathi, Modi, Nagari, Newari, Oriya, Rajasthani, Sarada, Armenian, Sinhalese, Arabic, Persian, Pushto, Javanese, Turki, Burmese, Chinese, Siamese, Tibetan etc. The materials used for the manuscripts are also varied: palm and palmyra leaves, barks of different trees, papers of various grades.

Sanskritic Manuscripts

The manuscripts cover the period from 7th c. A.D. down to the 19th century. These are useful source materials to illustrate the development of the Indian scripts (especially Bengali, Nagari etc.). The colophons and post-colophons contain information relating to socio-economic conditions of the people.

Besides, they help us to fix the chronology of the Royal dynasties of India. Where the inscriptions fail to ascertain dates and chronology, the manuscripts may throw some light, provided a thorough critical study of these and their colophons and postcolophons were made.

Some of the rare Sanskrit manuscripts may be mentioned here:

- Brihati,
- Amrita Vindu,
- Kiranavali,
- Charucharya,
- Nartaka Nirnaya,
- Parasika-prakasa,
- Sanskrita-ratnakara,
- Lalitavistara,
- Horoscope of a Muslim of the Mughal Court (1640 A.D.) A Deed of Mortgage (1639),
- Ramayana (Bengali) of Ramananda Yati,
- Vajrayana text (11th c.),
- A text on Buddhist Nyaya,
- Rigveda Padapatha,
- Laghu-Kalachakra-tika,
- Kalachakravetara,
- Kuttanimatam,
- Vajravalinama mannadalopayika,
- Ramacharita of Sandhyakar Nandi,
- Bhattikavyatika of Srinivasa, and
- Paragali Mahabharata.

The manuscript of Kubjikamatam is of the 7th Century A.D. The manuscript of Rigveda Padapatha, copied in 1362 A.D., is perhaps "the oldest manuscript of the Rigveda."

Islamic Section

Of the many Islamic Manuscripts there are some which are extremely rare and unique.

Of these only a few may be mentioned:

- Tahdhib Sharh As-Sab' at Mullaqat (early 12th c. Arabic),
- Qalaid al-Iquian wa Mahasin al-Ayan (12th c.),
- Kharidat al-Qasr (12th c.),
- Al-Jam Baynas as-Sahihin abridged version with autograph, (13th c.),
- A-Madkhul(13th c.),

- Tafsir-i-Quran (Persian, 13th c., important also for calligraphy),
- Tuhfat al-Ahbar fi usul at Hadith wa'l Akhbar (15th c.),
- Kitab al-I'lan (18th c.),
- Saha' if-i-Shara' if or Duraral Mansur (Persian, 19th c., an autographed copy), and
- Adab-i-Alamgiri (18th c.).

There are large numbers of illuminated and illustrated manu-scripts of different schools, many of which are unique for their calligraphy, delicacy of their lines, and elegance of composition and charming colour schemes.

These miniatures still afford glimpses of India's past achievements, Of these unique manuscripts (earliest belonging to the 10th Century A.D.) mention may be made of a few:

- Astasahasrika Prajnaparamita,
- Aparimitayurnama Mahayana sutra,
- Pancharaksha,
- Paramarthanama Sangati,
- Devimahatmya,
- Viveka Panchamrita,
- Bhagavatgita,
- Shahnama,
- Kullayat-i-Saadi,
- Suwaru'l aqalim,
- Farang-i-Aurang Shahi,
- Ain-i-Akbari,
- Diwan-i-Makhfi,
- Qissa-i-Nush-Afarin,
- Jamiut-Twarikh,
- Amir nama Tutinama,
- Iyar-i-Danesh,
- Bihar-i-Danesh,
- Tarjuma Mahabharata,
- Tafribul-Imarah (by Silchand, dedicated to J. H. Lushington), and
- Imaratut-Akbar (by Chitarmal for James Duncan).

Many scholars are using the collection for editing their texts and for translation in modern languages.

English Manuscripts

In the Library there are preserved a large number of old letters some of which date back to1784, just after the Society was founded. These letters were received by the Society from persons belonging to different walks of life, requesting information on such subjects as old and rare manuscripts, ancient monuments, coins etc.

Some among the writers of these letters were persons well known for their literary, scientific and other cultural accomp-lishments. These old files constitute important documents relating to the history of the Society, as also of many other scientific and humanistic organisations that were established in India either in the 19th or in the 20th century.

Urdu Manuscripts

The Society has a fine collection of about 234 Urdu manu-scripts many of which were received as a gift from the Fort William College.

Sino-Tibetan and Burmese Manuscripts

The Society has a complete set of Kanjur and Tanjur texts of the Buddhist scriptures and some extra-canonical works. These were collected by B. H. Hodgson and A. Csoma de koros. A section of the collection has been catalogued. There are over one hundred titles of Chinese books, some of which are rare and valuable for Chinese studies.

These cover almost all the subjects relating to Chinese Culture, Civilization and Science and Buddhism. Subjects covered include Classical Literature, Language. History, Geography, Topography, Philosophy, Religion, manners and customs, biography of scholars, sciences (Botanical, Astronimical, Zoological).

The Society has a valuable collection of about 162 Burmese manuscript written on parabaikes and palm leaf. The manuscripts deal with Buddhistic texts, Religion, History of the world and also of Burmja and Arakan, works on Gramour (including that of kaccayana) and Rhetoric, Buddhist cosmography, Astrology, Medicine etc.

Bengali Manuscripts

Other than Sanskrit, a few Bengali manuscripts have been found written by Bengali Brahmins residing in Varanasi. Parageli Mahabharat, Chuti Khan's Asvamedha Parva, and many other important manuscripts were purchased. Mss. donated by Justice Ramaprosad Mukherjee and Sri A Roy enriched the collection.

The society has 703 Bengali and 12 Assamese manuscripts in the collection. It comprises Asiatic Society's own collection, Government collection, Indian Museum collection and donors' collection. At present, the collection of Bengali manuscripts in the possession of Asiatic Society is rich in respect of number and rarity. The Society has manuscripts on Ramayana, Mahabharata, Srimadbhagavat, Mangala Kavyas, treatises on Vaisnava faith and its allied subjects. Folk literature, erotic verses and Vaisnaba Sahajiya Cult etc.

Rajasthani Manuscripts

The Society possesses very rare, valuable and important Rajasthani Manuscripts which date the pre-middle and middle years. The Society prepared and brought out a descriptive catalogue of Rajasthani manuscripts comprising 636 manuscripts.

RARE BOOK DIVISION

In 1978 the Council decided to open a Rare Book Division. The preliminarhy screening of the collection has since been started.

Among the earliest printed books mention may be made of the following:

- Julii Firmici Astronomicorum libri octo integri (Venice 1499),
- Kitabal-Qanum (Arabic/Romae 1595),
- Kripar Sstrer Arthabhed (Bengali in Roman Character, Kisbon 1743);
- S. Purchas's Purchas: His Pilgrimage (London, 1 61 4),
- N. Halhed's Grammar of the Bengal Language, (Hooghly, 1778),
- Malabar and English Dictionary, (Madras, 1779),
- Rasamanjari (Sanskrit, Banaras, 1791),
- Ram Ram Bose's Lipimala (Bengali, Serampore, 1802),
- The Ramayana 3 vols, (Bengali, Serampore, 1803),
- Hitopadesa (Sanskrit, Serampore, 1804),
- Colebrooke's Grammar of the Sanskrit language vol. 1 (Serampore, 1805).

2

The Functions in the University and its Library

RESOURCE SHARING

The sharing is a need-based activity framed around the age-old concept of give and take. In general it is as old as the civilization. In "the field of libraries we might trace the history of resource sharing since their inception in various forms *viz.*, shared cataloguing, library cooperation, interlibrary loan and union catalogue etc.

The term library resources include any and all of the materials, functions and services, which constitute a modern library system. It is amalgamation of people, processes, ideas, materials and money which forms the substance of a library and can be described as its resources.

Resource sharing is a sort of implied agreement amongst participating libraries wherein each participant willing to share its resource to other members and in turn are privileged to share the resources of its partners as and when the need arises.

At present time when the Computer and Communication Technology has gained the central role in all walks of life and drastically changed the way people think, communicate and do business, it became indispensable to computerise and network the libraries just to survive.

The entrance of these new technologies in library premises rescheduled the functioning of libraries and provided a new dynamic shape to the age-old concept of resource sharing. Lack of effective and efficient technology has been a major hurdle for resource sharing in India, besides the lack of co-operation among the participating libraries.

Now by the use of Information Technology, it became possible to create co-operative functional resource sharing library-network which is the—most important requirement at this juncture where the economic consideration, information explosion and specialized users needs are forcing the libraries to co-operate.

RESOURCE SHARING: NEED OF THE TIME

The increased growth, use and value of information generated the concept of information society or information oriented society. If we analyse the situation from invention of printing press to Internet, we find that the complete civilization is moving from generalisation to specialisation, whether it is growth and nature of subject, commodities or services.

In this era of specialization, the efficiency and efficacy of libraries will be measured by the services provided by them not by the physical collection they have. In this situation the sharing of the resources only may provide the variety of new information services, because in this era it is not possible for any library to accommodate the universe of knowledge physically within the library boundaries.

So the resource sharing became the need of the time to fulfill the ever-specialized user's information needs in cost effective manner as the main objectives of resource sharing are:

- Reduction in all round cast.
- Avoidance of unnecessary duplication of information materials and efforts.
- Possibility of developing specialised activities specifi-cally concentrating on some particular area. Maximum accessibility to information without losing the individual identity of libraries.

At present, specifically in case of Indian academic libraries, which are planning and going to adopt the Information Technology, the resource sharing is needed for:

- Retrospective conversion of their bibliographical data to electronic form.
  - To help less equipped libraries.
  - To reudce the cataloguing cost.
  - To share the valuable resources
  - Documents and information.
  - Technical expertise.
  - To decentralise information.
  - To boost the distance learning and more.

PROBLEMS, PROSPECTS AND PREREQUISITES

If we look at the usefulness and strength of resource sharing among libraries, we find a very enthusiastic picture, but on the other hand when we analyse the ground realities of the present situation of our academic institutions and libraries, it seems worthless to talk about these services and activities. We have to accept the realities to reform them as soon as possible, because the growth of IT will not leave space to do anything after some years.

The major problems to be eliminated before may be identified as:

- The required technology and needed organisational structures are not presently available to provide the required level of service, comparable to that available today without the concept of resource sharing.
- Resource sharing will effect the economics of publishing by increasing unit pricing as library orders decline. A substantial part of the prospective saving from resource sharing will thus evaporate.
- A large library may become more and more of a lender of materials, causing resource sharing to be a drain rather than a source of additional material.
- If all libraries turn to resource sharing, none will acquire sufficiently and have books to lend.

In spite of these lacunae we have started to move in the direction. At this stage it is essential to develop some sort arrangements to stream line the movement. Followings might be recognized the prerequisites of a functional resource sharing system.,

Infrastructure

It includes the installation of required hardware and software to create bibliographical, contents pages, abstracts and full text electronic databases and their networking. It is also needed to create various union catalogues and to develop efficient software to handle on-line users query. In addition to thcsc a sound document delivery system could also be needed to send the required information to its end user.

In nut shelta library wants to be part of resource sharing network should have to have computers, printers, modem, scanners, database creation and networking software of specified standards, telephone connectivity, network access, photocopying machines, fax and a reliable postal system. The cost effectiveness of resource sharing is diminished at the present, because it has to run in parallel with other running system.

Common Code of Conduct

Apart from similar software and networking protocols the participating libraries have to evolve a common code of conduct regarding the collection development and resource sharing. There are several basic agreements among libraries that must be developed to operate a co-operative resource-sharing network.

It includes:

- Agreement to share currently owned materials will protocols, limitations and priorities.
- Financial agreement, to safeguard the individual recognition of the libraries.

- Agreement on acquisition policies to ensure consistent development of holdings and to avoid redundancy.
- Agreement of record keeping to streamline and to ensure the smooth operations from acquisition to borrowing and lending.

Legal Copyright and Photo Copying Laws

It is noticeable that the resource sharing activities should violate the copyright and photocopying laws.

Trained Manpower

The establishment and organisation of resource sharing activities are not possible with out the competent, trained and dedicated manpower. At present it is needed to organise massive education and training programmes via different modes to fulfil the required need.

Aware Users

The user is the most important component of any system. Keeping in view this fact, participating libraries and nodal agency simultaneously have to develop and organise user education/orientation programmes in changing context, to ensure the maximum utilizations of the resource sharing activities.

In addition to above said prerequisites it is essential to adopt some professional ethics to run the system smoothly. There is no procedure to impose this idea on participating libraries, but it is worth noticeable that in future only those libraries will survive whose professionals will be guided by this idea.

CHARACTERISTICS OF A NETWORKED LIBRARY RESOURCE SHARING SYSTEM

Where there is a system there must be its users. The satisfaction of users should be the criteria to measure the effectiveness of the system. A sound library resource sharing system, whether it is automatic or manual should have following characteristics. These characteristics should be kept in mind to establish or remodel the networked system.

These checkpoints are also useful to measure the effectiveness of the existing resource sharing system:

- *Speed*: The resource sharing system should be speedy. It should be based on the latest means of data communication systems and programmes. It should be able to judge tile timeliness and urgency of user's information need, because the use of information depends on whether it is provided at right time or not.
- *Accuracy*: The resource sharing system should be able to locate and provide the accurate information. It should be reliable and error free.
- *Cost/Fee:* The information provided should be cost effective. It must be less than the original cost of document.

- *Staff Courtesy/Knowledge/Assistance:* The professionals engaged in the resource sharing activities should be knowledgeable and prompt to handle the queries. The speed and accuracy of manual resource sharing system depends on these professionals.
- *Consistency of Service and Reliability:* It must be consistent and reliable. The resource sharing activity should be adopted as an important component of present library system.
- *Communication (Provision for Status Reports):* The union catalogues should be able to provide the status report regarding availability of the document.
- *Delivery and Request Options:* The resource center should be able to deliver the needed document! information through required mode of delivery *i.e.* via e-mail, fax, courier or by post.
- *Self-service Options:* It will be easy to use, so that user can handle it without any problem. These character-istics should be considered as guiding principals to establish a new resource sharing system and to measure the efficiency and efficacy of existing one.

LIBRARY NETWORKING

The world has been witnessing a knowledge and infor-mation explosion during the past few decades. Over 10 million journal articles are published every year besides news items, editorials and articles that are appearing in popular print media. Information professionals who would be the leaders in the twenty-first century depend on information for their work.

Access to information holds the key to development. Libraries which are store houses of knowledge and information, and information centers which disseminate knowledge and information, form two important components of present day society.

While there is a deluge of information on one hand, the cost of collecting, processing, storing and disseminating information has been spiraling up on the other hand. This calls for heavy budgets for libraries even to maintain a reasonable level of acquisition of journals, books and reports. Estimates show that a three to fourfold rise in library budgets will be needed by AD 2000 to maintain the same acquisition level as in 1990.

Information buying power of libraries has been declining year after year. Because of this, resource sharing and cooperative functioning through networking have become inescapable for libraries and information centres worldwide. India is no exception; for that matter, it is even more necessary to network libraries in newly developing countries like India than in the developed nations.

Efficient resource sharing can be achieved by using the recent advances in information technology for realising a network of libraries. Information technology signifies the coming together of the disciplines of electronics, computer hardware and software, communications, artificial intelligence and human/machine interface.

During the last six to seven years, library and information activities in the country have entered a new era. Individual libraries are coming out of the proverbial "Berlin Wall"around them. They are trying to form a larger community in an effort to tackle the ever increasing demands for better services, quantitatively and qualitatively, in an environment already over strained by financial pressures. Forced, motivated, or logic driven, the librarians are coming out of their shell in large numbers.

This has resulted in discernible change in the information scenario. Now a large number of library resource sharing networks like the Metropolitan Area Networks, such as Calibnet (Calcutta), Delnet (Delhi), Bonet (Bombay), Punenet (Pune), Malibnet (Madras), Mylibnet (Mysore), Hylibnet (Hyderabad), Adne (Ahmedabad), and countrywide ones like ERNET (Educational and Research Institutions), Sirnet (CSIR Laboratories), Inflibnet (Universities and Research Institutions) and Desinet (Defence Laboratories), and sectoral ones like BTISNET (Biotechnology) and TIFACLINE (Technology *per se*) are under various stages of conceptualization, design and development.

A host of agencies, like the National Information System for Science and Technology (NISSAT), Dept. of Electronics, INSDOC/CSIR, DESIDOC/DRDO, DBT, NIC, and TIFAC/DST, are involved. Looking from the participant's side, it is common to find an institution participating in more than one network.

The ultimate goal of information/library networks is to interlink information resources in a metropolitan area, so that that users could access information irrespective of its location, format, medium, language, script etc.

Further, the development of such networks requires actions in several areas such as training, rationalization of information resource acquisition, diffusion of standards, preparation of union lists, generation of database services apart from setting up hardware, software and communication facilities. The concept of library networking to aid information resource sharing and support activities in libraries has become a real necessity.

The shortcomings observed are mainly related to two aspects:

- Non-availability of materials and services, and
- Efficient administrative control.

In India, the need for resource sharing has been well recognized but the technology options available until now were limited. NISSAT has taken up networking of libraries in Calcutta (Calibnet), Delhi (Delnet), Madras (Malibnet), Mysore (Mylibnet), Hyderabad (Hylibnet), Ahmedabad (Adnet), Pune (Punenet), and Bombay (Bonet). The present study highlights only some of the major library networks in India. Towards library networking activities in India NISSAT has taken the initiative for promoting resource sharing activities. These initiatives are aimed at ensuring better utilization of science and technology information resources, minimization of functional load of information centres and encouragement of motivational factors to a large extent by better means of communication.

NISSAT only goes to the extent of setting up general infrastructural facilities like network service centres including hardware, software, manpower and other organizational requirements, communication facilities etc. With a change in the development and implementation strategy, the participating institutions in a network are to arrange their own terminal hardware, software, manpower and data conversion.

DELNET

The limitation of financial resources and space for housing library collections in the libraries in Delhi led to the promotion of sharing of resources by automation and networking and establishment of the Delnet in 1988. NISSAT took the initiative in setting up Delnet. It has emerged as an important resource centre for the libraries in Delhi.

In Delhi the libraries have been growing very fast in number and site during the last four decades. They cater to specialized and general clientele and are of various types which include institutional libraries, research libraries, government libraries, public libraries, departmental libraries and libraries of the universities, colleges and schools. During the recent years, cumulative information has been increasing at a very fast pace and with it the increase in demands of the users. It has been noticed that in the era of information explosion the libraries in India are generally ill equipped to handle and retrieve information effectively.

The financial resources and the space for housing library collections are limited in almost all of the libraries. The option left with the forward looking librarians has been to promote the sharing of resources by automation and networking. Initially, 40 libraries were directly linked to the DELNET host system through e-mail to promote library mailing, interlibrary requests, transfer of files, exchange of messages, interlibrary services, etc. Side by side with the automation of participating libraries, the functions and services have also started.

Presently about 90 libraries are members of DELNET. Almost all participating libraries are now computerized by means of acquisition and fund accounting, cataloguing, circulation, serials control and local users services. Users are able to locate books and serials through Online Public Access Catalogue (OPAC). A union catalogue of current periodicals available in Delhi libraries, and a union list of current serials available in Indian libraries are available on online for Delnet participant libraries. A central database of Delnet has been created and made operational. This central database includes the library holdings of Delnet member libraries used as union catalogues of books/

monographs. Delnet provides access to the central union catalogue for books and monographs, efficient electronic mailing facilities to access databases of member libraries. It also proposes to develop a network for accessing CD–ROM databases available at member libraries in the near future. Delnet also provides CAS and SDI services, consultancy in library computerization, training and H.R.D. and assistance to libraries on standardization, local automation, retrospective conversion etc. Delnet is likely to emerge as a co–operative network incorporating all disciplines of science, technology, social sciences and humanities.

CALIBNET

The Calcutta Library Network (CALIBNET) was inaugurated on 21 December 1993. NISSAT, Department of Scientific and Industrial Research (DSIR), Government. of India, took the initiative in setting up CALIBNET, which has adopted a two way system for networking:

- The networking route with a library automation and networking through its own application software "Maitrayee" and
- The e-mail route connecting member libraries with on-line access to various databases within network and Internet access.

Calibnet established a high-tech resource base and provides the following services:

- Online/CDROM based global information search and retrieval services
- Full-text document delivery
- Database services

MALIBNET

The need for interconnecting libraries and information centres in Madras was visualized in the Indian National Scientific Documentation Centre (INSDOC) in 1991. Initially six major academic institutions were directly linked to the Malibnet host system. Two important databases have been created utilising the resources available in Madras libraries. One is a Directory Database of Current Serials in Madras covering 30 libraries, and the other is a Contents Database covering articles published in 300 journals available in Madras libraries.

Both these databases are continuously updated and also expanded. They are available for online-access to any user and the information is also supplied in diskettes and hard copy. Photocopies of articles from member libraries can be supplied within two days. Madras has about 60 important libraries besides information centres like INSDOC. About 15 of these libraries have a holding of well over 100,000 items. These libraries act as good resource centres on the network. As of December 1993, all the 60 libraries together invest about Rupees 8,000,000 on acquiring journals and books every year.

It is estimated that 40% of the information acquired is redundant. With the libraries networked and resource sharing implemented, each user on the network can get access to a vast amount of literature, and redundancy can be brought down significantly. A novel and unique feature of Malibnet is that the members will be permitted to offer their own innovative information services on the network. A membership in MALIBNET is open to universities, colleges, R&D institutions, industries and individuals.

Malibnet presently offers the following information services:

- Current serials acquired in about 60 libraries
- Full journal holdings of about 60 libraries
- Contents information of about 500 important journals
- Electronic mail including internet connectivity
- Door delivery system for document photocopies
- It also offers access to about 1000 international databases

MYLIBNET

It is the first library network established in a small city. The launching of MYLIBNET in association with Mysore city library consortium (MCLC) took place on 12th June 1995. There are 16 institutional members. The holding list of Mysore city libraries has been computerised and software has been developed to enable users to access the catalogue and information on-line. Mylibnet provides e-mail facilities to its members.

BONET

The Bombay Library Network (Bonet) was setup at the National Centre for Software Technology (NCST), Bombay, on 6 November 1992. The Network is sponsored by NISSAT. The aim of Bonet is to build a low cost library information system which can possibly be used as a model for future expansion of this service even outside Bombay.

Bonet also benefits significantly from the experience gained, and facilities created, by the Education and Research Networking (ERNET) project of the Department of Electronics, Govt. of India, assisted by the United Nations Development Programme (UNDP). Bonet is aimed at promoting cooperation between libraries in Bombay.

The focus is on inter-library activities, rather than on computerizing individual libraries, which will no doubt computerize their own operations and are likely to share their experiences with each other. Bonet offers training related to library computerization and networking, and speed up computerization of Bombay libraries. Bonet membership provides for access to its centralised catalogues and for E-mail among Bonet members. However, access to library related services outside Bombay in India and abroad would require use of ERNET.

The services offered through Bonet include the following:

- Consultation on standards
- Organized training for selected staff of participating libraries
- On-line catalogue of periodicals for the region
- On-line catalogue of books for the region
- On-line catalogue of preprints/reprints
- Inter-library lending of books and periodicals
- Inter-library request for photocopying
- Computer network support for book ordering
- Information retrieval services
- On-line document delivery of items (such as technical reports) made available by participating libraries in machine readable form
- On-line access to foreign databases, subject to the user's willingness to pay the costs incurred
- E-mail interface for inter–library queries
- E-mail facilities to order reprints from abroad, when necessary
- Dissemination of information, on new books etc, using E–mail, Bulletin boards, and SDI techniques
- Courier service for inter–library exchange of materials

Under Bonet the following databases were created:

- 25,000 items in a bibliographic database on computers and software technology
- Union catalogue of journals and other periodicals in libraries in the region
- Tables of contents of 250 Indian periodicals created by the national centre for information
- •• A number of CDROM databases have been mounted on a Novell Server for use to members

PUNENET

Presently, 30 libraries and 15 professionals from Pune city are accessing the Punenet through modem. The users not only access Punenet data, but also use the e-mail and internet facilities.

Following databases are available on Punenet for its members:

- Catalogues of holding of all member libraries
- Union catalogue of current periodicals in Pune libraries and information centres
- Publishers and book sellers database
- Database on international grants and fellowships in the health sciences
- Hard databanks in biotechnology
- Access to NICNET and databases available on NICNET *e.g.*, MEDLANS,AIDS database, US patent database

- Access to internet and various databases available on internet
- Patent information
- Union catalogue of books available in British libraries in India

ADINET

Ahmedabad Library Network (ADINET) was formally inaugurated in February 1995 when a memorandum of under-standing was signed between NISSAT and ADINET at Ahmedabad. ADINET has ten institutional members, five associate institutional members and two professional members. A centralized database has been created at ADINET which contains institute master, journal master and book databases. It also organized six work and training programmes. ADINET provided e-mail connectivity to 30 libraries of Ahmedabad.

INFLIBNET

Information and Library Network (INFLIBNET), a programme of the University Grants Commission, was launched in May 1991. The main aim of INFLIBNET is to establish a national computer-communication network to link libraries and information centres in universities, colleges, universities, UGC information centres, institutions of national importance, R&D institutions, etc., and thereby improve capability in information handling and services.

It is a programme for academic excellence to be achieved through establishment of a mechanism for information transfer and access to support scholarship and academic work. It facilitates pooling, sharing and optimization of scarce library resources in the country. As a major programme it helps modernize libraries and information centres in the country through application of information technology.

The National Centre of INFLIBNET is located in Gujarat University campus at Ahmedabad. At present, INFLIBNET aims at computerizing and networking of university/college libraries. Every year, INFLIBNET programme is identifying a number of university libraries for automation depending on the budget allocation. The selected institutions are given funds for procuring computer systems, retroconversion and networking. Application software for data entry and other library functions, library standards and formats, etc., are provided by INFLIBNET to the participating libraries.

Manpower development is an important part of the programme. Training courses for core library staff engaged in computerised library operations, have been conducted since 1992-93.

Development of suitable software, standards for various library operations and communication based services (*e.g.*, e-mail, bulletin boards) designing suitable network architecture and preparation of union catalogues of serials, books, non-book materials, and cooperation with other networking organisations like NISSAT, NICNET, etc., are other important activities.

Objectives of INFLIBNET

INFLIBNET is an autonomous institution and aims to provide a channel to the academicians and researchers for exchange of information from sources within the country and abroad:

- Modernize libraries/information centres in India
- Mechanization for information transfer and access
- Facilitate pooling, sharing and optimization of library resources
- Organize library services at macro level
- Speedy and efficient services to end users
- Promoting equity

The ultimate aim is to provide the end-users a mechanism for sharing and using information resources and for exploiting modern information technology.

Functions of INFLIBNET

- Aims to establish a nation-wide network for computer communication linking academic libraries and information
- Aims to establish a mechanism for information transfer and access to support scholarship and academic work
- Aims to organize library services at macro levels at affordable cost and maximise benefits providing speedy and efficient services to end users.
- Will include participants from colleges, universities, R&D institutes, institutes of higher learning, informa-tion centres, institutes of national importance and document resource centres
- Covers all disciplines such as science, technology, medicine, agriculture, fine arts, humanities, social science
- Will provide networking to members using available communication infrastructure in the country.

PROFESSIONAL ASSOCIATIONS IN LIBRARY AND INFORMATION SCIENCE

INDIAN LIBRARY ASSOCIATION (ILA)

Indian Library Association (ILA) was established on September 13, 1933, on the occasion of the First All India Library Conference held at Calcutta (now Kolkata). The ILA is the largest and renowned professional body in the field of Library and Information Science in India with a membership of more than 7000.

The main objectives of the Association are:

- Promoting library movement in the country,
- Developing Library and Information Science education,
- Training and research, betterment of library personnel,
- Cooperation at the national and international levels,

- Promotion of standards, norms, services and guide-lines, and
- Providing a forum for professionals and publication of materials.

INDIAN ASSOCIATION OF SPECIAL LIBRARIES AND INFORMATION CENTRES (IASLIC)

The IASLIC, acronym for the Indian Association of Special Libraries and Information Centres, was established on 3 September 1955 as a non-profit making national, professional body to:

- Promote the quality of Library and Information Services
- Foster mutual cooperation and assistance among the special libraries, scientific, technological and research institutions, learned societies, commercial organiza-tions, industrial research establishments as well as centres of studies in social sciences and humanities
- Improve the technical efficiency of the professionals
- Act as a centre of research and studies in special librarianship and documentation techniques
- Act as a centre of information in scientific, technical and other related fields of LIS in pursuance of the aforesaid objects.

INDIAN ASSOCIATION OF TEACHERS OF LIBRARY AND INFORMATION SCIENCE (IATLIS)

The idea of founding an association of library science teachers was floated at the Unesco Regional Seminar held at the University of Delhi in October 1960 and later on discussed at the following three seminars:

- All India Seminar on Education for Librarianship held at Banaras Hindu University (1963),
- All India Seminar on Education for Librarianship held at SNDT Women's University (1965), and
- All India Seminar on Teaching of Library Science held at Delhi University (1966). To elicit the opinion from teachers in library schools, a circular was issued by Prof Bashiruddin in collaboration with the late Prof. Das Gupta and P.N.Kaula from the Rajasthan School. At the Delhi Seminar in 1966, the same issue was reviewed but without yielding any result.

Mr *Derek Langridge*, principal lecturer, North Western Polytechnic School (England) delivered Sarada Ranganathan Endowment Lectures at DRTC, Bangalore on 'Teaching of Library Classification' from 15-19 December 1969. This provided a fortuitous opportunity to discuss the issue of having an organization for teachers of Library Science.

FORMATION OF THE ORGANIZATION

On 19th December 1969, a meeting of the teachers of library science attending the Sarada Ranganathan Endowment Lectures was convened by Mr.

P. N. Kaula at DRTC with Mr. C. K. Langridge in the chair. This was attended by teachers from several Library schools.

Dr. D. B. Krishna Rao asked Mr. P.N. Kaula to give his opening Address stating the purpose of the meeting. Mr. P. N. Kaula described the structure of Library education in the country and the need for having an association of teachers of Library science.He also stated the efforts made in the past and the interest shown by the teachers at the seminar.

Dr. D. B. Krishna Rao declared that the Indian Association of Teachers of library science be formed with an ad-hoc committee constituted for this purpose. Mr. Ganesh Bhattacharya proposed a vote of thanks. In the end a Committee was formed with Dr. D. B. Krishna Rao as its Chairman and Mr. P. N. Kaula as the Secretary.

Thus was born the Indian Association of the Teachers of Library and Information Science (IATLIS) a national professional organization to further the cause of library education in India. The General Body meeting of IATLIS was held on 21st December 1970 to adopt the draft constitution circulated to members earlier with Mr. P. B. Roy in the chair. The constitution was discussed and adopted unanimously.

THE REVIVAL

After the foundation meeting in 1969, the first 'National Seminar' was held in 1970 at DRTC, Bangalore with the blessings of Dr Ranganathan and dynamic leadership of Prof P.N.Kaula. Dr D.B.Krishna Rao, Padmasri Bashiruddin, Prof A.Neela-meghan, Prof M.R.Kumbar played a key role in the formative years of the Association.

However, the Association was remained dormant from 1973-80. In March 1980, Prof Kaula conducted an All India Seminar on Relevance of LIS Education to the changing needs of the country at BHU. At this Seminar IATLIS was revived with Prof Kaula as President and Prof Kumar as General Secretary. Since 1981 it was active once again and IATLIS Communication and several other activities were initiated by Prof Kumar. National Seminars are being conducted regularly since 1986.

AIMS AND OBJECTIVES

To promote exchange of ideas on education in library and information science, To promote research in education in library and information science, To promote the publication of books and periodicals on education in library and information science.

To hold conferences, seminars, and colloquia for the development and propagation of ideas on education in library and information science, to give consultation service on education in library and information science, to promote training of the teachers of library and information science in India, and to promote welfare of teachers of library and information science in India.

AMERICAN LIBRARY ASSOCIATION (ALA)

The American Library Association (ALA) is a non-profit organization based in the United States that promotes libraries and library education internationally. It is the oldest and largest library association in the world, with more than 62,000 members.

Founded by Justin Winsor, Charles Ammi Cutter, Samuel S. Green, James L. Whitney, Melvil Dewey (Melvil Dui), Fred B. Perkins and Thomas W. Bicknell in 1876 in Philadelphia and chartered in 1879 in Massachusetts, its head office is now in Chicago.

During the Centennial Exposition in Philadelphia in 1876, 103 librarians, 90 men and 13 women, responded to a call for a "Convention of Librarians" to be held October 4–6 at the Historical Society of Pennsylvania. At the end of the meeting, "the register was passed around for all to sign who wished to become charter members," making October 6, 1876 to be ALA's birthday.

In attendance were 90 men and 13 women, among them Justin Winsor (Boston Public, Harvard), William Frederick Poole (Chicago Public, Newberry), Charles Ammi Cutter (Boston Athenaeum), Melvil Dewey, and Richard Rogers Bowker. Attendees came from as far west as Chicago and from England.

The aim of the Association, in that resolution, was "to enable librarians to do their present work more easily and at less expense." The Association has worked throughout its history to define, extend, protect and advocate for equity of access to information.

Library activists in the 1930s pressured the American Library Association to be more responsive to issues put forth by young members involved with issues such as peace, segregation, library unions and intellectual freedom. In 1931, the Junior Members Round Table (JMRT) was formed to provide a voice for the younger members of the ALA, but much of what they had to say resurfaced in the social responsibility movement to come years later.

During this period, the first Library Bill of Rights (LBR) was drafted by Forrest Spaulding to set a standard against censorship and was adopted by the ALA in 1939. This has been recognized as the moment defining modern librarianship as a profession committed to intellectual freedom and the right to read over government dictates. The ALA formed the Staff Organization's Round Table in 1936 and the Library Unions Round Table in 1940.

The ALA appointed a committee to study censorship and recommend policy after the banning of *The Grapes of Wrath* and the implementation of the LBR. The committee reported in 1940 that intellectual freedom and professionalism were linked and recommended a permanent committee – Committee on Intellectual Freedom.

The ALA made revisions to strengthen the LBR in June 1948, approved the Statement on Labeling in 1951 to discourage labeling material as subversive, and adopted the Freedom to Read Statement and the Overseas Library Statement in 1953.

In 1961, the ALA took a stand regarding service to African Americans and others, advocating for equal library service for all. An amendment was passed to the LBR in 1961 that made clear that an individual's library use should not be denied or abridged because of race, religion, national origin, or political views. Some communities decided to close their doors rather than desegregate. In 1963, the ALA commissioned a study, *Access to Public Libraries*, which found direct and indirect discrimination in American libraries.

In 1967 some librarians protested against a pro-Vietnam War speech given by General Maxwell D. Taylor at the annual ALA conference in San Francisco; the former president of Sarah Lawrence College, Harold Taylor, spoke to the Middle-Atlantic Regional Library Conference about socially responsible professionalism; and less than one year later a group of librarians proposed that the ALA schedule a new round table programme discussion on the social responsibilities of librarians at its next annual conference in Kansas City.

This group called themselves the Organizing Committee for the ALA Round Table on Social Responsibilities of Libraries. This group drew in many other under-represented groups in the ALA who lacked power, including the Congress for Change in 1969. This formation of the committee was approved in 1969 and would change its name to the *Social Responsibilities Round Table (SRRT) in 1971*.

After its inception, the Round Table of Social Responsi-bilities began to press ALA leadership to address issues such as library unions, working conditions, wages, and intellectual freedom. The Freedom to Read Foundation was created by ALA's Executive Board in 1969. The Black Caucus of the ALA and the Office for Literacy and Outreach were set up in 1970. In June 1990, the ALA approved "Policy on Library Services to the Poor" and in 1996 the Task Force on Hunger Homelessness, and Poverty was formed to resurrect and promote the ALA guidelines on library services to the poor. The ALA archival materials, non-current records, are currently held in the University of Illinois archives. These materials can only be used at the University of Illinois.

MEMBERSHIP

ALA membership is open to any person or organization, though most of its members are libraries or librarians. Most members live and work in the United States, with international members comprising 3.5% of total membership.

GOVERNING STRUCTURE

The ALA is governed by an elected council and an executive board. Since 2002,Keith Michael Fiels has been the ALA executive director (CEO). Policies and programmes are administered by various committees and round tables.

One of the organization's most visible tasks is overseen by the Office for Accreditation, which formally reviews and authorizes American and Canadian academic institutions that offer degree programmes in library and information science.

The ALA's current President is Molly Raphael (2011-2012). Notable past presidents of the ALA include Theresa Elmendorf, its first female president (1911–1912), Clara Stanton Jones, its first African-American president (1976-1977), Loriene Roy, its first Native American president (2007-2008), Michael Gorman (2005-6), and Roberta Stevens..

Activities

The official purpose of the association is "to promote library service and librarianship." Members may join one or more of eleven membership divisions that deal with specialized topics such as academic, school, or public libraries, technical or reference services, and library administration. Members may also join any of seventeen round tables that are grouped around more specific interests and issues than the broader set of ALA divisions.

Notable Divisions

- ALA Editions (book publishing)
- American Association of School Librarians (AASL)
- Association for Library Collections and Technical Services (ALCTS)
- Association for Library Service to Children (ALSC)
- Association of College and Research Libraries (ACRL)
- Library Information Technology Association (LITA)
- Public Library Association (PLA)
- Reference and User Services Association (RUSA)
- Young Adult Library Services Association (YALSA).

Notable Offices

- Office of Intellectual Freedom (OIF)
- Office for Accreditation (OA)
- Office for Literacy and Outreach Services (OLOS)
- Office for Information Technology Policy (OITP).

Notable Sub-organizations

In 1970, the ALA founded the first lesbian, gay, bisexual and transgender professional organization, called the "Task Force on Gay Liberation", now known as the GLBT Round Table. On July 23rd, 1976, the Committee on the Status of Women in Librarian-ship was established as a Council Committee of the ALA on recommendation of the Ad Hoc Committee with the same name (which had been appointed by the President of the ALA in December of 1975) and of the Committee on Organization.

The Committee on the Status of Women in Librarianship works to "officially represent the diversity of women's interest within ALA and to ensure that the Association considers the rights of the majority (women) in the library field; to promote and initiate the collection, analysis, dissemination, and coordination of information on the status of women in librarianship; to coordinate the activities of ALA units which consider questions of special relevance for women; to identify lags, gaps, and possible discrimination in resources and programmes relating to women; in cooperation with other ALA units, to help develop and evaluate tools, guidelines, and programmes designed to enhance the opportunities and the image of women in the library profession, thus raising the level of consciousness concerning women; to establish contacts with committees on women within other professional groups and to officially represent ALA concerns at interdisciplinary meetings on women's equality; and to provide Council and Membership with reports needed for establishment of policies and actions related to the status of women in librarianship; and to monitor ALA units to ensure consideration of the rights of women."

In 1979 the Committee on the Status of Women in Librarian-ship received the Bailey K. Howard-World Book Encyclopedia-ALA Goal Award to develop a profile of ALA personal members, known as the COSWL Study. In 1980 the Committee on the Status of Women in Librarianship was awarded the J. Morris Jones-World Book Encyclopedia-ALA Goals Award with the OLPR Advisory Committee to undertake a special project on equal pay for work of equal value.

National Outreach

The ALA is affiliated with regional, state, and student chapters across the country. It organizes conferences, participates in library standards development, and publishes a number of books and periodicals. The ALA publishes the magazines *American Libraries* and *Booklist*. Along with other organizations, it sponsors the annual Banned Books Week the last week of September. Young Adult Library Services Association (YALSA) also sponsors Teen Read Week, the third week of each October, and Teen Tech Week, the second week of each March.

Awards and Honours

The ALA annually confers numerous book and media awards, primarily through its children's and young adult divisions (others are the Dartmouth Medal, Coretta Scott King Awards, Schneider Book Awards, and Stonewall Book Award).

The children's division ALSC administers the Caldecott Medal, Newbery Medal, Batchelder Award, Belpré Awards, Geisel Award, and Sibert Medal, all annual book awards; the Odyssey Award for best audiobook (joint with YALSA), and the (U.S.) Carnegie Medal and for best video. There are also two ALSC lifetime recognitions, the Wilder Medal and the Arbuthnot Lecture.

The young-adult division YALSA administers the Margaret Edwards Award for significant and lasting contribution to YA literature, a lifetime recognition of one author annually, and some annual awards that recognize particular works: the Michael L. Printz Award for a YA book judged on literary merit alone, the William C. Morris Award for an author's first YA book, the new "YALSA Award for Excellence in Nonfiction for Young Adults", and the "Alex Award" list of ten adult books having special appeal for teens. Jointly with the children's division ALSC there is the Odyssey Award for excellence in audiobook production.

The award for YA nonfiction was inaugurated in 2012, defined by ages 12 to 18 and publication year November 2010 to October 2011. The first winner was '*The Notorious Benedict Arnold: A True Story of Adventure, Heroism and Treachery* by Steve Sheinkin (Roaring Brook Press, November 2010) and four other finalists were named.

Beside the Alex Awards, ALA disseminates some annual lists of "Notable" and "Best" books. The annual awards roster includes the John Cotton Dana Award for excellence in library public relations. From 2006 the ALA annually selects a class of Emerging Leaders, typically comprising about 100 librarians and library school students.

This minor distinction is a form of organizational outreach to new librarians. The Emerging Leaders are allocated to project groups tasked with developing solutions to specified problems within ALA divisions. The class meets at the ALA Midwinter and Annual Meetings, commonly January and June. Project teams may present posters of their completed projects at the Annual.

Conferences

The ALA and its divisions hold numerous conferences throughout the year. The two largest conferences are the annual conference and the midwinter meeting. The latter is typically held in January and focused on internal business, while the annual conference is typically held in June and focused on exhibits and presentations. The ALA annual conference is notable for being one of the largest professional conferences in existence, typically drawing over 25,000 attendees.

Political Positions

The ALA advocates positions on United States political issues that it believes are related to libraries and librarianship. For court cases that touch on issues about which the organization holds positions, the ALA often files amici curiae briefs, voluntarily offering information on some aspect of the case to assist the court in deciding a matter before it.

The ALA has an office in Washington, D.C., that lobbies Congress on issues relating to libraries, information and communication. It also provides materials to libraries that may include information on how to apply for grants, how to comply with the law, and how to oppose a law.

Intellectual Freedom

The primary documented expressions of the ALA's intellectual freedom principles are the Freedom to Read Statement and the Library Bill of Rights; the Library Bill of Rights urges libraries to "challenge censorship in the fulfillment of their responsibility to provide information and enlightenment." The ALA Code of Ethics also calls on librarians to "uphold the principles of intellectual freedom and resist all efforts to censor library resources."

The ALA maintains an Office for Intellectual Freedom (OIF) headed by Barbara M. Jones, former University Librarian for Wesleyan University and internationally known intellectual freedom advocate and author. She is the second director of the Office for Intellectual Freedom, succeeding Judith Krug, who headed the office for four decades.

The OIF is charged with "implementing ALA policies concer-ning the concept of intellectual freedom," that the ALA defines as "the right of every individual to both seek and receive information from all points of view without restriction. It provides for free access to all expressions of ideas through which any and all sides of a question, cause or movement may be explored." Its goal is "to educate librarians and the general public about the nature and importance of intellectual freedom in libraries."

The OIF compiles lists of challenged books as reported in the media and submitted to them by librarians across the country. Its actions are not without controversy; for example, Nat Hentoff noted "An issue facing all members of the ALA is their leaders' shameful exception of the Cuban people's freedom to read."

Hentoff's characterization contradicts the ALA's official position on Cuba, which urges the Cuban Government "to eliminate obstacles to access to information" and expresses "deep concern" for political dissidents in Cuba.

In 1999, radio personality Laura Schlessinger campaigned publicly against the ALA's intellectual freedom policy, specifically in regard to the ALA's refusal to remove a link on its web site to a specific sex-education site for teens. Sharon Presley said, however, that Schlessinger "distorted and misrepre-sented the ALA stand to make it sound like the ALA was saying porno for 'children' is O.K." In 2002, the ALA filed suit with library users and the ACLU against the United States Children's Internet Protection Act (CIPA), which required libraries receiving federal E-rate discounts for Internet access to install a "technology protection measure" to prevent children from accessing "visual depictions that are obscene, child pornography, or harmful to minors."

At trial, the federal district court struck down the law as unconstitutional. The government appealed this decision, and on June 23, 2003, the Supreme

Court of the United States upheld the law as constitutional as a condition imposed on institutions in exchange for government funding.

In upholding the law, the Supreme Court, adopting the interpretation urged by the U.S. Solicitor General at oral argument, made it clear that the constitutionality of CIPA would be upheld only "if, as the Government represents, a librarian will unblock filtered material or disable the Internet software filter without significant delay on an adult user's request."

Privacy

In 2003, the ALA passed a resolution opposing the USA PATRIOT Act, which called sections of the law "a present danger to the constitutional rights and privacy rights of library users". Since then, the ALA and its members have sought to change the law by working with members of Congress and educating their communities and the press about the law's potential to violate the privacy rights of library users.

ALA has also participated as an *amicus curiae* in lawsuits filed by individuals challenging the constitutionality of the USA PATRIOT Act, including a lawsuit filed by four Connecticut librarians after the library consortium they managed was served with a National Security Letter seeking information about library users.

After several months of litigation, the lawsuit was dismissed when the FBI decided to withdraw the National Security Letter. In 2007 the "Connecticut Four" were honoured by the ALA with the Paul Howard Award for Courage for their challenge to the National Security Letter and gag order provision of the USA PATRIOT Act.

In 2006, the ALA sold humourous "radical militant librarian" buttons for librarians to wear in support of the ALA's stances on intellectual freedom, privacy, and civil liberties. Inspiration for the button's design came from documents obtained from the FBI by the Electronic Privacy Information Center (EPIC) through a Freedom of Information Act (FOIA) request.

The request revealed a series of e-mails in which FBI agents complained about the "radical, militant librarians" while criticizing the reluctance of FBI management to use the secret warrants authorized under Section 215 of the USA PATRIOT Act.

Copyright

The ALA "supports efforts to amend the Digital Millennium Copyright Act (DMCA) and urges the courts to restore the balance in copyright law, ensure fair use and protect and extend the public domain". It supports changing copyright law to eliminate damages when using orphan works without permission; is wary of digital rights management; and, in ALA v. FCC, successfully sued the Federal Communications Commission to prevent regulation that would enforce next-generation digital televisions to contain rights-management hardware.

It has joined the Information Access Alliance to promote open access to research. The Copyright Advisory Network of the Association's Office for Information Technology Policy provides copyright resources to libraries and the communities they serve.

SPECIAL LIBRARIES ASSOCIATION

Special Libraries Association (SLA) is an international professional association for library and information professionals working in business, government, law, finance, non-profit, and academic organizations and institutions. While Special libraries include law libraries, news libraries, corporate libraries, museum libraries, and medical libraries, many information professionals today do not actually work in a library setting. They actively apply their specialized skills to support the information needs of their organizations.

SLA was founded in 1909 in the United States. It is now an international organization with over 9,000 members in over 75 countries. SLA is organized by Chapters (geographic) and Divisions (topical) and special interest groups. The association has a CEO (employee of the association) and an elected President (mandate of one year).

Members of SLA typically possess a master's degree in library or information science. Given the rapid adoption of information technologies for selecting, analysing, managing, storing, and delivering information and knowledge, the average SLA member might be performing a range of services and employing a diverse mix of skills related to, but not exclusive of, library science. Association activities include conferences, professional education, networking and advocacy.

CHARTERED INSTITUTE OF LIBRARY AND INFORMATION PROFESSIONALS

The Chartered Institute of Library and Information Professionals (CILIP) is a professional body representing librarians and other information professionals in the United Kingdom.

It was formed in 2002 by the merger of the Library Association (abbreviated to LA or sometimes LAUK)–founded in 1877 as a result of the first International Conference of Librarians and awarded a Royal Charter in 1898–and the Institute of Information Scientists, founded in 1958.

Membership is not compulsory for practice, but members can work towards *Chartered Membership* which entitles them to the postnominal letters MCLIP, and subsequently towards *Fellowship* (FCLIP). Affiliated members can also obtain ACLIP upon completing certification.

Honourary Fellowship (HonFCLIP or FCLIP(hc)), a qualification akin to an honourary degree, is granted to a small number of people who have rendered distinguished service to the profession.

Functions

CILIP accredits degree programmes in library and information science at universities in the UK, including City University, London, Loughborough University, the Manchester Metropolitan University, the Robert Gordon University, the University of Sheffield and University College London.

CILIP is perhaps best known to the general public for awarding the Carnegie and Kate Greenaway Medals for children's books. CILIP publishes a monthly magazine, *CILIP Update with Gazette*, including listings of job vacancies. It also runs a publishing imprint, Facet Publishing.

There are several local branches across the United Kingdom, 28 special interest groups and over 20 organisations in liaison including such bodies as the African Caribbean Library Association, the Librarians' Christian Fellowship and the Society of Indexers. CILIP hosts a conference every two years called "Umbrella" (containing 'LA' the acronym of the Library Association). Umbrella 2009 was held in Hertfordshire and so was Umbrella 2011 (July 12-13 at Hatfield). The title is abbreviated from "Under One UmbrelLA" a Library Association event held every two years.

Role in LIS Education

CILIP's policy is to improve all aspects of professional practice through its work in education, maintaining a framework of universally recognised qualifications and providing a wide range of opportunities for CPD. In 2002 CILIP undertook a review of its qualifications framework. The new *Framework of Qualifications* was launched in April 2005.

It is designed to be flexible and adaptable, as the areas will evolve and develop over time to accommodate changing needs. It is appropriate to library and information professionals across the sector as a whole. As such it has a degree of overlap with the knowledge base of other professions.

The framework consists of four levels – certification, chartership, revalidation and fellowship. Certification provides recognition from the association for library and information work by para-professionals. Those who gain admittance to the Register of Certified Members are entitled to work towards Chartered Membership.

There are two categories of applicant for Chartership:

- Firstly para-professionals with over five years experience;
- Secondly those who have some evidence of training and have been working for two years.

Chartership is CILIP's standard for information professionals. Chartered members are entitled to use post nominal letters and describe themselves as qualified library and information professionals. All candidates for Chartership must work with a Mentor and demonstrate through their portfolio that they meet the required criteria.

Chartership is not an academic qualification but a recognition of the highest standards of professional practice. The individual makes a commitment to continued professional development. Normally applicants will have completed a degree in LIS and have been working for at least one year.

INTERNATIONAL FEDERATION OF LIBRARY ASSOCIATIONS AND INSTITUTIONS

The International Federation of Library Associations and Institutions (IFLA) is the leading international association of library organisations. It is the global voice of the library and information profession, and its annual conference provides a venue for librarians to learn from one another. The IFLA forum promotes international cooperation, research and development in all fields related to library activities. A very important and close partner of the IFLA is UNESCO. Several of the manifestos prepared by committees of the IFLA have been recognized as UNESCO manifestos. The IFLA is part of the International Committee of the Blue Shield (ICBS), which works to protect the world's cultural heritage threatened by wars and natural disasters, and whose Director General is currently Mr Julien Anfruns from the International Council of Museums (ICOM).

The IFLA was founded in Edinburgh, Scotland, in 1927 when library associations from 14 European countries and the United States signed a resolution at the celebration of the 50th anniversary of the Library Association of the United Kingdom. Isak Collijn, head of the National Library of Sweden, was elected the first president. The first constitution was approved in Rome in 1929 during the World Congress of Librarianship and Bibliography.

During the 1930s the first library associations from outside Europe and the US joined, these being China, India, Japan, Mexico and the Philippines. By 1958 membership had grown to 64 associations from 42 countries. A permanent secretariat was established in 1962. By 1970 there were 250 members from 52 countries. The secretariat was moved to The Hague in 1971. By 1974 IFLA membership had become virtually global with 600 members in 100 countries.

Membership criteria were expanded beyond library associations in 1976 to include institutions, *i.e.* libraries, library schools and bibliographic institutes. At this time, the word *Institutions* was added to the organisation's name. Since then further new categories of membership have been created, including personal affiliates. IFLA has now grown to over 1,700 members in 155 countries. It is headquartered in the Koninklijke Bibliotheek, the National Library of the Netherlands, in The Hague.

Mission

IFLA's objectives are:

- To represent librarianship in matters of international interest

- To promote the continuing education of library personnel
- To develop, maintain and promote guidelines for library services

Core Values

The objectives are informed by the following core values:

- The endorsement of the principles of freedom of expression embodied in Article 19 of the Universal Declaration of Human Rights
- The belief that people, communities and organizations need universal and equitable access to information, ideas and works of imagination for their social, educational, cultural, democratic and economic well-being
- The conviction that delivery of high quality library and information services helps guarantee that access
- The commitment to enable all Members of the Federation to engage in, and benefit from, its activities without regard to citizenship, disability, ethnic origin, gender, geographical location, language, political philosophy, race or religion.

Committee on Free Access to Information and Freedom of Expression (FAIFE)

One of the core activities of IFLA is the Committee on Free Access to Information and Freedom of Expression, which monitors the state of intellectual freedom within the library community worldwide, supports IFLA policy development and co-operation with other international human rights organisations, and responds to violations of free access to information and freedom of expression.

IFLA/FAIFE is a member of the International Freedom of Expression Exchange, a global network of non-governmental organisations that monitors freedom of expression worldwide. It is also a member of the Tunisia Monitoring Group, a coalition of 16 free expression organisations that lobbies the Tunisian government to improve its human rights record.

CONCLUSION

Following the launching of Delnet and Calibnet, the library automation and networking movement in India is surely catching on.

The objectives which are:

- Better utilization of funds through sharing of resources by creation of commonly usable data-bases and communication between libraries.
- Automating the functions of individual libraries at a local level for effective and efficient services to the users.

A number of benefits are being offered to member libraries of the particular networks. First, one gets access to a very large volume of literature without increase in the library budget because of the sharing of resources among the members. Secondly, the library budget can now be diverted to acquire the most important (even if expensive) information required by an institution, the other peripheral information being available on the network.

Third, one gets near real time access to about 1000 international databases apart from the electronic mail and remote log in facilities. There are plans of these networks to connect and share the resources in the near future. Nevertheless, the growth of these networks is slow. It is taking a long time to create and provide bibliographic databases of recognisable size, *e.g.*, DELNET took already ten years in creating bibliographic databases of reasonably good size. Without the databases neither could networks be made effective to achieve the goals nor could resource sharing be effective.

Finally it appears that prospects are quite favourable for development of networks for better information services and resource sharing in India. In this direction lot of work has to be done. Some of the problems faced by other developing countries are common to India too, including financial constraints, inadequate communication, non-availability of equipments, less awareness of the value of information, reluctance to development and non-coordination of various kind of activities, resource building, resource sharing and exchange of information and ideas, non-standardization operational procedure, lack of dedication, motivation and knowledge on the part of available manpower.

3

Departmental Collection

ACQUISITION OF ELECTRONIC RESOURCES DEALING WITH LICENSING ISSUES

The electronic publishing has a very short history, compared to traditional form of publishing. The first known form of e-publishing is in the early 1980s when plain text e-mails were sent to the subscriber via a mailing list. But, the subsequent technological advancements made a tremendous impact on the information cycle process of creation, gathering/production and dissemination of information, which in turn hugely influenced the electronic publishing itself. In 1994-95 the first e-journal was published and the distribution of e-journal turned out to be an instant success. Majority of the journals are now made available in digital form.

The publishers are now offering package subscription to electronic journals at highly reduced price as the publishing charges of e-journals have substantially come down, as compared to their print counterpart, which involved huge cost of printing and distribution. Subsequently, even bibliographic resources were brought in electronic form. Soon, e-books also made their presence. These developments made the libraries to seriously rethink their collection development and information delivery policies. While moving totally to electronic may be a distant possibility, a progressive shift from print to electronic, is being noticed.

MOVING FROM PRINT TO ELECTRONIC: *A CRITICAL ISSUE*

While the print and online versions have their own advantages and disadvantages. However, to put the subject in perspective, some critical remarks are made here. Print resources subscribed/ bought are physically available in the libraries and form an asset. Online resources subscribed/ bought on one-time purchase can only be accessed by users, as the digital content is held remotely at the publishers' end. This raises the issue of ownership *vs.* access and is a well debated point in the user and the librarians' communities. The fact, however, is that, in case of online resources, the libraries are currently dependent totally on publishers to access the subscribed/ bought content. This situation made the libraries to think in terms of ensuring perpetual access to the subscribed/ bought content. Of course, publishers too have their own concerns of protecting their content from misuse. It is, therefore, a mutual interest of both the publisher and the end-user to enter into an Agreement protecting each other's interests. This agreement is generally known as License Agreement.

LICENCE AGREEMENT AND ITS TYPES

A Licence agreement is a legal document and contract between the publisher and the institutional library. Both the parties agree to abide by the terms and conditions set in the agreement. There are basically three different kinds of site license agreements according to:

- The type of library,
- Product/ model, and
- Number of sites.

The agreements by the type of libraries include Academic/ Research, Government/ Corporate & Public and generally the variations are in terms of users, fees, etc.; The agreements by product/ model are based on the e-resources, such as E-journals, E-books and Bibliographic Databases. The agreements by site(s) are applicable according to the number of sites, such as single site, multi-sites and consortium. Although, the re-exist some Standard Licensing models, each publisher has his own Agreement and a close look at these indicate that there is a lack of consistency and standardisation. A few publishers have put up the copy of their site license agreement on their web site but others do not do so maintaining it as confidential document. However, signing of License Agreement has almost become mandatory. In fact, a well known publisher has a policy which stipulates that they will raise the invoice for an e-product only after the library signs the agreement. In a way, it is good that the library will know all the terms & conditions before buying the product. Other publishers send the agreement after the purchase order is raised and the payment is made. In such cases, it may be difficult to negotiate any changes in the clauses.

The terms and conditions of the site license agreement are heavily tilted in favour of publishers. However, except a few, the clauses in the Agreement are generally subject to negotiations. The job of dealing with such issues would be much simpler for those Organisations which have a Legal Cell. It is advisable to refer the document to that Cell. But, as is generally observed, many Organisations do not have such Units which make it imperative for the Librarian to take up himself the responsibility of examining the legal aspects in the Agreement. In that case, the librarian needs to be very cautious in studying various clauses in the Agreement. He/ she must ensure that the interests of his/ her Organisation are protected to the maximum possible extent. After going through the Agreements carefully, one has to first seek clarifications from the publishers on those points which do not seem to be very clear. Possible changes may be suggested to bring in more clarity. If certain terms are unacceptable, it is essential to request for changes/ amendments in the Agreement. Sometimes, it needs a hard bargaining and the librarians need to have strong negotiating skills.

KEY ISSUES IN THE AGREEMENT

Perpetual Access

Perpetual access is ensured by most of the publishers. But some publishers put a condition that the library should subscribe to at least one online journal or any online product of theirs. Otherwise, they will charge maintenance fee/ hosting fee. If the access is provided off-line, then they ask the libraries to bear the cost of production to provide the content on other electronic media, such as CDs/ DVDs, for local hosting. Some publishers prefer to use the term 'Continued Access' in place of 'Perpetual Access'. The terminological difference may have to be clearly understood. As one UK publisher puts it - the 'Perpetual Access' in their terminology refers to a limited period and the 'Continued Access' means indefinite period. Libraries need to ensure that their parent institution will not be put to disadvantage and take precautions to get inserted right terminology.

However, some publishers do not provide perpetual access at all to the subscribed content. If an online subscription is not renewed, the libraries will lose access even to the paid content. If that is the case, then the Licensing document must clearly state it. In such cases, the libraries need to think seriously about an alternative method of archiving either by continuing with print version or get archival year-end CDs/ DVDs, as offered by some publishers.

Withdrawal of Content

Publishers insert a clause that it reserves right to withdraw the content, which it no longer retains the right to publish or infringes copyright or defamatory, etc. While the last condition should be acceptable, the first two conditions may sometime put librarians in a fix. These situations may arise when a journal title is transferred to some other publisher. The new publisher may not permit the old subscribers to access this content, free. It is all the more critical if this content is substantial and/ or directly relevant to their users.

As a remedial measure, one can demand insertion of the following clauses - The publisher will make best efforts to convince the new publisher to provide access to the old subscribers or shall allow local hosting of such content. Also, if the withdrawal is substantial, then the publisher shall refund the amount proportionately.

Restrictions on Usage

Generally, publishers do not permit users to download entire journal issues and e-books. A standard condition to this effect may be found in License Agreement of all the publishers.

There are publishers who even put a restriction on the number of pages and chapters printable from e-books. The decision of the libraries to buy ebooks from such publishers depends on how comfortable they are with the restrictions imposed by the publishers. A few publishers do permit the licensee to make an electronic copy and a hardcopy for backup purpose. However, the libraries need to create necessary infrastructure to preserve the content on their local computer server.

Access to Archives through Third Party

In the event of a publisher deciding to wind up his operations or merge with another publisher, it is an obligation on the part of the publisher to make alternative arrangements to provide access to archive of the licensed materials concerned. This is where the third party arrangement comes into picture. Many publishers have made arrangements with some external agencies for the long time preservation of their digital archive. Some examples are LOCKSS, CLOCKSS, PORTICO, and National Library of Netherlands. In a trigger event, it becomes the responsibility of these agencies to grant access to the content to the subscribers. The libraries should insist publishers to incorporate in the agreement a clause specifying the names of the agencies with whom the arrangements are made to provide access to the content in the event of publisher closing his business. Some of these agencies offer paid service, but since the subscribers have already paid for the content earlier, it becomes a debatable point whether the libraries can afford to pay again for the same content.

Inter-Library Loan (ILL)

Providing a copy of an article to another library (not-forprofit, non-commercial) under ILL is generally permitted by most of the publishers, but with varying conditions. While the publishers expect subscribers to observe normal Copyright rules, some put specific restrictions on document delivery system. While one publisher permits only to send copies in print format, the other allows electronic transmission through secure network, but insists that the recipient library delete the file after printing a paper copy. Such clauses are non-negotiable and the libraries need to accept them, so long some form of ILL is permitted.

Governing Laws

Business of digital content is only three decade old. Like any other business, there is a possibility that disputes might arise especially in terms of copyright rules, access problems etc. If such disputes remain unresolved mutually, the aggrieved parties have no option, but to approach Judiciary. This gives rise to the problem of jurisdiction as the two parties belong to different countries. The agreement is generally governed by the laws of the country of origin of the publisher.

However, some publishers are flexible on this issue. While some agree to sort out the issue in the court of subscriber's country, others agree to the condition that the aggrieved party can approach their respective countries. Alternatively, some publishers also allow for an independent arbitrator mutually acceptable to both parties.

Fees

Fees charged by the publishers for e-books, online journal packages, etc. varies from library to library, depending upon size of the user community. However, publishers also offer price cap in case a library agrees to go for a multi-year agreement. The base price and the price cap shall form part of the Agreement and as such need to be stated explicitly.

Counter-signed Copy

Original copy of the agreement is generally in duplicate and the two signed copies are exchanged between the library and the publisher. However, the Agreements of some publishers have only the acceptance column which needs to be signed by the Library. In such a case, libraries should keep with them one copy of the agreement.

General Conditions

Some publishers incorporate a clause in the agreement, stating that the content of the Licensed Material is 'subject to change without notice'. If accepted, this allows the publisher to alter the subscribed/ purchased content without notice. In this case, subscriber will be totally in dark about the changes effected, including withdrawal of any content.

To avoid this, the librarians need to insist for change in the clause appropriately by changing it to 'subject to change with prior notice to the licensee' (*i.e.* library). This will protect the end-user from any loss of content, as the user will have time to copy and store the content locally. Some publishers also incorporate a clause that the contents of the License Agreement should not be disclosed to a third party without their consent.

While the publishers urging to maintain secrecy is understandable, it may be difficult for libraries to accept such a clause, especially for those organisations funded by State/ Central Governments, which, according to the Right to Information Act, may have to be disclose the content to those, who seek it. Therefore, it is essential that appropriate changes are demanded in the clauses.

USAGE PATTERN OF INFORMATION RESOURCES AT CSIR

The aim and objective of any Information Centre is to provide pinpoint, exhaustive, and nascent information to readers who use information for a variety of purposes. A library, therefore, is always adjudged good or bad on by its usage. This goal makes the collection development evaluation imminent. Considering the importance of such usage, an attempt has been made in this study to evaluate the current usage of literature at CSIR-National Metallurgical Laboratory, Jamshedpur, Jharkhand (Erstwhile Bihar).

The worth of a library collection can be judged through various methods like, circulation of documents, user survey, download analysis of literature, Citation/Reference analysis, etc. The present study, however, evaluates the library usage through reference analysis. Today, citation and ranking information are becoming key aspects of knowledge management in R&D Knowledge Resource Centers.

It helps to examine the changing user needs and products so as to understand and manage the information resources besides responding the user needs better. Effective collection analysis and assessment provides quantitative and qualitative data for evaluating the usefulness and utility of a library's holdings.

It assists with determining budget requirements by focusing attention on how well the library's collections in specific areas support the needs of the users and the institution as well. It also points out whether the institution's investment in the collection is being managed responsibly. The aim of such assessment is, therefore, to determine as to how well the collection supports the goals, needs, and mission of the library or parent organisation. The collection (both locally held and remotely accessed materials) is assessed in the local context. Evaluation seeks to examine or describe collections either in their own terms or in relation to other collections and checking mechanisms, such as lists. Both evaluation and assessment provide a better understanding of the collection and the user community. The major problem of research libraries all over the world today is deciding as to which serials should be subscribed to meet the needs of their specialised users without subscribing to any unnecessary journals.

The problem has been further aggravated recently by shortages of funds and subsequent cuts in library book budgets. In order to operate effectively, libraries must identify literature of high utility to their clients, and must acquire and organise the literature in such a way to ensure their optimal use. One of the generally accepted methods of scientific investigation is, indeed, to follow the scientific literature by the simplest means. Various sources are used by scientists to gather information, for example, through regular reading of all available texts, recommendations of colleagues and superiors, and references or citations in other related publications.

RESEARCH METHOD AND DATA

A total of 187 Research papers published in various formats like, SCI, Non-SCI, National proceedings, Internatioal proceedings and book chapters were identified by institutional affiliation.Fig.1 depicts the status of R&D publications, a maximum of 120 papers appeared in SCI was downloaded from Web of Science with complete reference data and the remaining 54 papers were scanned form Non-SCI journals, proceedings and book chapters. Thus, the total number of references cited in the 187 research papers was 3,825.

The average number of references per paper was 20. The availability of references was coded under the following four categories:

- Available in electronic form;
- Vailable in print form;
- Available in the open network; and
- Not available.

The bibliographic references in each article in the sample were first examined by classifying each citation into one of the following nine source categories by format of publications: books/monographs (includes chapters in a book, monograph series, sourcebook), journals (*i.e.* scholarly and academic serials in the form of print or online, articles 'in press' with journal title cited), periodicals (*i.e.* magazines, newspapers, working papers, Newsletters), conferences proceedings (proceedings, seminars meetings, workshops, forums), unpublished (*i.e.* unpublished manuscripts, thesis/dissertation, documents, reports/documents, unpublished test and short communications), reference sources (*i.e.* government documents, dictionaries, handbooks, encyclopaedias) reports (*i.e.* published reports by institutions or corporations), web documents (documents retrieved from the internet via the worldwide web with Uniform Resource Locator (URL) provided, and others. 'Conference proceedings' was designated for compilations of papers presented at conferences or symposia that were not published as a regular issue of a journal.

CONSORTIA MODELS FOR NETWORKING
SOME ISSUES ON CSIR CONSORTIA

The word consortium has been derived from Latin, meaning association or partnership. In general a Consortium could be described as a group of organisations who come together to fulfil a common objective that usefully requires co-operation and the sharing of resources, and need to have a clear mutual goal in order to ensure their success. Various definitions are there in different dictionaries on consortium but almost the meaning is same in the context of library. An e-journal consortium means the collaborative acquisition of access rights to electronic databases and journals and the aim of is to achieve what the members of the group cannot achieve individually. Journals play a major role in the R&D but unfortunately the number and cost of journals are increasing at very high speed. Number of journals and their costs has increased by threefolds every 15 years and 226 per cent, respectively. During the last 20 years in terms of dollars, this may be further compounded by currency conversion whereas the increase in library 1 budget was only 110 per cent during the same period. In another study by the Association of Research Libraries in USA, it was found that average CPI (Consumer Price Index) for US increased by 73 per cent during 1986-2004, but the research libraries expenditure for journals 2 increased by 273 per cent during the same period due to the increase in number of research scholars, institutions and global competition.

The estimated number of STM (Science, Technology and Medicine) journals is about 25,000. Out of this 15,000 journals are peer- 3 reviewed and 12,000 are in e-form. All types of libraries/information centres are not in a position to subscribe all the information resources required by their users. Not even a single library can meet the thrust of knowledge required by all the readers from its stock of information to the full extent.To solve this, libraries have started library cooperation, *i.e.* inter-library loan (ILL), resource sharing, and library consortium, etc. For the past four centuries, dissemination of information was done through print media alone, but now the electronic media has taken over this mean of communication. Basic purpose of the consortia is sharing of resources, money, and manpower. In the digital context, it is the access to information rather than holding information. 'Collection building' concept has changed to 'Connection building' with the help of Information and Communication technologies (ICT).

Access to the e-resources and the subscription amount is shared among the participating libraries. Significant price reduction can be achieved through consortium and individual libraries in the consortium will have collaborative acquisition of access rights to databases and e-journals. Library consortia's have become powerful negotiating parties and incorporating their own clauses in the contracts with the publishers and just no longer signing the standard contract texts provided by the 4 publishers.

TYPES OF CONSORTIA

The types of consortia identified are generally based on various models evolved in India in Variety of forms depending upon participations' affiliation and funding sources.

- *Open Consortia*: This type of consortia is very flexible and it is the wish of members of consortia can join and leave any they please. INDEST Consortium is an example to this.
- *Closed Group Consortia*: This kind of consortia emerges either by affiliation and collaboration among them like CSIR, DAE, IIM Consortium. The formation and operation of the consortia guidelines and its administration are fairly simple and easy.

- *Centrally Funded Model*: In this model, consortium will solely depend on the parent body. A few examples are CSIR, INDEST, UGC-INFONET and ICMR Consortia, etc.
- *Shared-budget Model*: In this model the participating libraries take the lead and form the consortium. IIM and FORSA are examples of this model.
- *Publisher Initiatives*: The Emerald Full-Text Library published by the Emerald Publishing Group (formerly MCB University Press) is recent example. Here, the consortium members will get deep discount price to the participating libraries.
- *National Consortium*: This is a model perceived at national level which includes member libraries from one country.

BENEFITS OF CONSORTIUM

Some of the important advantages of the proposed library consortium are as follows:

- Main advantage of e-journal consortium is, it checks the space problem, shelving, binding, lending, and related aspects of member libraries.
- Instead of user coming to the library, the library is available at the user's desktop/laptop virtually all the time (24/7). Available 24 hours a day, 7 days a week.
- It saves the time of the user since instant access will be available after every updating unlike the shipping time, missing issues, and mutilations. etc., which prevail in respect of print media.
- Consortium builds communication among different libraries and avoids duplication of core journals.
- Consortium provides high quality literature and faster document delivery service, *i.e.*, it provides a wealth of relevant resources readily available and helps in facing the challenges to have a meaningful presence in this digital era to its users.
- It is easy to assess the areas of interest of users so that efficient services can be provided by the concerned librarians through usage statistics given by the publisher.
- The consortium have been offered better terms of licenses for use, archival access and preservation of subscribed electronic resources, which would not have been possible for any single institution and facilities to build up digital libraries.
- Helpful to provide better library services like CAS and SDI.

BOTTLENECKS OF CONSORTIUM

- Absence of a printed copy of Journals and lack of archiving and back files availability.

- Require training of staffs in handling electronic documents etc.
- A consortium requires high initial investments in licensees and infrastructure, internet connectivity, and other accessories.
- Copyright problems. Problems like copyright/ excess downloads from the publisher.
- Content provider/publisher combines both essential and non-essential journals as a package. Whereas in print collection, the selection is done by subject expert(s) and only journals of core area are subscribed. Therefore, measures have to be taken to avoid unwanted items and recall the most relevant items.

GROWTH OF CONSORTIA IN INDIA

The new technology or the modern information technology has made the task of resource sharing very simple and convenient. The new technology brings forward to the information field many products and services which have changed the nature of fundamental library objectives and operations. Over the last 2 decades, the libraries have witnessed the impact of information technology that has been affecting the structure of the services to a great extent. Library networks have grown mostly during the last 30 years in different geographical environment in order to cater the specific needs of the users. In the U.S., there has been a proliferation of them. In the developed countries, resource sharing networking was started long back, *e.g.* the growth of the network in the U.S., can be traced from mid 1960. USA is the birthplace of library networking and by now libraries in each state are networked to local, regional and national network.

On the other hand, the growth of library networks in India can be traced to the initiatives made by NISSAT in establishing 6 CALIBNET in 1986 and DELNET in 1988 and other networks like UGC/INFLIBNET has established UGC-INFONET Consortium, Digital Library in Engineering Science and Technology (INDEST) Consortium of all Indian institute of Technologies (IITs), Indian Institute of Science (IISc) and a few other institutions which include RECs, NITs, IIMs, etc., the Forum for Resource Sharing in Astronomy and Astrophysics (FORSA) is a consortium of Raman Research Institute (RRI), Indian Institute of Astrophysics (IIA), Tata Institute of Fundamental Research (TIFR), Inter-university Centre for Astronomy and Astrophysics (IUCAA), National Centre for Radio Astrophysics (NCRA), and Physical Research Laboratory (PRL) subsequently.

CSIR CONSORTIUM

The Council of Scientific and Industrial Research (CSIR), a public-funded organisation, is India's largest R&D organisation established in 1942 with a chain of 37 National laboratories and institutes. CSIR is carrying out the research work in various disciplines all over the country.

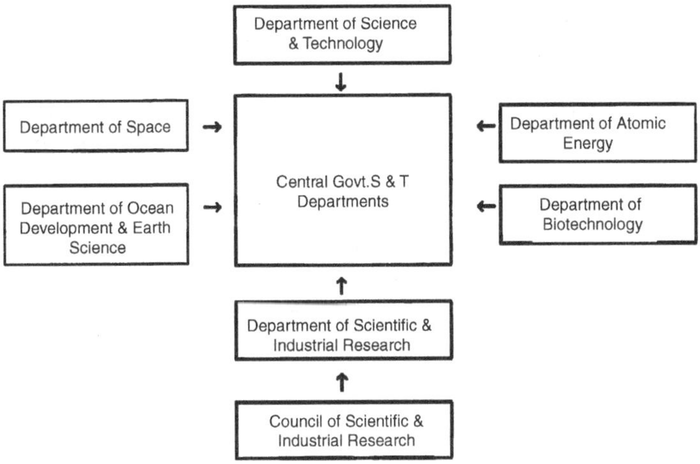

Fig CSIR Orgnisational Structure

NEED FOR THE CONSORTIUM

There has been a constant decrease (66 per cent) in the journals base of CSIR laboratories over the last decade, which necessitated its libraries to find out alternate solution to make available R&D information.While laboratory size, areas of work and number of researchers vary, it is desirable to have comparable and adequate information 7 resources irrespective of the size or strength of the laboratory.

OBJECTIVES OF THE CONSORTIUM

- The primary objective of the overall programme focuses on enhancing the visibility and impact of CSIR research output internationally in terms of papers and patents.
- This will be attempted by providing access to maximum possible e-resources to the researchers.
- To provide CSIR & S&T staff electronic access to global knowledge with continues to subscribe existing e-resources.
- To expand the information base of CSIR and provide divergent nature of contents of information to CSIR users subscribe to additional e-resources.

E-JOURNAL CONSORTIUM

The Director General set up a study group in April 2001 to collect/study and compile information to the journals subscribed by the CSIR labs. After several deliberations the eth journal Consortium project finally took shape as a Network Project of CSIR under 10 Five Year Plan with a budget layout of Rs 11.79 crores for the plan period 2002-2007 targeting to access 4500 e-journals. E-Journal consortium is being coordinated centrally by CSIR's National Institute of Science Communication and Information Resources (NISCAIR) as nodal agency for implementing the Consortium, with a task force team established with senior scientists from CSIR laboratories and also negotiation committees to negotiate and finalise the agreements with the publishers in providing required e-journals, databases, etc., for CSIR's constituent laboratories.

The heads of the libraries of the participating labs are designated as 8 the nodal officers to implement the Consortium access to e-journals at their respective labs. CSIR e-Journal Consortium strengthens its library resources by pooling, sharing and providing electronic access services like e-journals and international databases to its scholars and scientists. On 10 June 2002, CSIR signed an agreement with M/s Elsevier Science to 9 access around 1500 world class e-journals. NISCAIR has coordinated well by constituting different committees like Core Committee, Negotiating Committees, etc., for effective implementation of the consortium. 'Electronic plus' price model was chosen to maintain the print collection of the individual institution libraries irrespective of the duplicate and triplicate subscriptions from the same publisher and paying an extra amount of 9 per cent of the print to ScienceDirect at the beginning of the project.

This extra amount is varied subsequently in the following years based on effective negotiations by the concerned committees. Usage statistics is being provided by the publisher to the individual institutes for effective monitoring of the consortium. Archival issues pertaining to past five years are also being provided by the concerned publisher as per the agreement. E-Journals and other document requirements of the constituent laboratories have been put forth by the nodal officers to coordinating agencies. The coordinating agency prepares the financial document and gets the money from CSIR negotiation committees to allocate this money to different publishers based on the suggestions received from the nodal officers. In this way it receives 10 more than 4000 e-journals. CSIR Consortium has proved to be a great success and its impact can be measured in terms of revenue savings, usage of e-journals in terms of downloads and contribution of articles in international journals, etc. Substantial revenue has been saved, and significant growth in number of papers and IF (Impact Factor) have been achieved.

Quantitative as well as qualitative improvements have been achieved in the years following the access to e-journals through the Consortium. Continual and steep increase in the number of downloads has also been recorded. In this way CSIR became a leading institutions of the world and the contribution of CSIR researchers in international journals have raised. The 11 National savings on this account is around Rs. 535 crores. Upgrading the CSIR information system is proving effective in meeting its researcher's divergent nature of information requirements.

ELSEVIER CONTEXT

To fill the lack of information in the CSIR laboratories, decided to subscribe e-journals of Elsevier by individual laboratories and sharing these resources among the CSIR laboratories.

The coordinating agencies suggested subscribing only the unique journals and avoiding for the duplication for maximum possible so that sharing of e-journals shall be easier through the CSIR network.

As scientific literature is exploding, publishing has become an increasingly profitable enterprise.

The competition in the publishing world is very fast, with even old scientific societies turning to commercial publishers, to bring a degree of professionalism of producing and marketing their journals.

As journals multiply and costs increase, libraries must worry about budgets and coverage. Problems are compounded by growing costs of maintaining both print and online subscriptions and issues related to continuing electronic access to back files.

Large publishing houses like Elsevier Science and Springer-Verlag are beginning to monopolise the world of science journals, which arises a situation that 12 promotes a seller's market. CSIR Consortium did not agreed to the price hike proposed by publisher and termed it as unreasonable and gave a counter proposal for consideration of the publisher.

However, access to ScienceDirect was stopped in April 2008 as the agreement was not renewed between the CSIR Consortium and the publisher due to failure of negotiations with the regard to price hike by the publisher. In this way after 2008 CSIR laboratories were felt the necessity for a strong networking among their constituent laboratories.

SUBSCRIPTION TO JCCC@VIC: *J-GATE CUSTOM CONTENT FOR CONSORTIA*

After this CSIR entering into JCCC for exchange of holdings of individual CSIR laboratories on inter library loan basis but problems with JCCC are it is a platform which is common to all for accessing information which becomes a great problem to serve the users. As CSIR laboratories are scientific in nature so their members are also dealing with scientific field, but it is difficult to analyse the member of JCCC. It becomes a question mark in their authenticity in identification.

NAL CONTEXT

For possible solution NAL (National Aeronautics Limited) compile a union catalogue for CSIR laboratories and it has come forward flood the updated union catalogue with the cooperation from the member CSIR libraries, an alternatives mode to avoid JCCC.

EXPERIENCE NETWORK WITH DST

After seeing the experience of CSIR consortium with the publishers, DST (Department of Science and Technology) has also decided to join with CSIR consortium for their e-journal subscription.

NATIONAL KNOWLEDGE RESOURCE CONSORTIUM FINAL SOLUTION

Open Consortium- Consortium of S&T institutions, will help to expand the information base will strengthen the negotiating power, develop uniformity across different departments.

NISCAIR should perform a leading role to bring other S&T organisations under Consortium. CSIR going to interconnected all the scientific laboratories with powerful computer networks with one CSIR slogans and the solution is formation of National Consortium of Scientific Departments and named as National Knowledge Resource Consortium (NKRC).

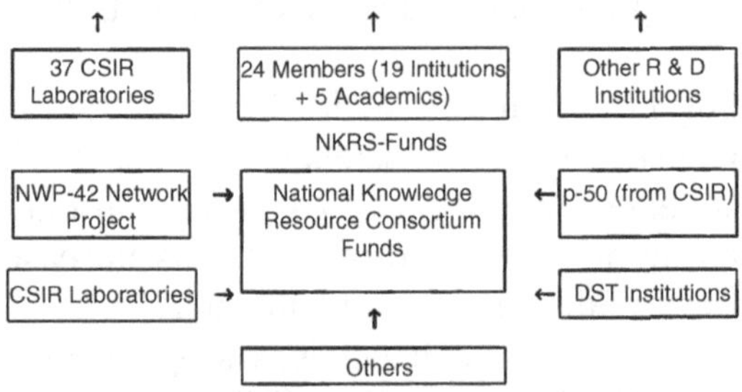

Fig. National Knowledge Resource Consortium

COLLECTION DEVELOPMENT AND MANAGEMENT POLICIES

The libraries are now functioning as Information or Knowledge Centers, resource centers, which disseminates required pinpointed information to the users. Libraries collect the information published in various forms *e.g.* books, periodicals, thesis, patents etc. and organise it in helpful sequence. The heart of the library is in its collection. The main purpose of the collection is to serve the needs of users and organisational aims in better ways. Libraries have to develop the collection keeping in view the users need and demands and hence the collection development in the library must be proper.

Traditional Libraries have some set of rules framed for the collection development but not operative, but now due use of ICT, revolutionary changes have been observed in the library practices including collection development. The framed rules are not appropriate and suits to the changing practices and hence majority of the libraries in the developed countries have formulated the collection development policies to build the proper and useful collection in the libraries which supports to the needs of the users. Similarly the change in format from print to digital made the issues to develop new policies or to amend the existing policies to suit the environment. In digital media acquisitions the process is different due to change in format and pricing structure as compared to previous methods followed in libraries. Collection development is the main activity of any library and hence librarians are now focusing more in this area. To maintain the proper collection in libraries there is a need to develop policies or amend to the existing to suit the emerging trends in publications and acquisition methods. The increase in digital media publication and usage the collection development policies for the digital information resources are required to be developed.The process of the collection development covers selection and de-selection of the resources.

Collection development or management involves activities like collection management programme, collection development policy statement, collection assessment, funding and budgeting, selection and de-selection, preservation, and resource- sharing projects. It is very clear from the statement made by Verzosa that collection development process is a complex process involving various activities but its advantages are more to have a proper collection.

WHAT IS COLLECTION DEVELOPMENT

The purpose of collection development pointed out by Melvil Dewey was to provide 'The best reading for the largest number at the least cost'. ALA defined a very suitable definition for collection development as "A term which encompasses a number of activities related to the development of the library collection, including the determination and coordination of selection policy, assessment of needs of users and potential users, collection use studies, collection evaluation, identification of collection needs, selection of materials, Planning for resource sharing, collection maintenance and weeding."

ALA Glossary State that "Library Collections will contain all types of registered information, including printed materials of all formats, audio-visual materials, visual material, materials used with computers, graphs and three-dimensional materials and ways to access the electronic information" Harold Libraries Glossary defined "collection developments as the process of planning a stock acquisition programmed not simply to cater for immediate needs but to build a current and reliable collection over a numbers of years to meet the objectives of the services." These definitions clearly indicate the need of collection development in information growing age. If libraries need to provide qualitative services then qualitative collection is to be made available in the library irrespective of forms and formats.

WHY PROPER COLLECTION DEVELOPMENT

Collection of the documents in the library is the prime task as it is the power house of information resources. There are many factors involved to have proper collection development like.

- Information explosion and Information overload
- Limited and shrinking library budgets
- Increasing users demands for pinpointed qualitative information resources due to specialisation
- Multiple forms and formats of the information resources including digital
- Increase in prices of documents all the times
- Shift in demand of users from collection based services to information and access based services
- More usage of Internet based e-documents

Since digital, internet resources, databases and e-publications are increasing and simultaneously the use in academic and special libraries are also increasing continuously. Growth in literature made necessary to manage proper collection.

Objectives and Purpose of Collection Development

The main objectives and purpose behind collection development are:

- Fulfil the user needs by proper collection
- To support the teaching learning and research endeavors
- Periodically review the collection for weeding
- To provide nascent and relevant information
- To acquire the best and useful literature to the core group of the users

Collection Development policies allows the library personnel's to develop proper collection and based on this value added services can be provided to the users. The purpose of the collection development policy is to provide guidelines for day to day acquisition and withdrawal decisions, resource allocation and long range planning of collection needs keeping in mind the library mission, activities, organisational needs and interest etc.

TECHNIQUES FOR PROPER COLLECTION DEVELOPMENT

For proper collection development for any library, a detailed written collection development policy is necessary. The policy clearly specifies the organisational requirements, goals and the user needs in specific. The Library committee formed for the proper development and progress of the library consist of the expert members from the various faculties who can contribute in formulating the proper collection development and designing the policies. It is also necessary to look in to the policies formulated by the other libraries and the policies prepared by LC and ALA etc. Library collection development policy should be in clearly spelt out in a written form. The American Library Association's collection development policies assumed that a written collection development policy is a desirable tool that enables selectors to work with greater consistency towards defined goals. The following aspects need to be considered basically while developing policy:

- Users needs and demands
- Review the organisational needs and objectives
- Review the standard, core, border and peripheral subject areas
- Conduct use and users studies for user behaviour and need analysis
- Try to cover the sources which disseminate maximum access to current information in the area
- Take the help of techniques like citation analysis, impact factor, bibliometrics and scientiometrics studies, information audit, information behaviour of users etc
- Resource Sharing practices be initiated at various level including consortium
- Evaluation techniques must be adapted
- Trial access for the databases for certain period and get the feedback from the users before subscription
- Initiate the OA and IR project for protecting IP of organisation
- Analyse strengths and weakness of the collection regularly
- Apply management techniques for quality procurement

Many libraries have developed collection development policies but these are informal in nature and no concrete policies are developed except larger organisations.

The collection development policy is required due to multidisciplinary subjects, procurement of epublications. Policy is a guideline to act on. To prepare a policy for any library a review of different standard collection development policies becomes useful to draft a policy.

REVIEW OF EXISTING COLLECTION DEVELOPMENT POLICIES

The basic elements while formulating the collection development policy for any library was discussed in the conferences also and the output presented in the National Conference on "Putting Knowledge to Work: Best Practices in Librarianship" 1-2 May 2009 151-152 highlighted following issues.

- *Organisational Objectives*: The nature of the organisation, its function, objectives and the purpose must be considered at the initial level.
- *Users*: It is necessary to review the needs of the users of the library especially from the organisation, their main area of concern, projects under taken, information resources covering the general aspect about the stream as well as the specialised needs of the users in the area of research. Real and potential needs of the users must be covered.
- *Level of collection*: The collection may satisfy the needs of the experts as well as a common man whose interest is to read for the entertainment and knowledge addition. (Maslow's need based

triangle). There is a need to focus on the current and future needs of the organisations.

- *Subject Coverage*: It is necessary to fix the core subjects in which organisational collection must be deep and updated. The peripheral subjects can be developed based on the priority as well as need based collection or even can be shared with other organisations (Resource Sharing). Hence collection assessment must be evaluated based on the area and subjects of core importance.
- *Type of Information Sources*: While selecting the information recourses it is necessary to provide the access to the literature published in the area which is covered by the secondary information sources. It is necessary to provide maximum access to the users rather than owning the information resources. To make the collection economic on demand acquisition can also be preferred in case of peripheral area or can be obtained from ILL.
- *Budget*: Allocation of the budget must be proper and as per the usage. The budget of any library is not adequate to get all the literature published and hence policies must be fixed keeping in mind the usage and cost effective factors. Resource sharing activity will also help in reducing the expenses in case of peripheral research area.
- *Forms in which material must be acquired*: It is necessary to fix the form in which documents can be acquired. A policy stating the forms (print, digital, non print etc) to be procured must be detailed. However the acquisition must always be cost effective to adjust in the budget allocated.
- *Services provided*: Many libraries provide services to the users from the organisation as well as from different institutions. For this purpose the acquisition must be qualitative.
- *Users and use studies at frequent Intervals*: It is necessary to evaluate the usage of the acquired material. If the material is less used it must be weeded or stacked in parallel.
- *Policies for the preservation of the resources*: Preservation of the literature is the objective of the library. The heritage of the knowledge is useful for the future generation and hence modern tools and techniques may be used.

IFLA POLICY FOR COLLECTION DEVELOPMENT

The IFLA suggested following points in its collection development policy:

- Must be a written Policy covering procedure for selection, de-selection planning (future), public relations, weeding, retaining, preservation etc
- Covers general, narrative and subject profiles

- Use of collection evaluation methods
- Use of collection depth indicators
- Language (English, Primary and predominantly used as per need and country language)
- Policy implementation and revision

The first elements of a collection development policy will be a mission statement of the library, the purpose of this policy and the audience to whom it is addressed. General area covers current focus or also retrospective acquisitions; the resource types (monographs, periodicals, theses, gray literature, maps, etc.); languages; formats (printed, nonprint or electronic); special sources of funding (a grant or gift from a donor); the policy regarding gifts and any special policies regarding maintenance (weeding, discarding, preservation) of the collection; and size of the collections.

Collection evaluation is based on quantitative and qualitative measures:

- Quantitative Measures reveal size, age, use, costs and other numeric data. Examples of quantitative measures include inventory, or shelf list measures to determine actual title or volume counts, by segment or subject area. Median age or similar measures indicate the currency of the materials. Amount expended for acquisitions in a segment or subject area per year illustrates the ongoing commitment to develop that area. Percentage of titles owned by a library when compared to a standard list shows the breadth and depth of the collection. Use statistics (including internal library use and ILL) are both collection and client-centred.
- Qualitative measures are obtained through subjective evaluation and involve the professional judgment of librarians, appraisal from subject experts, or the opinion of customers. These techniques include impressions of the condition, character and appropriateness of a section of the collection. Another qualitative technique is the judgment made by comparison of one subject in the collection to a similar subject in another library, or to a subject bibliography.

Collection depth indicators indicated are: current collection level, acquisition commitment and collection goal. Indicators define out of scope, minimum information level, basic information level, study and instructional support, research level, comprehensive level etc Each institution, including its community and other constituents, is unique.

Therefore, its policy statements will be unique. The policy statements should reflect this particular library and the community it serves.

ALA POLICY

ALA covers following standard elements in its policy developed for academic libraries (College)

- *Standards* 1: Mission, Goals, and Objectives of institution
- *Standard* 2: Collections: including print materials in all formats, audiovisual materials, sound recordings, materials used with computers, graphics, and three dimensional materials.
- A formula is also presented in terms of collection development in the policy
- *Standard* 3: Organisation of materials: Library collections shall be organised by nationally approved conventions and arranged for efficient retrieval at time of need. The processing methods need to be applied for this purpose.
- *Standard* 4: Staff: The staff shall be of adequate size and quality to meet the library's need for services, programmes, and collection organisation.
- A staff formula is also presented in the policy
- *Standard* 5: Services: The library shall establish, promote, maintain a range and quality of services that supports the academic programme of the institution and encourage optional library use.
- *Standards* 6: Facilities: The library building shall provide well-planned, secure and adequate housing for its collections and personnel; secure space for users and staff, and space for the provision of services and programmes. A formula is also presented to calculate the space for per vol/Per Sqft.
- *Standards* 7: Administration: The college library shall be administered in a manner which permits and encourages the fullest and most effective use of available library resources.
- *Standard* 8: Budget:
- The library director shall have the responsibility for preparing, defending, and administering the library budget in accord with agreed upon objectives. These standards provide the guideline for formulating the policy.

UNIVERSITY GRANT COMMISSION (UGC) COLLECTION DEVELOPMENT POLICY

The UGC policy stated following points for collection development:

- Library Committee and its constituents (Chairman, member secretary, members, student representative)
- Library Collection norms based on courses, students and faculty
- Technical Processing.
- Library Finance
- Library Services
- Library Personnel
- Physical Facilities

AICTE COLLECTION DEVELOPMENT POLICY FOR ENGINEERING COLLEGE LIBRARIES

All India Council for Technical Education (AICTE) has formulated norms or policy for development of library collection including number of titles and their volumes, number of national and international journals including e-resources made available through INDESTAICTE. The main elements covered with formulas are:

- Collection of Books and Journals (Print Reading Material)
- Collection of Electronic Resources (e-journals and e-books etc)
- Library Personnel and Library Building

LIBRARY OF CONGRESS. COLLECTION DEVELOPMENT POLICIES

The Library's Collection Development Policy is a guide for materials to be added to the Library's permanent collections. The Collection Policy Statement (CPS) governs the Library's collection development and acquisition efforts. The statements implement the Library's responsibilities to serve. The policies provide a plan for developing the collections and maintaining their existing strengths.The highlighted points in to this policy are:

- *Collecting Levels*: Out of scope no need to buy, minimum level, basic information level, instructional level, research level, comprehensive level
- *Collection Overviews*: Scope, research strength,
- *Selection Guidelines for Electronic Resources*: Evaluate contents, add value, server reliability, judicious use of multimedia, adherence to copyright and fair use guidelines, provision of links to source for the plug-in-software, organisation and ease of navigation, presence of search and help features, procurement of Standard Fee based resources with permanent retention.

From the analytical study of the collection development policies it is understood that minimum components to be considered are:

- *Selection*: Covers purpose (free or purchased) teaching, learning, research and needs of staff and students; responsibility (Staff and librarian), Format (Print or digital), Language, special collections
- *Allocation of resources*: Considerations based on need based requirements and on demand procurement and provide more access to information than possession.
- *Collection maintenance*: Retention policies considering usage, main stack, parallel stacking, compact storage, weeding, retro-conversion etc are properly applied for better management and reduction in cost.
- *Preservation*: Rare and useful collection is to be retained for longer use and needs proper preservation manual or converting to digital

- *Access*: open access or authority permitted to consult in case of rare and confidential.
- *More use of e-publications*: The print media is shifting to e-publications and databases and more use is observed in the present generation.
- *Network based resources and consortium arrangement*: These are also to be considered while planning collection economically
- *Resource sharing and IR initiatives*: Open access and IR and resource sharing initiatives need to be considered

There is a need to develop proper collection in different forms. Collection development policies are to be framed for digital collection also as these documents may increase in the collection including acquisition and resource sharing policies.

The policies need to be revised regularly. Policy supports to customer-focused needs, so that library users have access to current, relevant and authoritative information in their preferred format.

4

Library Finance

INTRODUCTION

In this chapter we first present the data compiled and discuss their validity. Then Trends over the eight-year period are established. Expenditure is then analysed 'per capita' - to normalise the results between large and small countries. Most CEE States show very low levels of resources in financial terms. The reason of this may be due to currency conversion problems, but much can be attributed to lower standards of living and of national resource in the economy of those states. To understand this better the main data are, finally, analysed as a proportion of Gross Domestic Product (GDP) devoted to library resources.

METHODOLOGY

The most comprehensive and reliable Expenditure data are provided for materials. It is unusual for library managers not to have a materials budget, so figures on materials expenditure are generally maintained and reported. The cost of rebinding and preservation activity is often not included with expenditure on new books. 'Servicing' operations - special physical labelling and reinforcement plus catalogue cards or records - is often done by the supplier and included here: but sometimes it is done by library staff and charged to a general account. Data on staff expenditure are usually available - although there can be comparability problems where payroll is managed by a parent sponsoring department rather than by the library itself.

There are also different practices regarding the inclusion or exclusion of the costs of recruitment, staff training - though it is now generally accepted that indirect items - pensions, social security, etc. - need to be included. Figures for total revenue expenditure are less complete: many returns give expenditure on materials and on staff but not total expenditure. There are comparability problems with various overhead items - particularly premises, security, refurbishment, and computer systems. For these reasons comparisons between Materials and Staff figures are generally more reliable and these possible pitfalls must be kept in mind when making comparisons. However, there has been little change in accounting procedures and conventions during the period, so the percentage change calculations can be treated with confidence.

INFLATION

While in real terms expenditure has increased significantly - the precise percentage depends on the index of general price inflation selected for the calculation. This varies significantly between countries - as is shown in Table. However, between 1991 - 1997 general price inflation in most Western European states varied within the 15 - 20 per cent range. The composite EU Consumer Price Index published in the Eurostat Yearbook 1997 gives 18.7% between 1991 and 1997 - with the rate of inflation slowing markedly since 1995. For our purposes inflation between 1991-98 is taken as about 20 per cent. Inflation in the price of books can be taken as within the same range but periodical prices increased by a vastly greater percentage. So, in broad terms, reported overall increases of expenditure above 20 per cent can certainly be treated as genuine increases in real terms.

Trends

There has been greatly increased activity in Tertiary Libraries and lack of growth - overall - in the Public Library sector, with modest growth in National Libraries. The obvious expectation from this is that levels of expenditure have increased more in the Tertiary sector than in others. Here we look at the situation overall - and at the main trend results as given in Table 6.1.

Table 6.1. Main Trends in Financial Results.

		Expenditure	
	1991 € millions	**1998 € millions**	**%age change**
Staff	5,007	6,697	34
Materials	2,342	3,121	33 Electronic information
317	528	67	
Total Revenue Expenditure	10,347	13,965	35
INCOME ITEMS	382	648	70
Fees and Charges			
Other' (i.e.special funds)	432	1,034	139 **CAPITAL**
PAYMENTS	487	695	43

Since staffing costs represent the largest part of the budget, expenditure on staff has increased at a rate reflected by the charge in total expenditure. The total expenditure on conventional materials also shows an average increase, but this average conceals an estimated + 64% for Special Libraries, + 40% for Tertiary, + 27% for National, + 33% for Schools, and only + 1% for Public Libraries. As anticipated the data show a dramatic 67 per cent increase in expenditure on Electronic Materials.

This is heavily concentrated in the Tertiary and Special Libraries sectors - and Special Libraries are more fully represented in these statistics than ever before. It is significant, however, that the 1998 results show Electronic Information still at only 15 per cent of total materials expenditure - so confirming that conventional materials are still dominant. Capital payments are reported by only a minority of states and are affected by inconsistent accounting both within and between states.

The increase reported in Capital Payments contains some impressive investment in National Libraries during the period. No separate figure is necessary for total income, as all library organisations balance their books – at least over a number of years.

Perhaps the most surprising revelation in this set of statistics lies in the specifically identified 'Income Items'.

The magnitude of the increase in Fees and Charges - 70 per cent - is impressive, and the pattern is virtually universal across all countries. At this strength this is a new trend.

It would be interesting to explore how far it relates to income from conventional services and how far it is associated with new electronic resources and networked provision of materials. The even larger increase in 'Other' income will relate to specific grants for development and modernisation as well as to diversified funding sources. Again it would be interesting and important to have more detailed information on this - now that these statistics establish the magnitude of this trend.

The net result of these 'Income Items' is that they now cover 12 per cent of total library expenditure - the balance coming from regular institutional sources.

Countries and Sectors

We present here a number of 'Cross Sector Total' tables covering the main financial variables. Each table consists first of the 1998 data entered onto the database for each country. Three dots (...) shows that no satisfactory information was provided for that feature in that country. The next part contains the grossed up estimates for All States and for regions and geographical areas. The 'Response%' gives the proportion of the All States grossed up figure that is represented by actual data. Finally percentages are calculated to show, for this feature, the relative strength of each sector overall - which have already been presented in Table.

MATERIALS SPEND

Table 6.2 summarises the available data - uncorrected for population or for living standards. This gives a useful indication of the size of the library market for suppliers of print materials. The returns are particularly comprehensive for the Tertiary sector. The data in table take no account of country size.

Table 6.2. Materials Costs (€ 000s).

0	National 1	Tertiary 2	Public 3	Special 4	Other 5	School 6	1998 Total 7
Bulgaria	98	391	450	240	158	79	
Czech Republic	495	3,253	4,485	...	0	...	
Estonia	385	1,049	2,860	272	702	809	
Hungary	382	...	3,630	6,553	...	...	
Latvia	261	281	849	...	77	...	
Lithuania	232	436	960	340	264	3,942	
Poland	382	7,932	...	...	...	...	
Romania	190	...	798	...	0	...	
Slovak Republic	176	1,008	962	...	...	6	
Slovenia	...	3,844	6,116	...	0	5,566	
Austria	1,352	26,526	5,038	...	...	...	
Belgium	...	14,408	23,238	...	...	...	
Denmark	2,155	13,831	46,576	4,801	0	16,197	
Ireland	344	10,754	7,131	...	0	...	
Finland	735	14,259	32,928	1,497	...	...	
France	...	57,044	100,661	...	...	...	
Greece	...	...	...	...	...	...	
Iceland	...	...	1,492	...	0	...	
Italy	...	65,603	...	...	...	...	
Liecht-enstein	...	...	...	...	0	...	
Luxembourg	...	...	...	...	0	...	
0	**1**	**2**	**3**	**4**	**5**	**6**	**7**
Netherlands	1,396	32,180	...	55,114	0	...	
Norway	424	16,468	15,505	6,385	0	...	
Portugal	336	7,600	2,310	3,685	22	...	
Spain	2,047	49,883	22,575	35,053	4,365	...	
Sweden	710	23,184	40,985	2,200	...	...	
Switzerland	733	...	...	...	0	...	
UK	19,675	175,985	179,920	327,452	0	76,161	
Germany	32,725	198,427	86,406	94,623	...	...	

All States	98,752	779,841	761,850	900,389	14,574	565,555	3,120,961
CEE	2,566	27,560	32,470	52,412	2,257	75,041	192,306
EU	94,999	708,594	686,870	831,036	12,317	480,480	2,814,296
EFTA	1,187	43,687	42,510	16,941	0	10,033	114,358
Northern	4,052	68,738	137,486	15,269	466	38,356	264,367
Europe							
Central Europe	72,538	542,317	456,069	662,916	5,198	304,879	2,043,917
Southern Europe	19,597	141,226	135,826	169,791	6,653	147,278	620,371
Baltic States	878	1,767	4,669	20,296	1,043	6,427	35,080
Eastern Europe	1,688	25,793	27,801	32,116	1,215	68,614	157,227
Response total	65,151	724,346	585,875	538,215	5,588	102,760	2,021,935
Response%	66	93	77	60	38	18	65
Sector proportions	3.2	25	24.4	28.8	0.5	18.1	100

In order to produce figures that are more comparable between countries, these data have been presented on a 'per capita' basis in Table 6.3. The base for this table is not the sector's 'Target Population to be served': while this can be satisfactorily calculated for Tertiary, School and Public library clientele, there are severe difficulties in arriving at meaningful figures for the National and Special Library sectors. So in the interests of comparability the base here is Total Population.

Table 6.3. Materials Spend Per 1,000 Population (€ 000s).

0	National 1	Tertiary 2	Public 3	Special 4	Other 5	School 6	1998 Total 7
Bulgaria	11	45	51	27	18	9	
Czech Republic	48	316	436	...	0	...	
Estonia	252	686	1,869	178	458	529	
Hungary	38	...	359	648	...	...	
Latvia	102	110	332	...	30	...	
Lithuania	63	118	259	92	71	1,065	
Poland	10	207	...	...	...	...	
Romania	8	...	35	...	0	...	
Slovak	33	188	180	...	...	1	

Republic							
Slovenia	...	1,976	3,144	...	0	2,861	
Austria	169	3,319	630	...	...	...	
Belgium	...	1,488	2,400	...	...	...	
Denmark	422	2,707	9,115	940	0	3,170	
Ireland	99	3,101	2,056	...	0	...	
Finland	146	2,836	6,549	298	...	...	
France	...	1,031	1,819	...	...	...	
Greece	...	...	...	...	...	...	
Iceland	...	...	5,587	...	0	...	
Italy	...	1,159	...	...	...	...	
0	**1**	**2**	**3**	**4**	**5**	**6**	**7**
Liechte-nstein	...	...	...	...	0	...	
Luxembourg	...	...	...	...	0	...	
Netherlands	95	2,181	...	3,735	0	...	
Norway	97	3,765	3,545	1,460	0	...	
Portugal	33	748	227	363	2	...	
Spain	53	1,299	588	913	114	...	
Sweden	81	2,647	4,679	251	...	...	
Switzerland	107	...	...	...	0	...	
UK	345	3,085	3,154	5,740	0	1,335	
Germany	411	2,490	1,084	1,187	...	...	
All States	206	1,627	1,589	1,878	30	1,180	6,510
CEE	24	261	308	497	21	711	1,822
EU	262	1,956	1,896	2,294	34	1,326	7,768
EFTA	103	3,788	3,686	1,469	0	870	9,916 Northern
Europe	172	2,920	5,841	649	20	1,629	11,231 Central
Europe	308	2,305	1,939	2,818	22	1,296	8,688 Southern
Europe	170	1,227	1,181	1,476	58	1,280	5,392
Baltic States	113	227	600	2,606	134	825	4,505
Eastern Europe	17	264	285	329	12	702	1,609
Response total	...	...	...	...	...	...	...
Response %	...	...	...	...	...	...	...
Sector proportions	3.2	25	24.4	28.8	0.5	18.1	100

So, in 1998, European libraries spent on conventional materials □3.121 billion - and this represented an average of □6.5 per capita. A number of conclusions can be drawn from table:

- With the exception of Estonia and Slovenia it appears that the level of expenditure is very much lower in CEE states than in EU states. How far this is due to lack of economic wealth in those states generally - and how far to low resources devoted to libraries.
- In the EU States there is a tendency for high spending countries to spend at high levels in all sectors. The lower spending countries, on this 'per capita' basis, appear to be Portugal, Spain and France - with Scandinavian countries spending most.
- Again in the EU States there is much more homogeneity in the Tertiary sector than in Public Libraries.

The very high expenditure figure for UK Special Libraries stands out as quite exceptional.

This could be the result of either:

- More comprehensive and innovative statistical analysis,
- Exaggeration in the statistical estimating and/or
- A more developed information economy in the UK - particularly with respect to libraries in industry and commerce.

Table 6.4. Staff Expenditure (€ 000s).

0	National 1	Tertiary 2	Public 3	Special 4	Other 5	School 6	1998 Total 7
Bulgaria	315	636	2,808	259	785	444	
Czech Republic	1,586	...	12,175	...	0	612	
Estonia	1,853	1,266	3,944	489	620	1,121	
Hungary	3,422	...	17,186	...	...	...	
0	1	2	3	4	5	6	7
Latvia	697	451	3,265	...	295	...	
Lithuania	1,241	1,174	6,635	759	322	...	
Poland	3,081	12,703	...	...	...	...	
Romania	555	...	2,656	...	0	...	
Slovak Republic	1,005	...	3,904	...	...	...	
Slovenia	...	...	10,927	...	0	8,100	
Austria	13,125	...	...	...	...	...	
Belgium	...	24,698	124,273	...	...	...	
Denmark	12,313	34,062	183,781	10,516	0	20,841	

Ireland	2,011	22,250	28,183	...	0	...	
Finland	4,951	26,400	125,322	7,198	...	...	
France	...	126,698	530,943	...	...	...	
Greece	...	...	...	...	...	...	
Iceland	...	...	3,580	...	0	...	
Italy	...	104,480	...	...	...	...	
Liechte-nstein	...	...	...	...	0	...	
Luxem-bourg	...	...	...	...	0	...	
Nether-lands	...	...	...	...	0	...	
Norway	...	...	61,386	...	0	...	
Portugal	4,075	4,732	10,358	7,908	858	...	
Spain	10,407	82,664	87,790	52,444	25,460	...	
Sweden	10,047	54,680	157,034	10,899	...	...	
Switzerland	6,139	...	...	...	0	...	
UK	91,000	298,768	662,676	547,430	0	188,576	
0	**1**	**2**	**3**	**4**	**5**	**6**	**7**
Germany	84,495	240,319	477,250	67,986	...	...	
All States	372,581	1,209,703	3,348,022	1,253,91	760,041	453,134	6,697,398
CEE	14,012	28,530	105,038	11,701	4,109	83,165	246,555
EU	332,297	1,131,053	3,080,070	1,215,475	55,932	356,853	6,171,680
EFTA	26,272	50,120	162,914	26,741	0	13,116	279,163
Northern Europe	47,368	135,134	531,102	39,279	7,403	120,809	881,095
Central Europe	259,889	825,443	2,085,673	951,791	14,807	214,303	4,351,906
Southern Europe	51,312	220,596	626,209	251,146	33,722	34,857	1,217,842
Baltic States	3,791	2,890	13,843	1,460	1,237	4,744	27,965
Eastern Europe	10,221	25,640	91,195	10,241	2,872	78,422	218,591
Response total	252,318	1,035,981	2,516,076	705,888	28,340	219,694	4,758,297
Response %	68	86	75	56	47	48	71
Sector proportions	5.6	18.1	50.0	18.7	0.9	6.8	100.1

Further study is called for - and the encouragement of more data collection in this area. Comparisons with the situation in large countries in the Western Hemisphere would also be pertinent.Comparing Tertiary with Public library materials expenditure at the country level is enlightening. States can be broadly placed in three categories:

Public Double Tertiary	Public = Tretiary	Tertiary Double Public
Bulgaria, Czech Republic	Slovak Pepublic	Austria
Estonia, Latvia	Solvenia	Ireland
Lithuania, Belgium, Denmark,	Norway	Germany
Finland, Sweeden, France	UK	Spain

There are a number of possible explanations for this:

- Historical emphasis in developing one sector earlier than another;
- Unequal allocation of resources;
- Public libraries in some countries taking on a major role for students;
- In some countries the public using academic libraries for some Non Fiction and Reference material.

These point either to institutional differences in the scope of each sector or to abnormal resource allocation. It is important to establish which is the main feature.

This is not the place to speculate on particular situations - but the contrasts are so unexpectedly large that the reasons for these differences deserve serious consideration by policy makers in the states concerned. The low Tertiary results suggest the possibility of intellectual deprivation through inadequate provision of scientific and technical journals in the academic libraries of smaller or poorer countries - though this may be made good where national library is a major academic library *e.g.* Slovenia, Slovak Republic and Estonia.

While the newly compiled data on Special Libraries is incomplete and more subject to errors of estimation than more established statistical series, the data from Hungary, the Netherlands, Spain and the UK suggest that the level of expenditure on Materials may be as high, or even higher, in the Special Libraries sector than in Public and Tertiary libraries. Data from the School Library sector is much more sparse - sufficient only to point to the need for more data in what is an important area. The estimates of 28.8% for Special Libraries and of 18.1% for School Libraries must be treated with considerable caution at this stage: but their size certainly alters the perspective in which these sectors have traditionally been regarded.

EXPENDITURE ON STAFF

The response here is not quite as complete as for Materials expenditure. Comparing the two heads a very much higher proportion is spent on staff in public libraries (50% of all staff expenditure) - and to a lesser extent in national libraries. This largely reflects the much higher prices required for materials in the Tertiary and Special Library sectors compared to Public and School Library sectors. A simple but interesting ratio can be derived by combining Expenditure on Staff with Staff Numbers to give the data contained in table Staff Expenditure per Member of Staff.

Table 6.5. Staff Expenditure Per Member of Staff (€ 000s).

	National	Tertiary	Public	Special	Other	School	1998
0	1	2	3	4	5	6 7	Total
Bulgaria	957	...	...	...	...	...	
Czech Republic	3,573	...	2,803	...	...	...	
Estonia	3,527	2,541	2,689	3,109	4,770	2,098	
Hungary	6,337	...	4,428	...	...	...	
Latvia	1,557	1,365	1,718	...	2,953	...	
Lithuania	2,009	1,817	1,612	1,745	2,119	...	
Poland	3,397	1,924	...	...	...	...	
Romania	1,580	...	530	...	...	...	
Slovak Republic	3,573	...	2,803	...	...	...	
Slovenia	...	...	14,100	...	...	10,384	
Austria	42,613	...	...	...	...	...	
Belgium	...	34,786	31,541	...	...	...	
Denmark	38,941	38,101	35,347	26,965	...	17,966	
Ireland	29,569	29,666	21,679	...	...	...	
Finland	27,519	23,943	29,888	28,791	...	...	
France	...	32,621	25,843	...	...	...	
Greece	**...**	**...**	**...**	**...**	**...**	**...**	
0	1	2	3	4	5	6	7
Iceland	...	...	...	...	...	...	
Italy	...	...	...	...	...	...	
Liecht-enstein	...	...	...	...	...	...	
Luxem-bourg	...	...	...	...	...	...	
Nether-lands	...	...	...	...	...	...	
Norway	...	...	32,286	...	...	...	
Portugal	12,853	5,029	7,149	6,173	9,431	...	
Spain	20,013	17,970	15,962	16,544	17,320	...	
Sweden	34,525	34,895	30,037	33,230	...	...	
Switz-erland	59,482	...	...	...	...	...	

UK	31,347	22,982	25,656	30,413	...	36,265	
Germany	38,582	25,936	25,251	10,665	...	...	
All States	24,456	19,559	19,791	20,009	7,996	7,822	99,632
CEE	3,049	1,895	2,341	1,129	981	1,792	11,187
EU	32,629	25,474	25,863	23,775	16,842	33,054	157,637
EFTA	57,665	20,982	31,250	22,694	...	18,171	150,762
Northern Europe	41,605	29,908	31,801	27,309	16,826	27,266	174,715
Central Europe	34,272	25,875	26,034	24,748	16,826	35,492	163,246
Southern Europe	26,753	21,272	22,780	20,247	16,852	33,229	141,134
Baltic States	2,383	1,960	1,850	1,856	3,239	1,650	12,938
Eastern Europe	3,402	1,888	2,440	1,069	755	1,801	11,354
0	**1**	**2**	**3**	**4**	**5**	**6**	**7**
Response total	•••	•••	•••	•••	•••	•••	•••
Response %	•••	•••	•••	•••	•••	•••	•••
Sector proportions	24.5	19.6	19.9	20.1	8.0	7.9	100

It should be remembered that the data requested here are the average cost per member of staff and not staff salaries, *i.e.* they should include social security and other indirect costs incurred by the employing organisation. But, with these reservations, the table will point to variations in staff salary levels.

A number of observations can be made:

- First, one value of these ratios is their use to check and query data supplied - to reveal transposition or categorisation errors and to get wrong data corrected.
- Generally there is consistency within a country where the figures for the main sectors show relatively low variation.
- The fact that the Special Library ratios mostly correspond to the norm gives confidence to them.
- The low costs in the few Schools figures may reflect less qualified personnel employed in Schools libraries – or failure to apply the FTE formula to part time staff.
- The above average levels in National and Special Libraries are no surprise given the technically advanced work requirements there and lower proportions of unqualified staff employed.

Again, however, it is clear that most of the CEE States and Portugal are showing very low figures. How far are these to be explained by low salary levels for librarians and how far by the low standard of living in those countries' economies? One approach to answer this question lies in relating library salary levels to the countries' Gross Domestic Product (GDP).

The table 6.6 shows "Employee Expenditure per member of Staff" related to each country's Per capita GDP - adjusted for Purchasing Power Parity to take account of the lower cost of goods and services in some countries.

Table 6.6. Librarian Salary Levels Related to GDP 1998 €s.

Economy	National Libraries	Public Libraries	National		
Capita	GDP Per Staff	Employee Expenditure Per Member of	As Proportion of GDP Staff	Employee Expenditure Per Member of	As Proportion of GDP
1	2	3	4	5	6
Bulgaria	4,352	...	...	957	0.22
Czech Republic	12,351	2,803	0.23	3,573	0.29
Estonia	6,391	2,689	0.42	3,527	0.55
Hungary	8,391	4,428	0.53	6,337	0.76
Latvia	4,656	1,718	0.37	1,557	0.33
Lithuania	5,006	1,612	0.32	2,009	0.40
Poland	7,879	...	...	3,397	0.43
Romania	4,955	530	0.11	1,580	0.32
Slovak Republic	9,536	2,026	0.21	2,879	0.30
Slovenia	13,867	14,100	1.02	...	...
Austria	25,342	...	...	42,613	1.68
Belgium	26,237	31,541	1.20	...	...
Denmark	27,643	35,347	1.28	38,941	1.41
Ireland	25,597	21,679	0.85	29,569	1.16
Finland	23,794	29,888	1.26	27,519	1.16
1	2	3	4	5	6
France	25,369	25,843	1.02	...	...
Greece	14,452	...	...	...	...
Iceland	26,163	...	...	...	...
Italy	23,315	...	...	...	...
Liechtenstein	32,231	...	...	...	...
Luxembourg	35,767	...	...	...	...
Netherlands	24,505	...	...	...	...

Norway	28,706	32,286	1.12	...	...
Portugal	16,698	7,149	0.43	12,853	0.77
Spain	18,525	15,962	0.86	20,013	1.08
Sweden	22,827	30,037	1.32	34,525	1.51
Switzerland	28,706	...	...	59,482	2.07
UK	24,124	25,656	1.06	31,347	1.30
Germany	24,416	25,251	1.03	38,582	1.58
All States	20,089	19,791	0.99	24,456	1.22
CEE	7,464	2,341	0.31	3,049	0.41
EU	23,344	25,863	1.11	32,629	1.40
EFTA	28,657	31,250	1.09	57,665	2.01
Northern Europe	25,219	31,801	1.26	41,605	1.65
Central Europe	24,848	26,034	1.05	34,272	1.38
Southern Europe	20,354	22,780	1.12	26,753	1.31
Baltic States	5,158	1,850	0.36	2,383	0.46
Eastern Europe	7,644	2,440	0.32	3,402	0.45

Per capita GDP is taken here to indicate the relative cost of living and labour cost in each country. 'Salary levels' are given for Public Libraries and for National Libraries - those being the sectors with most complete responses on the database. As an example we find that, in Estonia, Public library staff cost 2,689-6,391 = 0.42 (or 42%) of average labour costs: National Library staff cost 3,527-6,391 = 0.55 (or 55%) of average labour costs. In the average for All States the cost of public library labour equates almost exactly to the European average but labour costs in National Libraries are 22% above the European average. When comparing CEE to EU and EFTA it is obvious from the individual country data that the CEE ratios are very much lower. The calculated averages are:

	Public	**National**
CEE	0.31	0.41
EU	1.11	1.40
EFTA Norway	1.12	
Switzerlant		2.01

So these statistics show:

- That library salaries are much below country averages in CEE states,
- That they are somewhat above country averages in EU states, and
- That in both sectors they are higher in national libraries than in public libraries.

Thus, not only are the CEE states less wealthy economies, but the cost of library staff is below average within those countries. In layman's terms librarians earn less than half the average salary in CEE States, but they are paid slightly above average in EU States - and will above average in Northern Europe. An important corollary of this state of affairs is that there is less incentive in economic terms to introduce labour saving automation in the CEE states - since labour costs are relatively low already.

TOTAL REVENUE EXPENDITURE

Comparisons between EU and CEE financial statistics are greatly complicated by the different economic conditions pertaining. To a lesser extent this also applies to comparisons between Mediterranean states and Northern Europe. This is the reason why, for most purposes, it is more valid to concentrate on the operational, non financial. However, for completeness, the data on Total Revenue Expenditure is presented in another 'Cross Sector Total' table and the 'per capita' results (per 1000 total population).

Table 6.7. Total Revenue Expenditure (€ 000s).

1	National 2	Tertiary 3	Public 4	Special 5	Other 6	School Total	1998 7	0
Bulgaria	488	1,342	3,481	550	1,389	527		
Czech Republic	4,951	...	29,536	...	0	...		
Estonia	3,416	2,539	8,757	1,041	1,753	2,026		
Hungary	...	...	29,914	...	...	...		
Latvia	1,844	938	6,528	...	591	...		
Lithuania	3,312	2,004	11,284	1,284	820	...		
Poland	8,962	26,331	...	...	...	...		
Romania	955	...	4,864	...	0	...		
Slovak Republic	2,987	...	7,656	...	...	316		
Slovenia	...	9,697	23,493	...	0	14,290		
Austria	16,977	...	33,955	...	...	...		
Belgium	6,162	45,864	...	...	...	...		
Denmark	19,104	57,694	304,652	17,625	0	37,892		
Ireland	3,318	37,083	47,393	...	0	...		
Finland	11,502	57,202	218,681	11,618	...	...		
France	...	235,364	...	...	...	...		
Greece	...	...	...	...	...	...		
Iceland	...	...	7,459	...	0	666		

Italy	6,841	242,976	...	...	...	...	

1	2	3	4	5	6	7	
Liechtenstein	...	...	...	...	0	...	
Luxembourg	...	...	...	...	0	...	
Netherlands	...	...	...	...	0	...	
Norway	16,884	48,069	99,953	15,544	0	...	
Portugal	6,875	13,194	14,787	12,623	1,079	...	
Spain	17,061	142,524	125,414	93,746	36,372	...	
Sweden	17,378	99,945	327,907	15,581	...	...	
Switzerland	11,149	...	...	...	0	...	
UK	205,583	588,822	1,211,735	1,205,000•	287,902		
Germany	139,868	...	787,475	...	...	...	
All States	757,230	2,780,005	6,279,359	2,969,001	105,469	1,073,461	13,964,525
CEE	39,925	84,437	246,126	77,460	9,745	169,693	627,386
EU	665,332	2,496,377	5,763,733	2,812,544	95,724	879,605	12,713,315
EFTA	51,973	199,191	269,500	78,997	0	24,163	623,824
Northern Europe	91,057	318,330	1,060,630	79,579	10,941	168,640	1,729,177
Central Europe	531,802	1,875,606	3,829,170	2,224,444	28,194	547,006	9,036,222
Southern Europe	94,446	501,631	1,143,433	587,518	56,589	188,122	2,571,739
Baltic States	8,581	5,757	28,923	26,347	3,229	11,778	84,615
Eastern Europe	31,344	78,681	217,204	51,113	6,516	157,915	542,773
Response total	505,617	1,611,588	3,304,924	1,374,612•	42,004	343,619	5,977,364
Response %	67	58	53	6	40	32	43
Sector proportions	5.4	19.9	45.0	21.3	0.8	7.7	100.1

Notes:

• Calculated by adding the average 38% to {Materials + Staff Expenditure}

There is little in the results for individual countries that has not already been noted in the analysis of Materials and Staff expenditure.

Table 6.8. Total Revenue Expenditure Per 1,00 Population €s.

0	National 1	Tertiary 2	Public 3	Special 4	Other 5	School 6	1998 Total 7
Bulgaria	56	153	397	63	158	60	
Czech Republic	481	...	2,869	...	0	...	

Estonia	2,232	1,659	5,722	680	1,146	1,324	
Hungary	...	...	2,957	...	...	...	
Latvia	721	367	2,553	...	231	...	
Lithuania	895	542	3,050	347	222	...	
Poland	233	686	...	...	...	...	
Romania	42	...	213	...	0	...	
Slovak Republic	558	...	1,430	...	...	59	
Slovenia	...	4,984	12,074	...	0	7,345	
Austria	2,124	...	4,249	...	...	...	
Belgium	636	4,736	...	...	...	...	
Denmark	3,738	11,290	59,619	3,449	0	7,415	
Ireland	957	10,693	13,666	...	0	...	
Finland	2,288	11,377	43,493	2,311	...	...	
France	...	4,253	...	...	...	...	
Greece	...	...	...	...	...	...	
Iceland	...	...	27,937	...	0	2,494	
Italy	121	4,293	...	...	...	...	
1	**2**	**3**	**4**	**5**	**6**	**7**	
Liechtenstein	...	...	...	...	0	...	
Luxembourg	...	...	...	...	0	...	
Netherlands	...	...	...	...	0	...	
Norway	3,860	10,990	22,852	3,554	0	...	
Portugal	677	1,298	1,455	1,242	106	...	
Spain	444	3,713	3,267	2,442	948	...	
Sweden	1,984	11,409	37,432	1,779	...	...	
Switzerland	1,625	...	...	...	0	...	
UK	3,604	10,321	21,240	21,222	0	5,047	
Germany	1,755	...	9,882	...	...	...	
All States 800	1,580 2,333	5,800 734	13,100 92	6,194 1,609	220 5,946	2,240	29,134 CEE 378
EU	1,836	6,890	15,909	7,763	264	2,428	35,090
EFTA	4,507	17,273	23,370	6,850	0	2,095	54,095
Northern Europe	3,868	13,524	45,058	3,381	465	7,164	73,460
Central Europe	2,261	7,973	16,278	9,456	120	2,325	38,413

Southern Europe	821	4,360	9,938	5,106	492	1,635	22,352
Baltic States	1,102	739	3,714	3,383	415	1,512	10,865
Eastern Europe	321	805	2,223	523	67	1,616	5,555
Response total	•••	•••	•••	•••	•••	•••	•••
Response %	•••	•••	•••	•••	•••	•••	•••
Sector proportions	5.4	19.9	45.0	21.3	0.8	7.7	100.1

Here it is the grossed up totals that are particularly important - as they provide the best estimate available of the magnitude of library services in Europe overall. The grand total estimate is that, on average, □29.1 are spent per head of population on library services. Of this □6.5 go on traditional Materials and □14.0 on Staff. Compared to an EU estimated average of □35 per head of population the estimates for Eastern Europe are □5.6 and for the Baltic States □10.9. There is again a wide spread between countries. Of the four countries that replied for all sectors the lowest was □0.9 per head and the highest □86.

These overall estimates are of limited value since there are such wide differences between each sector, and because the statistical validity of the data is much better for some sectors than for others, and because of exchange rate complexities.

Analysis at the sector level is therefore more valid and of more interest - and it is that on which most of this report concentrates. Within the EU States we see the same pattern of low spending and high spending countries with a wide gap between the Nordic highs and the Mediterranean lows.

There is also a very wide range within the CEE group of countries - which would be even lower but for the relatively high and complete results reported from Slovenia and Estonia. There are two further hypotheses suggested by these results - which can only be established after further study.

- There is a correlation between countries with the most complete statistics and those with the most developed services.
- Small countries have to devote relatively more resources to libraries since they do not benefit from economies of scale to the same extent as large countries.

Both these hypotheses deserve further investigation: but it is particularly recommended that more complete statistical reporting is given a high priority by agencies funding library and information service development.

LIBRARY RESOURCES AS PROPORTION OF GDP

This leads into the next stage of analysis - to explore what proportion of the economic wealth of Europe is devoted to libraries - how far variation is due to lack of economic wealth in individual states generally - and how far to a low proportion of that wealth is devoted to libraries. Table shows Total Revenue Expenditure as a proportion of GDP adjusted for Purchasing Power Parity.

Table . Total Revenue Expenditure as Proportion of GDP and PP €s Spent Per Million GDP.

0	National 1	Tertiary 2	Public 3	Special 4	Other 5	School 6	1998 Total 7
Bulgaria	13	50	132	22	49	14	
Czech Republic	42	...	291	...	...	...	
Estonia	349	271	970	106	179	208	
Hungary	...	...	469	...	...	...	
Latvia	156	88	615	...	55	...	
Lithuania	179	111	654	69	44	...	
Poland	30	87	...	...	...	...	
Romania	8	...	43	...	...	...	
Slovak Republic	59	...	150	...	...	10	
Slovenia	...	485	1,049	...	...	536	
Austria	91	...	388	...	...	...	
Belgium	31	181	...	...	...	...	
Denmark	148	476	2,530	135	...	268	
Ireland	37	496	548	...	...	...	
Finland	96	503	2,154	97	...	...	
France	...	196	...	...	...	...	
Greece	...	...	...	...	...	...	
Iceland	...	...	1,069	...	...	167	
1	**2**	**3**	**4**	**5**	**6**	**7**	
Italy	32	190	...	...	...	...	
Liechtenstein	...	...	...	...	...	...	
Luxembourg	...	...	...	...	...	...	
Netherlands	...	...	...	...	...	...	
Norway	306	597	797	237	0	...	
Portugal	48	90	97	96	7	...	
Spain	29	242	211	180	59	...	
Sweden	96	557	1,691	87	...	...	
Switzerland	62	...	...	...	0	...	

UK	152	428	880	...	...	209	
Germany	85	...	488	...	...	...	
All States	79	289	652	308	11	111	1,450
CEE	51	107	313	98	12	216	797
EU	79	295	681	333	11	104	1,503
EFTA	157	603	816	239	0	73	1,888
Northern Europe	153	536	1,787	134	18	284	2,913
Central Europe	91	321	655	381	5	94	1,546
Southern Europe	40	214	488	251	24	80	1,098
Baltic States	214	143	720	656	80	293	2,107
Eastern Europe	42	105	291	68	9	211	727
Response total	•••	•••	•••	•••	•••	•••	•••
Response %	•••	•••	•••	•••	•••	•••	•••
Sector proportions	5.4	19.9	45.0	21.3	0.8	7.7	100.1

On average 0.145 per cent of GDP was spent on libraries. Only four countries provided data for all six sectors, and they ranged from a low of 0.03 per cent to a high of 0.36 per cent. As elsewhere it is best to concentrate on those sectors that are comprehensively reported - National, Tertiary and Public; the EFTA totals should be disregarded as only one EFTA state provided data. While the CEE average of 0.08% is well below the 'All States' 0.145%, when we look at the Baltic States separately we find that their proportion of GDP devoted to libraries is actually above average (0.21 per cent). It is Eastern Europe (0.0727 per cent) and Southern Europe (.1098 per cent) where library spending - proportionate to GDP - is significantly below average. Policy makers in every country, and those interested in a particular sector, should benefit from studying this table - in addition to the ratios per head of population. Relating sector expenditure to the 'All States' average per sector may be even more valuable than focus on the overall average.

5

Succession Planning and Development Process

PHASE I: IDENTIFYING AND ASSESSING TALENT

One of the key aspects of any succession management and development process is talent identification. In this phase of the process, you identify employees with the potential (often called "high potentials") for success in filling key roles, including leadership, and develop a talent profile for each. This process is completed by a succession planning committee—the leadership team or a subset of it convened for this purpose—and should always include the library director and HR director.

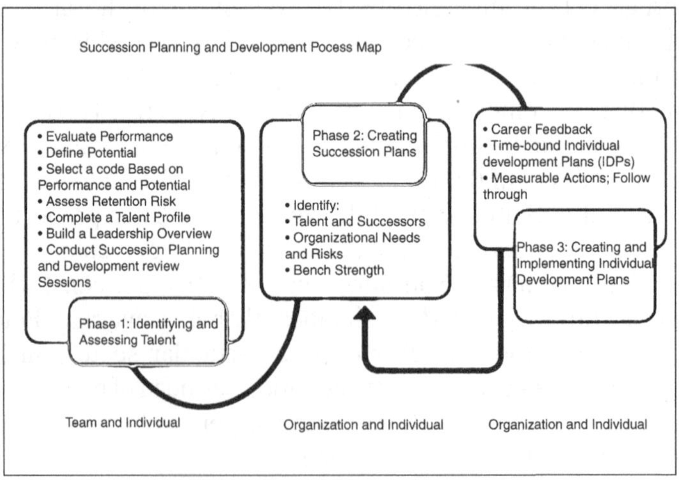

Fig. Succession Planning and Development Process Map.

There are several ways for the library to proceed as it assesses talent:

- The first choice point involves scope. Will identification and assessment be made of all library employees? Will talent profiles be created for all? In the alternative, will it be limited to target groups of employees by level (*e.g.*, all first-line managers)? Will the talent review focus only on leadership and star employees brought to the committee by HR, a library manager, or leader? Successful talent reviews have been conducted in all of these ways. Choosing the first or second option helps ensure that no one falls through the cracks because they are not visible or have a personality difference with their boss. Regardless of which method you chose, it is advisable that you begin the talent review process with senior leadership and other key positions, because these positions are usually hardest to fill and are staffed with employees most likely to retire in the shortest time frame.

- The second choice point pertains to who completes this first level of talent review; that is, who (specifically) compiles the information to create the individual talent profile. Should it be done by the employee's manager or supervisor and then brought to the succession planning committee for review? In the alternative, should the committee as a whole review staff under consideration and complete the profile together? In large library systems where leadership is not likely to be aware of the abilities and potential of most staff members, it is suggested that managers conduct the first level of review and bring their completed talent profiles to the succession planning committee. If the library is small enough that most members of the succession planning committee have a picture of the staff, even if it is just the top layers of staff, you will benefit from having the input of all. Numerous perspectives are likely to broaden the picture painted of the individual.
- The third choice point involves the composition of the committee that performs the second level of review—the succession planning committee. This group should always include the library director, the HR director (if the library is large enough to have one), and a group of senior leaders. They are responsible for the activities in phases 1 and 2 of the succession planning and development process and work from a focused agenda to complete their work. The HR director typically chairs the process and ensures that pre-session work (such as first-level talent reviews, if done by managers) is completed.

Once these choices have been made, leaders complete the following steps for each employee under review, producing a completed talent profile for each employee.

EVALUATE PERFORMANCE

The first step of assessing talent requires an accurate, completed performance appraisal for each employee. It would be shortsighted to build a talent profile on potential alone; performance ratings/profiles must be included as well. You should easily be able to translate the following definitions to your own form and process.

If you do not have an appraisal form, you may wish to consider employees as high, medium, and low performers in terms of the following definitions (and then develop a form and a process):

- *High-performing employees* are rated "exceeds expectations." They consistently meet and often exceed goals, consistently meet and often go beyond expectations defined in competencies, and are viewed as outstanding performers.
- *Medium performers* are often rated as "fully meets expectations." Most of the members of your workforce are likely to fall into this category: employees who fully meet expectations, consistently meet most goals, consistently perform at a satisfactory level in most areas, and may exceed expectations in some.
- These employees perform all aspects of the job with minimal errors and exhibit most of the competency behaviours. Others rely on these employees to perform all aspects of their jobs with a high degree of proficiency. These performers do have some room for performance growth.
- *Low performers* do not meet the expectations of the job. Though these employees may perform some aspects of the job well, they need improvement.

In this process, each employee is identified as a low, medium, or high performer. This rating will be combined with a rating of potential in the next step before it is entered into the individual talent profile.

DEFINE POTENTIAL

In this next step the library determines the ability and motivation of individual staff members to take on new or more senior roles in the short and long terms. According to many library directors, this is one of the most difficult aspects of the process. But by conducting this review systematically and globally (*i.e.*, throughout the library system), leadership can obtain a picture of its entire workforce and examine employees' potential and possibilities for development, change, lateral transfer, or promotion. During this step, leadership and HR are able to focus on the individual's key talent and ability for growth and increased contributions within the library system. Leadership should be keyed into looking for high-potential employees. But what is, who is, a "high-potential employee"? Employees with high potential are the library's future leaders and holders of key positions.

Broadly, they are the members of your workforce who are able and willing to advance two or more levels in the library, are possible candidates for key positions, or have not yet reached a plateau in their career. High potentials are not the same as stars. Although being rated as a star or as exceeding expectations (or whatever language the library uses to identify those in the top performance category) in the employee's current job is usually a prerequisite to identification as a high potential, not all stars are necessarily high potentials; advancement and leadership potential involve criteria other than current performance, not the least of which are ability, aspiration, and engagement.

Every library identifies its own key positions, yet experience shows us that many are at a loss about defining "high potential." What follows is a way for library leadership to view the differences between low-, growth-, and high-potential performers based on ability, aspiration, and engagement. Start with these definitions and view them as a draft. Feel free to alter and add, so that you create criteria and a narrative that fit your culture. You may find criteria more applicable than ability, aspiration, and engagement, or your culture may suggest different definitions or language for them.

Some possibilities include prior leadership experience, education, learning agility, assessment against competencies (often reviewed in the performance management process), leadership ability based on the library's leadership competencies, risk-taking ability, and project management experience. The definitions below can help you assess the potential of each employee in terms of ability, employee aspiration, and how engaged each is in her job and with the library.

But first, before you review employees, here are some tips:

- Be objective.
- Be future oriented; do not focus on the past year.
- *Ask*: Is this employee capable of moving to the next level (*e.g.*, branch manager if presently a librarian, youth coordinator, or subject specialist) or to a leadership or department head role?
- Does this employee consistently demonstrate competencies at the next level (high potential), sometimes demonstrate the next level of competencies (growth potential), or not demonstrate competencies at the next level (low potential)?
- Ensure that you hold no biases, like recency (basing an opinion of most recent performance) or halo-or-horns effects stemming from a positive or negative experience potentially from years ago. There are other biases you might have about individual employees as well. Maybe she is not like you in temperament, personality, or style. Maybe she comes from a different culture; reminds you of your mom, dad, or child; is of a different generation, nationality, gender, level of ability, or sexual orientation—or doesn't laugh at your jokes. We tend to want to hire, promote, and work with people who are like us—but such an approach seriously limits the candidate pool (and, of course, can be illegal). Reflect on your thoughts and feelings about the individuals you are reviewing

for potential. Separate feelings from facts about performance and potential as a star employee, high potential, or upcoming library leader. Talking with a trusted colleague or HR about employees has helped many reviewers separate potential biases from employees' actual ability and performance.

- *The leadership team should ask*: Does the employee demonstrate competencies, knowledge, skills, and abilities at that next level? How do you know this? Do performance evaluations document it? What about performance as a member of a key team or committee? Do her projects come in on time and within budget? Does she have a role as an informal leader in the library? How does she use that influence? Do other employees ask her to be assigned to their committees or projects? What comments on the performance appraisal, about actual situations, are indicative of the competencies needed to move to additional challenges in your organisation?
- Finally (and especially where there are gaps), do not rely only on anecdotal evidence. Many of the shelf objective and job-related assessments are available for evaluating the potential of individual employees. Results provide the library, as well as the individual, with important feedback as well as input into a development plan.

After reflection, leaders determine each employee's potential for growth or expanded roles within the library as low, growth, or high (L, G, H), using the following definitions (or something like them):

- Low-potential employee:
  - *Ability.* May be a solid performer with consistent execution but has not demonstrated the capacity for growth in terms of a larger volume (*e.g.*, larger branch) or role (*e.g.*, reference librarian to adult services supervisor).
  - *Aspiration.* May not have the motivation or interest to advance or transfer laterally into other positions; does not actively seek and may not be open to development, feedback, and opportunities.
  - *Engagement.* May not appear to be happy with the library system or its future plans, or infrequently goes above and beyond.
- Growth-potential employee:
  - *Ability.* Has solid competencies in current job; occasionally exhibits the knowledge, skills, and competencies needed for the next level or another job; is smart; exhibits high emotional intelligence (*e.g.*, self-awareness, self-regulation, empathy) as well as strong social and interpersonal skills.
  - *Aspiration.* Conveys the motivation and ability for development and advancement; insightful about own ability and seeks feedback from others.

- *Engagement.* Is committed to the library, excited about challenges and new directions, often goes above and beyond.

- High-potential employee:
  - *Ability.* Has a track record of results and leadership that is clearly superior to peers; demonstrates the knowledge, skills, abilities, and competencies of the next level; is smart, analytical, thinks systemically and critically; possesses a high degree of emotional intelligence and social and interpersonal skills.
  - *Aspiration.* Demonstrates the motivation, drive, and ambition to rise in the library; aware of own strengths and limitations, actively seeks development.
  - *Engagement.* Values and enjoys being part of the library; is excited to be involved in projects; often goes above and beyond.

SELECT CODE BASED ON EMPLOYEE'S PERFORMANCE AND POTENTIAL

At this point you have determined a rating for performance (low, medium, or high) and one for potential (low, growth, or high). Now it is time to determine a code that takes both ratings into account. Coding makes it much more likely that staff are evaluated consistently and on the same terms.

<table>
<tr><td colspan="2" rowspan="2"></td><td colspan="4">Potential</td></tr>
<tr><td colspan="2">Low</td><td>Growth</td><td>High</td></tr>
<tr><td rowspan="3">Performance</td><td>High</td><td colspan="2">Key Contributor–KC</td><td>Emerging Talent–ET</td><td>Promotable–P</td></tr>
<tr><td>Medium</td><td colspan="2">Key Contributor–KC</td><td>Key Contributor–KC</td><td>Emerging Talent–ET</td></tr>
<tr><td>Low</td><td>New Hire–NH</td><td>Action Required–AR</td><td>Improvement Required–IR</td><td>Improvement Required–IR</td></tr>
</table>

Fig. Charting Performance and Potential.

Use the matrix shown in table to integrate the employee's performance and potential and to select an appropriate code for succession planning. To complete this matrix, simply identify an employee's performance (low/medium/high) and potential (low/growth/high) and then choose the category where performance meets potential. You can use the code definitions to confirm alignment with your view of the staff member's talent and potential with the library.

Each box on the matrix has a code that acts as a kind of shorthand to describe the employee's performance and potential:

- *Promotable (P)*: Excellent performer; has a history of high performance ratings and consistently exceeds expectations; high-potential employee; has taken on more responsibility; is ready for next level position; seeks a promotion.
- *Emerging Talent (ET)*: Excellent performer; typically given high performance ratings by manager or supervisor; shows growth potential; can take on more responsibility; promotable within 12–24 months; lateral transfer within 8–12 months.
- *Key Contributor (KC)*: Consistent performer and well placed in current position; management should provide individual with committee or other assignments to see how employee responds. Manager should value the person in this position and support her efforts.
- *Improvement Required (IR)*: Inconsistent performer; may lack knowledge, skills, abilities, competencies, or motivation in one or more areas; could become a concern requiring action if performance does not improve; not promotable; performance improvement plan should be in place.
- *Action Required (AR)*: Poor performer in current role; transfer if appropriate position in library system can be found or ask to leave; time line for action is required. *New Hire (NH)*: Too new to rate; usually less than six months in current position.

Now you are ready to transfer the code that identifies the employee in terms of performance and potential onto the talent profile form. There is no box labeled NH for new hires, since, they are considered too new for leaders to assess performance and potential accurately. You might also want to use the table matrix, or some variation of it, to get a picture of all members of a unit or classification of employees at once. For example, you might place all librarians, or all staff from one unit, on the matrix to get a picture of emerging and potential leadership. This approach circumvents the possibility of staff with potential falling through the cracks, since, everyone is considered systematically. You will be surprised at how many quiet shining stars emerge through this methodical exercise.

Current Performance			
	High	Steady Producers Strategy: Keep Turn Over Low, Keep Them Motivated and Productive where they are,	Stars Strategy : Keep Turnover Low Accelerate Development.
	Low	Deadwood Strategy: Convert to Steady Producers. Terminate them If they can't be Salvaged	Question Marks Strategy: Convert to Steady Producers Terminate them if they can't be Salvaged.
		LOW	High
		Future Potential	

Fig. Charting Performance and Potential Alternate Grid.

Another way to classify employees by performance and potential is through use of a performance/potential grid using the following definitions: *Stars* are the "exceed expectations" performers who are perceived to have high potential for future advancement.

They are a key source to replace incumbents in key positions:

- *Steady Producers* also exceed expectations in their performance in the current position, but they are not identified as having strong potential to fill key positions at the library. Since, they are still highly productive, the strategy is to capitalise on their skills and knowledge and keep them productive and motivated.
- *Question Marks* are poor performers in their current position, but they might have potential in another position or in the future. The best strategy for working with these employees is to focus on improving their performance, ideally to turn them into stars. Consider coaching, mentoring, or job rotation to help improve performance and productivity.
- *Deadwood* are poor performers seen as having little potential for growth at the library. Because of retirements, layoffs, limited expansions, and budget cuts, fewer of these performers are left in most libraries. Where they do exist, supervisors should be coached to help them improve productivity or to ease them out.

ASSESS RETENTION RISK

Now that talent has been identified, there are still a few steps remaining. One is to assess the degree of risk that the staff person might leave the library in the next year. It is suggested that you identify the level of risk as high, medium, or low (H, M, L) and enter it on the individual talent profile.

High risk implies that the manager or others believe the person will not be in her current job for the next year, medium that she may not be, and low that she likely will remain in her current position for the next twelve months. Your reason for selecting a high/medium/low risk factor can be based on knowledge you have or on your intuition. Some examples of risk based on knowledge include these: employee might be promoted or given a lateral position or developmental position; might make known that she is seeking to leave the library, or is interviewing elsewhere; is having performance problems; spouse is relocating. Examples of risk factors based on intuition are the managers' (or employees') perception of readiness for the next level; leaders' perception of risk or fit; perceived satisfaction with direction in which the library is going; and satisfaction with current job, peer group, or supervisor. The risk factor selected, along with the rationale for it, should be discussed at the succession planning committee meeting. Examples of other factors, which may or may not be based on knowledge and yet should be considered, are dissatisfaction with compensation or benefits; recently passed over for a promotion; personal or family issues; dissatisfaction with job rotation assignment (*e.g.*, to branch farther from home); does not feel included by peer group or recognised by manager; dissatisfied with potential for career growth or communications flow; does not agree with the direction in which the library is heading based on its recent planning process; feels lacking in the information or training needed to be successful; does not feel challenged and empowered to make a meaningful contribution to the library; does not feel recognised and appreciated for contribution to the success of work group or the library; does not feel part of an effective, diverse, and winning team; and, most important, does not have a good, mutually respectful relationship with supervisor.

COMPLETE THE TALENT PROFILE

The next step is to complete the talent profile forms to create in-depth, individualised profiles. You have already entered results from the assessments you have completed to date regarding performance, potential, and risk. Now be sure you have collected information from prior performance reviews and the individual's résumé. The completed profile serves as basis for discussion in the succession planning committee meeting.

BUILD LEADERSHIP OVERVIEW

The next step is to create a talent summary of the library's leadership team or any group under consideration (*e.g.*, all branches, all librarians). You can create the overview from the information listed in the individual talent profiles. The resulting overview provides a comprehensive, high-level view of top talent and the multiple leadership opportunities available.

CONDUCT SUCCESSION PLANNING AND DEVELOPMENT REVIEW SESSIONS

The succession planning committee meets to review employees with an eye towards growing leaders and providing development opportunities to maximize their potential at the library. At the review sessions, the committee uses the completed individual talent profiles and leadership overviews to move into phase 2 of the process—creating succession pans.

PHASE II: CREATING SUCCESSION PLANS

Leaders create succession plans on the basis of organisational needs, goals, and priorities as well as individuals' performance, potential, ability, and motivation. To accomplish this, they utilise the documents completed in phase 1 to prioritise needs and potential candidates to fulfill these needs. Leadership evaluates library needs in the future through the risk assessments and anticipated retirements to identify bench strength and internal candidates for positions. At this point, leadership has already identified key positions, including those in leadership. From their risk and retirement analysis, they know which positions may become vacant. High-potential employees are identified, and developmental needs are at least identified. Now is the time to identify successor candidates. When considering successor candidates, start by asking the following questions: How would this position further develop the employee being considered? Would the employee be interested in this opportunity?

Table is a sample of a succession planning report summary for leadership positions. It builds on the leadership overview prepared for the review sessions.

Employee	Position/Title	Location	Talent Code	Development Needs	Recommended Next Position	Timing	Notes
Jenny Fir	Deputy Director	Central	KC	Current position:managing four generations			
Jane Tree	Director, Public Services	Central	P	Executive coaching to Improve understanding of impact of Behaviour on individuals and groups	Deputy Director	12 Months	
John Oak	Manager, Central and Outreach	Central	ET	Experience with Building projects And facilities management	Director, Public Services	9-12 months	
Harry Maple	Director, Research and Strategy	Central	KC	Excellent in Current role:does not seek Promotions Does not hold an MLS		Not at this time	
Annie Pea	Manager, Community Branches	Central	ET	Leadership development presentation skills	Manager, Central and Outreach	18+ months	

One easy way to assess bench strength, to see if the library can fill vacancies from within with relative ease, is through replacement charting or planning. Replacement charting was the original goal of succession planning before it broadened out to include talent development and building a pipeline of employees ready to fill vacancies. Replacement charting indicates one or more successors for key positions and also helps to create a management inventory for the library. Smaller libraries may not need this at all, but larger libraries will find it useful.

Table. Replacement Charting Using a Demand Forcast.

Table. A

Key Leadership Position or Knowledge Base Needed	Primary Skills and Knowledge Required until	Approx. Months
Central Library Director	• Knowledge of librarianship • Well-developed leadership/coaching skills • Networking within community	60

Table. B

Three potential Successors, in order Of Readliness	Rate Successors' Readlines Level[a]	Strengths	Developmental Experiences Needed
• Central Director Knowledge of • Librarianship Well-developed • Leadership/coaching skills • Networking within community			
Anni Reference	1	Strong leadership skills Strong reference skills	Community networking
John smith	3	Good reference skills	Community Networking Leadership/coaching skills
Jerri Frank	4	Good communicator, Networker	Leadership/coaching skills

Table is one format for a replacement chart. It lists the positions in the hierarchy. Successors are identified under each position with a notation as to readiness to take on the higher-level job. The number "1" identifies those ready for the promotion immediately, number "2" those ready in six months, and so on. Those identified as successors should be both stars and high potentials, or those with a talent profile coded Promotable and Emerging Talent. If they are not, review why the selected code was assigned; is the identified successor truly a successor or just a fill-in in the event of vacancy? In either event, plan to create a robust individual development plan for those identified as replacements (unless there is indication of interest being limited to filling the position only until a replacement is located internally or externally).

PHASE III: CREATING AND IMPLEMENTING INDIVIDUAL DEVELOPMENT PLANS

TALENT DEVELOPMENT

A good understanding of where employees fall in the matrix is not where developing talent stops—it is actually where it begins. The critical work comes from providing feedback and developing staff. Although each employee is different, each more or less fits into one of the nine matrix categories according to performance and potential.

Still, it is not sufficient merely to identify an employee by category; providing useful and insightful feedback is key to talent development. How managers and leaders approach each employee and their individual situations requires thought. It calls for honest feedback of potential along with a meaningful conversation about the individual's career growth and development.

Here are some things to think about, tips for development, and talking points for managers and leaders to reflect upon when giving feedback to:

- Promotable/high-potential employees,
- Emerging talent,
- Fully successful key contributors, and
- Employees requiring performance improvement.

Do not forget that every employee, regardless of category, is different; it is the manager's role to consider the needs and motivations of each employee, how they receive and internalise feedback, and to act accordingly.

Promotable/High- Potential Employees

Key Considerations

The primary challenge in working with high-potential employees is to communicate that they are valued without prematurely raising expectations about promotions. These employees often want to see that they are making measurable progress towards their career goals. As a result, they actively seek additional responsibilities that broaden skills or offer new challenges. They may need help from you to modify their sense of urgency for promotion.

Here are several ideas for working with them:

- Give frequent reassurance that you and the library regard them highly.
  - Do not make promises about promotions or next assignments unless the situation is very clear.
  - Most libraries are unable to provide compensation increases that align with this level of performance. But, to the extent you can, provide salary increases, incentives, and awards commensurate with performance. In addition to or in lieu of monetary recognition, provide recognition to such employees in the manner they want to receive it.

- Make sure the employee understands the competitive nature of promotion decisions when there are others equally or better skilled. In other words, there are no assurances; no employee is anointed to fill the position of another.
- Assess retention risks and develop a specific plan if appropriate and allowable within civil service or other rules.

Tips for Development

- Help the employee create and implement a vigourous individual development plan.
- Establish frequent one-on-one sessions to discuss career goals and progress in meeting IDP goals. Openly discuss concerns the employee may have about the future. This is particularly important to members of generations X and Y.
- Develop "stretch assignments" by delegating projects or responsibilities you are currently doing (in the important, not mundane, areas).
- Look for opportunities for the employee to get broader visibility and "showcase" her talents (*e.g.*, task force assignments, presentations to library leadership or the board of trustees).
- Allow the employee to stand in for you at meetings or provide backup when you are out of the office or on vacation.
- Encourage the employee to present at state and national library conferences and to get involved in these (and other) organisations to develop talents, learn new skills, get exposed to other ideas, and take on leadership roles in a non-work environment. Encourage volunteer work with local non-profit groups of any type as well as participation in Rotary, chamber of commerce, or other business associations.
- Identify cross-functional developmental (lateral) moves or rotational assignments.
- Arrange a mentoring relationship with a well regarded, successful internal or external leader who can assist in targeted developmental needs.
- Ask the employee to participate in 360-degree feedback or other developmental assessments to gain more insight into career strengths and developmental needs.
- Partner with a coach for targeted developmental needs or prepare for the role in a promotional assignment.

Suggested Talking Points

- It is important to spend some time with you specifically to have a conversation about your career goals and aspirations.

- You are highly regarded by me and other leaders throughout the library. You continue to be an excellent performer—always delivering results in a manner that is congruent with our library's goals, mission, and values. For example (insert appropriate examples). You continue to expand the scope of your responsibilities, and your work is consistently high quality (again, insert examples—be they the quality of responses to reference questions, helping a page team leader work out schedules, forming a partnership with the local day care center, etc.). These are exactly the types of characteristics we look for in our future professionals/ leaders (as appropriate). (It is critical to use specific examples of the employee's observed behaviour so that she understands exactly what you value.)
- Based on your performance, it is appropriate to begin considering other opportunities for you to enhance your career within our library. Just to check, is that something you want? If so, let's talk about what those possibilities might look like (and really listen to what is being said).
- Now let's discuss how to align your IDP properly with where you would like to see your career heading.
- Please keep in mind that your performance (both results and behaviours as articulated in the competencies—the what and the how) in your current position is one of the most important factors in determining future advancement. We encourage you to continue providing the exceptional performance you have been demonstrating.
- It is also important for us to ensure that we have a qualified individual who is ready to move into your position. Let's talk about who may be a potential successor for you and what we need to do to get her ready (if appropriate).
- What other questions do you have for me? How can I support you in your development? What else could I be doing to help make your work more satisfying and for you to feel that you are learning and growing?
- We will continue to have this type of dialogue on a (insert frequency) basis as a part of our regular meetings. I look forward to our future discussions.

What is it like to be identified and developed as key talent? Succession planning has been a key initiative at OCLC for more than ten years. George Needham is vice president of Global and Regional Councils at OCLC. He went through the first and more recent talent management and succession planning programmes at OCLC and is also someone who identifies and manages others. We asked him to remember being identified as someone with high potential and being invited to participate in the first programme. He paused for a few seconds to reflect, and I could hear the feeling in his voice: "It was an honour to learn that my boss feels that way. It was a heady feeling." Very appreciative of the opportunities, he said that it made him feel valued and very loyal. He worked harder, stayed longer, and now gives back by developing others.

Emerging Talent

Key Considerations

The primary challenge in working with emerging talent is to convey that they are valued without prematurely raising expectations about growth opportunities.

Development plans for these staff members should include activities that help clarify their growth or performance potential:

- Give frequent reassurance that you and the library hold them in high regard.
- Avoid absolute promises about promotions or next assignments unless the situation is very clear.
- Most libraries are unable to provide compensation increases that align with this level of performance. But, to the extent you can, provide salary increases, incentives, and awards commensurate with the performance. In addition to or in lieu of monetary recognition, provide recognition to this employee in the manner she wants to receive it.
- Make sure the employee understands the competitive nature of promotion decisions when there are others equally or better skilled. Create teams of highly talented peers to accelerate growth and elevate the level of performance.
- Consistently assess retention risks and develop specific plans, if appropriate.

Tips for Development

- Ensure that a vigourous IDP exists and is being implemented.
- Establish frequent one-on-one meetings to discuss career goals and progress in meeting those goals. Openly discuss concerns the employee may have about her future.
- Develop "stretch assignments" by delegating projects or responsibilities you are currently doing (in important, not mundane, areas).
- Look for opportunities for the staff member to get broader visibility and "showcase" her talents (*e.g.*, task force assignments, presentations to library leadership or the board of trustees).
- Allow the employee to stand in for you at meetings or provide backup when you are out of the office or on vacation.
- Identify cross-functional and other developmental assignments.

- Arrange a mentoring relationship with a highly regarded, successful internal or external leader who can assist in targeted developmental needs.
- Ask the employee to participate in 360-degree feedback or other developmental assessments to gain more insight into career strengths and developmental needs.

Suggested Talking Points

- It is important to spend some time to have a discussion with you regarding your career.
- You know that you are well regarded by library leadership and me. You continue to be a very strong performer—consistently delivering results in a manner that is consistent with library values (insert appropriate examples of observable behaviour). You demonstrate the desire and capacity for further development and growth. Just to check, is that something you want?
- Let's talk for a moment about your career interests.
- Now let's discuss how to align your IDP properly with where you would like to see your career go.
- Please keep in mind that your performance (both results and behaviours) in your current position is one of the most important factors in determining future advancement. We encourage you to continue providing the high level of performance you have been demonstrating.
- What other questions do you have for me? How can I support you in your development? What else could I be doing to help make your work more satisfying and for you to feel that you are learning and growing?
- We will continue to have this type of dialogue on a (insert frequency) basis as a part of our regular communication. I look forward to our future discussions.

Key Contributor

Everyone eventually reaches a level beyond which promotion would be ill advised (for both the individual and the library). This limitation does not imply poor performance in the current position.

Typical types of key contributor:

- Strong individual contributor who may be well placed in her current assignment, whether cataloger, circulation clerk, or department head.
- Employee who prefers to remain in her current role. Not everyone wants to rise in the library hierarchy; sometimes overachiever leaders forget that.

- Staff member with limited experience in broader, more strategic, or big-picture roles or tasks and little or no desire to gain more.
- Staff member with limited ability, or desire, to supervise or manage others.
- Employee who is simply not as qualified as others in the position in the library.

Key Considerations

Regardless of the scenario, your conclusion is that for the time being the present position is the one for which the individual is best suited. Your role is to manage the employee's career expectations constructively.

Here are several ideas on how to provide feedback to these members of the workforce (most employees are likely to fall into this category):

- Regularly recognise contributions the employee is making (especially directly following the initial career discussion).
- Gain a clear understanding of the real reasons behind the employee's desire (if any) for career advancement. Is the motivation income growth, a position or title of "importance," professional recognition, the need for continued challenge and growth, or something else? Acknowledge these needs and develop an understanding that they may not be met immediately or that an alternative way of meeting them may need to be determined.
- This is critical because these are good, solid employees who are contributing a great deal to the library and are successful in their roles. There are likely many opportunities to meet all but the desire for increased income. Point out opportunities for expansion of current responsibilities and the room for growth in compensation without a promotion.

Tips for Development

- Ensure that an appropriate IDP exists and is being implemented.
- Establish regular time to discuss career goals and progress in meeting those goals.
- Openly discuss concerns the employee may have about her future.
- Identify what the employee is "best at" and leverage that skill in other parts of the library.
- Provide opportunities for the staff member to "showcase" her skills.
- Assign special projects or "stretch assignments" that provide challenge and visibility both functionally and cross-functionally.
- Use the employee to help train new staff in her classification or below.
- Allow the employee to stand in for you at meetings or provide backup when you are out of the office or on vacation.

- Consider a job rotation to provide appropriate technical skill or leadership experiences.

Suggested Talking Points

- I want to have a discussion regarding your performance and career growth.
- As you know from our past performance discussions, you have made numerous important and significant contributions in your position as (insert job title). You are a solid, highly successful performer with consistent execution (or insert applicable comments and applicable examples of observed behaviour).
- We believe it is in your best interest—and the library's—to continue to challenge you to develop your skills and competencies in your current position.
- I am committed to helping you continue to grow and develop in the direction that best suits you and the library. I look forward to working through the details with you as part of your IDP.

Employees Who Require Improvement

Key Considerations

Employees who require improvement may fall into this area for several different reasons. In general, this employee is either not meeting expectations from a performance standpoint or is exhibiting low growth potential in terms of ability or motivation to succeed. The main point of focus is to discuss the sustained improvements required to remain in the position and with the library. In some cases, a lateral move into another position may be the appropriate solution.

If so, keep in mind that at some point this employee was likely seen as having potential and good job performance. She may even have been promoted at some point.

You need to reassure her of your commitment to work with her to improve performance. You should also assess factors that could cause this individual to lose motivation and leave the library rather than improve performance and stay.

Tips for Development

- Develop and implement a healthy performance improvement plan. The plan should be time bound with specific measurable actions.
- Establish check-in meetings to discuss career goals and performance progress.
- Openly discuss concerns the employee may have about her future.
- Identify what the employee is "best at" and leverage that skill.

- Provide structured on-the-job training with a trainer, peer, or supervisor.
- Engage the employee in appropriate education- based programmes.

Suggested Talking Points

- I want to respond to your questions about your potential for career growth here at the library.
- As you know from our past discussions, I have several concerns regarding your performance. Specifically, you are not demonstrating (insert appropriate skills, observable behaviour, etc).
- Your most concentrated effort right now needs to be focused on improving and sustaining your performance in the areas I just mentioned.
- I sincerely want to see you turn this situation around. Therefore, I will work with you to create a targeted plan that incorporates (insert appropriate tactics).
- We will meet on a biweekly basis to discuss your performance plan objectives and progress. As your performance improves, we can talk more specifically about your career growth.
- Aside from the steps that I have mentioned, how else can I support you in your development? What do you specifically need from me?

FEEDBACK STYLES

In the context of career development discussions and feedback, it is important to know the person to whom feedback is being given and to account for personal style, needs, and motivations when planning these conversations. The literature and anecdotal evidence point to the ways members of different generations view and seek feedback.

INDIVIDUAL DEVELOPMENT PLANS

Development plans are based on thoughtful feedback, the individual's career interests, and organisational needs. A time-bound development plan assists in closing the skill and competency gaps between an employee's current role and her next position, be it a lateral or promotional opportunity. By creating an IDP, managers are able to identify specific activities and opportunities for each individual on their staff. Once you have assessed the employee's potential and performance, consider what key experiences would most benefit them in reaching their career goals.

These experiences serve as the framework for the IDP and must include the what, how, and when of activities to ensure that the employee is making progress towards her next position.

An IDP is essentially a learning contract that conveys what learning gap is being filled (*e.g.*, what competency or skills are acquired), what the employee will learn, how she will learn it, and how this learning is to be demonstrated.

A few tips:

- It is critical that managers understand staff members' needs and desires, as well as the needs of the library, when identifying activities for the development plan. Employees own their development plan, so you should work with them on a regular basis to foster their development and prepare them for career growth.
- To create IDPs, managers and employees must conduct the following two activities: First, determine a lateral career move or the next-level position on the basis of career goals. Then, jointly identify the gaps in the employee's current role to the skills, knowledge, abilities, and competencies needed in the next-level position or to enhance performance in the current position. It is possible that the employee's next career move will not be within your organisation, perhaps because you do not have an opportunity for her when she is ready. Yet IDPs are for everyone, whether they are "growing in place" or preparing to move up or move on.
- We suggest that, once the areas of development to focus on have been determined, development activities should be structured to include a variety of approaches, including on-the-job experiences (70 per cent), relationships (20 per cent), and education (10 per cent).

Identify and schedule specific time-bound (*i.e.*, six to eighteen months) activities that provide the employee with an opportunity to demonstrate competence or to work to close the gap between her current position and the next (lateral or promotional) position. Activities and time line should be captured in the employee's development plan. Do not just assume that, once it is completed, you and the employee can check off the IDP box. Rather, managers and employees should schedule regular conversations to check progress, reevaluate activities, and provide feedback, support, and recognition.

Progress towards completing the IDP should be a regular component of each performance review. IDPs are useful for staff at all levels, independent of whether they have been identified as candidates for a succession planning programme. OCLC is a good example of an organisation with both a strong succession planning programme and a strong focus on individual career development for *all* employees. At the County of Los Angeles Public Library, every librarian (levels 1–5) is interviewed by her boss in July of each year.

They discuss the librarian's career goals and how the library, and the manager, can help the librarian reach them. These discussions are separate from and in addition to the performance management process and conversations surrounding it. The assistant director of public services reads all plans. Margaret Donnellan Todd, the county librarian, reports several additional outcomes to this method of development planning. First, managers get to know the librarians, even all new level 1s. They are able to discuss how realistic or inconsistent with performance an employee's goals are, then use this occasion to reinforce any changes in performance needed for the librarian to proceed with her career goals.

This is not always a matter of poor performance or attitude. Todd shared a story about a manager who told a librarian that she could not be promoted or developed unless some changes were made. However, this librarian is creative with an artistic (rather than managerial) temperament. She decided to alter her career goals rather than change.

SUCCESSION PLANNING FOR THE LIBRARY DIRECTOR

Many library boards and local governments across the country will be going through a search process for a library director over the next five to ten years—some more than once. Some boards and local government officials will be putting their heads in the sand to avoid thinking about this issue; others will peek up slowly, until they willingly engage in the process. It is, after all, their most important function. Why is it so difficult? It is not hard to answer this question. It is about change, it is about real work, it is about risk, challenge, and uncertainly. It is also about evaluation and assessment.

There will be more meetings, more dialogue, and a need to talk honestly and look at yourselves—as leaders—and at your organisation—as an important entity in your community or educational institution. It is hard: change is hard, and costly, and frightening—and it the most important activity the members of a board will undertake. While fraught with challenge, this period is also filled with opportunity if you take the time to pause and reflect before rushing to fill the vacancy.

Our values are reflected in our belief that the board's role is to set policy and that the library director, with staff, is responsible for implementing policy. Further, research and our experience have taught us that trustees should steer far away from micromanaging the library; the most important task of the board is to recruit, retain, evaluate, provide feedback to, engage in dialogue with, and support the library director—as well as to terminate the library director if warranted. There is no more important function. The library board, to support your efforts in director succession planning. If your library does not have a governing board—if, for example, a university search committee or city or county hires the director—many of the principles that follow still hold true.

We hope you are reading this before you have to hire a new library director, because the most effective boards are thinking and planning ahead in order to stay ahead. They are looking at ways to capitalise on the inevitable opportunity they will have to shape the library and search for the new. They may even be working with retiring directors to create new models for succession that could bring the library new benefits and create a win for everyone. There *will* be many retirements in the next five to ten years as baby boomers leave our libraries. It will be a very competitive time. We are not seeing a plethora of members of the Generation X community ready and waiting in the wings, their boards, or other governing bodies plan for the inevitable, be proactive, rise to their fiduciary responsibility, and continue to meet community needs. But if you find yourselves with a hiring emergency. It offers a step-by-step emergency plan for succession that you, your departing director, HR department, and city or county leadership should become very familiar with.

WHY PLAN

The primary purpose of an effective succession plan for a library director is to facilitate a seamless transition to the new director. A commitment from the board of trustees or other governing body to a timely planning process ensures that the library makes this transition most effectively and successfully, so that the transition appears seamless to the library's community stakeholders. There are many decisions to make, prompted by many questions.

These questions are about time lines, responsibilities, and desired outcomes— all of which guide the planning process. To be most effective, the process must be systematic and suited to your library's specific needs. In other words, what follows is *not* in and of itself a succession plan for your library director. There is no one single cookie-cutter plan. Rather, to be effective, the board of trustees, with staff support, must engage in a dialogue that responds to key questions. There is no one right answer to these very delicate questions. What is important to note is that the *process* is a critical aspect and can make or break a succession. The other crucial and often neglected aspect of a leadership change is that it is a *transition* and needs to be considered holistically, not as a one-day or one-time event. The questions and issues we build into the following outline for succession planning address both of these aspects of recruiting a library director, helping to make the transition a smooth and successful one. Our outlined plan is broken into three major phases: preparation, recruitment, and transition.

PHASE I: PREPARATION (WHEN YOU HAVE TIME TO PLAN)

During this first phase the library has an opportunity to take stock, reflect on the past, anticipate and plan for the future, and identify the competencies needed by the incoming library director. Keep in mind that each library needs different competencies of its director at different points in its life cycle as well as in accordance with changing community, staff, governance, or other needs. Libraries facing a union drive, major fund-raising or bond challenge, building projects or construction difficulties, technology overhaul, political upheaval or contentious board relations, low staff morale, or other challenges require unique skills sets of their director. Be very honest, first to yourselves and then to your candidates, about your needs and the knowledge, skills, abilities, and competencies required of the director entering your system. Do not skip over the preparation aspects of this process. When a library hears that its director is leaving, it is too easy to just rush into the hiring phase. Do that at your own peril. Remember: sometimes you have to go slow to go fast. The work you do in the preparation phase provides a foundation that enhances the success of the library and its incoming director.

If you are open, you will see many opportunities in this time of transition. Not rushing, and taking the time to look forward, will help you hire the right leader, one who has the competencies to bring the library to new phases of growth in line with its strategy.

GETTING STARTED: SHOULD YOU USE A CONSULTANT

In recent times many libraries, large and small, have been engaging search consultants or transition consultants. Some consultants generally focus their attention on helping the library recruit a new director. Some assist the board of trustees to ascertain the needs and expectations of the library or to prepare for the arrival of the new director. Some help the library build internal and board capacity so that it is in stronger shape before welcoming the new director. Others recommend working through the roles of the board and director so there is an easier transition and both can hit the ground running in an effective and healthy manner (yes, this includes eliminating practices of micromanagement, promoting open communications, creating a performance plan, and other forms of open feedback and dialogue). In a few cases, "houses are cleaned," with ineffective or inattentive staff and board members being retired early or otherwise asked to leave prior to the new director coming on board. There are pros and cons to retaining the services of a consultant.

Why retain a consultant:

- Unlike library staff, the consultant is an expert experienced in the search or transition process. She can also provide an unbiased perspective, and the library is the beneficiary of best practices learned from her research and experience with other organisations. A consultant who specialises in libraries (academic or public) knows, and has connections with, many of the most effective leaders in the country—some of whom may never consider applying for a position advertised in a journal but would respond to a phone call from a respected colleague.
- A consultant can help provide an objective assessment of a library's situation and help identify issues library leadership may not have been able to articulate effectively.
- The board of trustees may desire a fresh look at the library's strategy, its structure, and the nature and scope of the position of library director.

- You may recognise the need for external help with the transition, because you do not have the time to devote to a search or for other reasons.

Why conduct the search in-house:

- Members of the board of trustees and staff have the expertise and time to conduct the search and design a transition process.
- Consultants are an extra expense.
- Board members may see every candidate fresh by not having relationships with potential candidates.
- Your staff or board members have been active in the state and national library associations and personally know or are aware of potential candidates.
- An external consultant cannot know the details of your situation as well as you do.

PRIMARY TASKS OF THE PREPARATION PHASE

In this phase, you begin looking at yourself and your library. Taking the time to assess the library's strategy, culture, and governance honestly supports and guides the succession planning process. It also helps your library board's capacity building and development process.

Identify Library Vulnerabilities

This is an excellent time to take a realistic look at the state of the library and to design and implement strategies where they are needed. For example, this might be the time to create a position of deputy or assistant director—perhaps a step the director had been avoiding.

Or it might be a good time to create an advisory board for marketing, or fund-raising—if the assessment identifies these as areas of weakness. Ensure that the library's financial and HR systems are in order, so that the library's daily operations can run smoothly during any period of interim leadership.

Solidify the Management Team

This is also a time to think about staffing in light of what is required to achieve the strategic direction. For example, suppose there is a gap in marketing competencies at the staff and leadership levels, and strategies to move the library forward indicate a need for marketing expertise. In that case it would be appropriate to establish a plan to develop these competencies in the senior staff, agree to hire a senior staff person with these competencies, or retain the services of a marketing consultant.

You may realise some salary savings in the turnover of the director position, and now is the time to use whatever financial flexibility is associated with her departure. But whether the changes you need cost money or not, consider what changes should be made in leadership, systems, staffing, or structure to ease the director's transition into your library and her ability to hit the ground running. Also at this time, the board should ensure that there is staff or board backup for key director functions.

It is also critical that administrative systems (especially financial and human resources) are in order, so that the library can operate effectively during the transition to a new director, which often involves a period when the library must function with interim leadership.

Assess Staff for Leadership Potential

Whether or not you have a succession plan in place, you should ask:

- Are there current employees who have the potential to fill any given position? Now? After a formal training and development process?
- Are these employees interested and motivated to pursue this growth opportunity?
- Will the succession planning process in which your library is engaging put in place a formal training and development process to cultivate these new leaders?

Identify the Library's Broad Strategic Directions

Where are you in implementing the strategic plan? How are your customers and partners responding? Is the annual performance evaluation for the director tied to progress measured against your strategic initiatives? Is there a process for the new director to provide input to the plan?

Build the Board's Leadership Abilities

Is your board operating at an optimal level? Is there a job description for the trustees? Does the board have trouble making decisions or working through conflict? Is there agreement about the kind of authority you are prepared to give the next director and what kind of accountability mechanisms you should consider to ensure responsible board oversight? Assess board governance practices and organisational health, looking at mission, vision, and strategic and operational planning processes.

This is an ideal time to build the leadership capacity of the board and its members.

A board member with organisational or board development skills can do this, although you might prefer to use an objective outsider to help you address these often complex, difficult, and very human issues. Using a consultant to interview the departing director as well as individual board members in confidence can really assist the process of moving ahead quickly. The consultant can use this information to help move the board forward in its thinking about roles, relationships, and how board members can individually and collectively support the library and its director.

Back Up the Library Director's key Relationships

Too often we find that the library director is the only person who knows key elected and appointed government officials, important community leaders, grantors, and executive directors of other partners. This is the time to make sure that staff and board members also know and have connections with these leaders.

Prepare a Communications Plan

This is one of the most important steps. Communications to all key stakeholders (city/county officials, higher education leadership, board of trustees, Friends of the Library, library foundation, community leaders, and staff) should be ongoing, sincere, and transparent. Updates at each step in the process are critical. Connect with stakeholders (internal and in the community); talk to them about their needs and expectations for a new director in your community.

Determine by whom and how communication will be handled. Board members may develop the plan or assign communication responsibilities to a board committee or staff member to be coordinated. The communications plan you prepare now will be used regularly and often with staff, board members, and all stakeholders is to keep them up to date on the status of the search and transition.

It should utilise all of your library's communication channels, such as your web site and intranet, newsletter, and news releases.

Ultimately, it will:

- Announce why the director is leaving and highlight her many accomplishments.
- Announce the formation of a search committee.
- Invite community input regarding possible attributes for success, candidates, and organisational priorities.
- Circulate the profile and encourage applicants to apply.
- Provide status reports.
- Announce selection of the new director and let the community know how they can meet her.

At every milestone in the process, your communications plan should answer these questions: who needs to know what is happening, and how do we tell them?

Set Financial Parameters

Discuss possible financial and budgetary issues for the succession (hiring costs, severance package costs for the exiting director, training and development and compensation package for the new director, fee for a search or transition consultant if used).

Deal with the Personal and Professional Barriers for the Departing Director

Issues might be the degree to which the director is emotionally and financially prepared for retirement or the best exit strategy to make all parties feel good about the ending. You will want to help make the departing director's transition as easy as possible, especially if she is appreciated throughout the community and has served for a long time. Set a fixed departure date. Everyone needs to be able to move forward, and there is much work to do. Or, you may even decide to continue some new kind of working arrangement with the departing director, redefining what retirement means. In that case, all parties want and need clarity about what the new arrangements and roles are—and are not. Make plans now for when and how you will say good-bye, publicly and graciously, to the departing director. Celebrate her successes and contributions.

PHASE II: RECRUITMENT AND SELECTION

PRIMARY TASKS OF THE RECRUITMENT AND SELECTION PHASE

As soon as the library director announces her intention to leave the system and sets a date for so doing, the recruitment and selection process begins.

Develop an Up-to-Date Job Description

Although your inclination may be to reach for the departing director's job description, resist the temptation. Instead of looking to the past and what was, focus on the future. Look forward towards the library's aspirations and then shape the job, and job description, around your current and future leadership needs. What are the core values, beliefs, and assumptions about how the library operates that are important for the new director to understand? What are the "nonnegotiable" behaviours that the director should uphold and nurture? What current processes and activities create the most frustration, confusion, or dysfunctional behaviour within the library that the board wants the director to change? Does the new director need to fit the current culture, or is she expected to change it? How? Completing a profile of the ideal candidate helps you update the library director's job description as well as recruitment materials such as job postings.

Craft a profile by answering these questions:

- What are the desired experiences and qualifications of the director?
- How are your library's values and needs matched to the director?
- What is exceptional about your library and why is *this job* a wonderful opportunity?
- What leadership skills and competencies are unique to the library's needs and challenges?
- What are the key attributes needed (*e.g.*, visionary, seasoned manager who provides stability and structure, turnaround expert,

transformational change agent, entrepreneur, community builder, strategic thinker/actor)?

- Does the new director have to be a librarian?
- Does she need to be politically astute?
- Does she need to have skills in fund development?
- Does she need to be skilled in working with a union?
- How does the director attend to the board's feelings and needs?
- How does the director envision changes in organisational functioning?
- How does the director communicate and interact with the board?

Appoint a Selection Committee

Such a task force, appointed by the board, might be composed of members of the board as well as key constituents such as county elected or appointed officials, the school system superintendent, the director of the county's literacy group, the head of the United Way, a teenager, and a representative from the chamber of commerce.

The library's HR director staffs the committee process. The charge for this group is very specific: identify and prioritise the key competencies, knowledge, skills, and abilities that the next library director should possess *before* advertising the position. Input from the library's key constituencies is important to this process. Ultimately, the full board will interview the final two or three candidates.

When finalists are brought in for interviews, the selection committee members will attend public presentations or meet and- greet sessions and provide feedback to the board, to help them make a better decision. Should you use staff in the recruitment process? There are differences of opinion about how and to what extent staff should be involved in the leadership selection and transition process. We believe, again, that staff should be kept informed and that ongoing communication is important to staff at all levels, but that they should not play a deciding role in selection. We strongly support Tom Gilmore's thoughtful perspective: "The only universally wrong step a board can take (and many do) is not to have thought through how the staff will be involved and be kept informed at all stages of the process." Gilmore suggests that staff should be very involved in assessing the library's strategic challenges and identifying the characteristics needed of the director as well as in recommending candidates and resources for recruitment.

Staff should also be invited to meet the final candidates, often as part of an interview process, and provide their advice and input. However, the final selection should not be made by staff; that is a decision to be made by the board of trustees. In general, we agree that staff should not serve on the search committee. If your library has an HR director, it would be appropriate to ask her to staff the process and work directly with the members of the search committee.

If not working with a search or transition consultant the HR director should, at a minimum, support the search committee by engaging in the following tasks:

- Work closely with the committee chair throughout the process in a support capacity.
- Issue invitations to serve on the search committee, prepare agendas (with committee chair), and arrange for meeting room space, refreshments, and so forth.
- Take notes at meetings; send to committee members.
- After search committee conversations, draft the job description and other collateral public relations materials.
- Help prepare the communications plan for staff and community.
- Advertise the job opening as appropriate, for example, in *Library Journal, Library Hotline.*
- Determine how and when candidates will receive communications throughout the process, and who will communicate with candidates.
- Screen résumés against established criteria.
- Prepare summaries of highly qualified candidates for the search committee.
- Provide sample interview questions and any other preparation needed by interviewers.
- Schedule telephone screening interviews on behalf of the search committee.
- Schedule and arrange interviews for finalists.
- Check references.
- Suggest, based on data, a fair and equitable compensation and benefits package for the person selected. Determine who will handle the offer and salary negotiations.

The HR director must act with the highest integrity and utmost confidentiality throughout this process. You may wonder if another staff member could take on this role. The answer is possibly, and probably not. In our experience, general staff are accustomed to and respect the barrier of silence from HR staff about all personnel issues. They do not have the same expectations of other staff, nor are other staff members accustomed to this level of confidentiality.

Keep in mind that the confidentiality extends beyond your library. Many applying for the position will not make their interest known at their present workplace. Recruiting at this level must be handled delicately and with the utmost confidence. Many high-potential and highly visible candidates working in other libraries will not apply unless confidentially can be guaranteed unless and until they are named as a finalist. There are other considerations as well.

Consider the plight of one system that did not have a full-time HR manager. With the resignation of the library director, the library's four senior managers were asked to function as a team in an "interim director" role. We worked with this team to help them clarify roles, responsibilities, and expectations.

The group worked together rather effectively—until a shift in roles occurred. One of the team members was assigned by the board to work with the search consultant and staff the search committee. Although this individual was capable, other team members became jealous and insecure because they were not privy to the same information as their colleague. This made for a less than effective process and also affected the team's longer-term working relationships.

Plan the Search, and Search

Plan a national, or at least regional, search. To assist with this, the board asks the library director and senior staff for a list of five to ten key library leaders to talk with who either might be interested in the job or could recommend other viable candidates. Through conference attendance and journal reading, staff and board members also keep an eye out for current and emerging leaders. The library announces the position vacancy formally, using a variety of communications channels including its web site, statewide and national electronic discussion lists, and professional journals. The library's public relations staff helps by developing a piece that sells the position, the library, and the community to potential applicants. Note the individual responsible for each recruitment step. Add more time, because a search always takes longer than one thinks it will. The board can take advantage of any additional time to plan and prepare adequately.

Identify an Interim Library Director

This should not be a candidate for the permanent position. Establish a separate job description for the interim position that articulates scope, boundaries, duties, and responsibilities. If the interim director is a member of the library's senior staff, the library should provide a salary supplement in the form of a separate check or temporary pay increase (rather than part of base pay).

Communicate

It is critical to begin implementing the communications plan you began to develop in the preparation phase so that all of the library's key stakeholders—both internal and external—are kept informed throughout the process.

PHASE III: TRANSITION

Trustees need to be aware that a leadership transition is a time of stress and anxiety for staff, especially senior staff. They will have many questions that are rarely articulated: What is my role? Will she like me? Will she bring in her own leadership team? Will I have a job here? Will I like and be a part of any changes in direction or strategy? Where will I fit in? Is it time for me to get off the bus? Rumors fly and water cooler chatting increases substantially. Having a schedule, sticking to it, and communicating regularly help to allay the anxiety.

Another thing that reduces staff anxiety is helping the leader get off to a good start—ensuring that she too has a smooth transition. Board members set the tone for that transition and for how they will work with the incoming director. From the time they offer the job and begin negotiating a salary and employment agreement, they are beginning to orient the new director to the culture of the organisation. Thus, they must give some thought to structuring the kind of orientation that serves their board, the library, and the new director well.

Considering these questions can help:

- Who on the board will serve as the director's primary contact for management and coaching? How—and how often—will the board expect to hear from or meet with the director?
- Who on the board can help introduce the director to community partners, university or local government department heads, and other valuable people outside the library? How can the board pave the way for the director to establish her new network of connections?
- What role should senior (or other) staff take in orienting the director?
- What are the performance goals and expectations for and with the newly hired director at three, six, and twelve months? What mechanisms will be used to review performance and share feedback?
- How quickly can the new library director be scheduled to go through the same orientation process that all staff attend?

Remember that your new director will have a list of tasks to undertake shortly after coming on board that will be a part of her orientation to the job, the staff, the community, and the board of trustees. These important activities include (if a public library director) meeting local elected and appointed officials, community leaders, partners, fenders, media representatives, and local and statewide library directors. She will also want to meet all staff quickly, especially those who report directly to her, and visit all branches; spend time reviewing the budget, policies, HR policies, strategic, facilities, marketing, technology, and other important library documents; meet with all board members one-to-one and as a group; and review bylaws, the trustee manual, and other relevant documents.

Be prepared to help your new director into each of these tasks. Finally, don't forget that there is another element to being new in a community. If you have ever moved to take a new job, whether across town or across the country, you know that your orientation to the community is not complete until you find a trustworthy auto mechanic, the best bakery, a good handyman, a great hairdresser, the physicians who take your new health insurance plan, and so on. Your new director will not really feel at home until she knows the territory, so be sure to let her know that, when she needs a local recommendation, you stand ready to help.

EMERGENCY SUCCESSION PLAN

Sometimes a surprise happens: the director lets you know, with little or no warning, that she is leaving the job for another opportunity, family issues, health, or other reasons. In the worst case, she has been struck by a bus or challenged by a major illness, and there is little time to prepare. That is why it is important to have in place, at a minimum, an emergency plan. The trustees of one of our academic library clients made the mistake of not worrying about succession planning since, the library director, who was 60 years old, said that he was planning to stay for another five years, at least until age 65. They did not want to upset the director, whom they valued highly, by raising the issue of succession planning before he was ready for it. And what happened? They were surprised—and so was he! His daughter had triplets, and he and his wife decided to move cross-country to help her.

The moral is clear: every library should have at least an emergency plan for library director succession at all times. An emergency succession plan ensures the continuous coverage of executive and administrative duties critical to the ongoing operations of the library and its services to its customers or patrons and fenders, political officials, and others by outlining policies and procedures for the temporary appointment of an acting executive director. There are several key components to such a plan. It should identify the priority functions of the library director, both the general functions of a library (or any) leader as well as tasks that are exclusive to your library.

Second, the plan should specify what happens in the event of a short- or long-term absence of the library director. This includes notification of trustees, the process that the board or board president begins once notified, the compensation and authority of an acting director and provisions for recruiting a new director. Another component of the emergency succession plan should be the identification of one or two senior staff members capable of appointment to the position of acting or interim director. If the board decides to divide the functions of the director, these should be clearly delineated in writing.

If necessary, any provisions for cross-training staff to help them fulfill priority director functions should be made. Such cross-training should begin with the adoption of the plan. Finally, a communications plan and protocol should be outlined, including categories of constituents (*e.g.*, public officials, customers) who should be personally notified, how (in writing, personally, by phone) and by whom (the board, interim director, other), and in what time frame.

If the succession plan has to be implemented in an emergency, the board should ensure that the following are in place:

- Board members who have experience in search/transition.
- Senior staff member(s) or others who can serve as interim director.
- An up-to-date job description for the position of interim or acting library director.
- A key contact list to notify individuals and communicate plans/status.
- Written procedures for conducting a search (with and without a search firm) and for the selection process.
- Identification of a key spokesperson for the library board.

ADDITIONAL STORIES OF LIBRARY SUCCESSION PLANNING AND DEVELOPMENT PROGRAMMES

FRESNO COUNTY PUBLIC LIBRARY

- The Vision of the library is that Fresno County residents of all ages will have free access to library services and materials to enhance the quality of their lives and further life-long learning.

This vision from the mission statement of Fresno County Public Library (FCPL) is to be taken seriously; Fresno's population is expected to experience tremendous growth. To support this increase, most of the county's branch libraries as well as central will need to expand. Libraries will need more materials, computers, and meeting rooms to better serve their communities and experienced, competent staff to support them. Karen Bosch Cobb, county librarian, joined FCPL in 1972 and has served as director since, 2003.

Like so many library directors and county librarians, she looked around at the management team and saw that many could be retiring within close proximity of each other—and perhaps sooner rather than later. The FCPL succession management and talent development experience has been coloured by past good fortune. In 1998 a sales tax measure resulted in amasing growth for the library. New positions were created, new services and programmes offered. The library grew from 143 to 320 staff members in a relatively short time. Prior to 1998 many of these positions were filled by baby boomers, who are a large group of the library's formal and informal leaders. After 1998 new entry-level librarians filled many new positions.

Bosch Cobb spoke of a variety of strategies the library utilises to develop leaders, including executive training through Info people, the Urban Libraries Council Executive Leadership Institute, and California State Library Eureka Leadership Institute; special salary upgrades during leaves of absences; responsibility charting; serving on task forces and committees; shadowing managers; taking on lead responsibilities; growing its own librarians through the use of librarian trainee classification; participation in community leadership opportunities; one-on-one coaching to help staff seeking a promotion develop a résumé and prepare for interviews; and staff forums.

STAFF DEVELOPMENT

Bosch Cobb believes in committing time, energy, and money to continuous staff development. Opportunities were identified that would develop competencies in FCPL staff, with the California Library Association's (CLA) personal and professional competencies used as a starting point. Training is one of the ways to develop these and other competencies; both internal and external training opportunities are available. FCPL employs a fulltime training coordinator librarian, Camille Turner, who both offers programmes and helps staff find the appropriate learning forums. Turner graduated from Infopeople's Master Trainer Programme, which added skills to her repertoire of facilitating staff development.

Four librarians have completed Urban Libraries Council's (ULC) Executive Leadership Institute (ELI) programme. Their projects included supporting the rural community and working with the business community to create an awareness of how the library can support economic development; developing homework centers; and expanding world language services. Two fellows of the ELI programme are currently members of the library's management team. In addition, two other librarians attended the Eureka Leadership programme, completing a joint customer service and culture-altering project now called "People First!" Staff members regularly attend workshops and webinars sponsored by the statewide Infopeople library staff training initiative. Over twenty employees participated in Infopeople's Building Leadership series of monthly classes, and many learn from OCLC and ULC conferences, seminars, and materials. ULC provided a grant to allow seven employees to attend library school.

GROWING OUR OWN

One example of growing your own is a librarian trainee programme in which paraprofessionals (library assistants) who have a bachelor's degree are selected to work under the direction of a librarian as they attend library school. Librarian Trainee is a provisional classification and incumbents must complete eligibility requirements for a Librarian I within three years to retain employment with Fresno County. These employees receive pre-professional training, mentoring, and work experience while in the programme. The goal is to promote trainees to the Librarian class when they have successfully completed an MLIS or MLS programme.

The Friends of the Library supports the programme by offering scholarships of up to $2,500 for those attending library school. Fresno also promotes staff development by encouraging involvement with committees and projects in the CLA and ALA as well as attending conferences. Not only does this help build staff members' professional development, the library generally benefits from the knowledge and experiences gained through participation.

Bosch Cobb talked about outreach as an important component of the library's mission and sees not one but three libraries: the physical branches, the virtual library, and the library in the community.

Because the library in the community is so vital, staff members are encouraged not only to take library services to the community but to take on leadership positions in local non-profit and other agencies as well as attend local leadership programmes (such as Fresno Leadership). FCPL's tactic for filling promotions is a bit unusual. In this system, by library practice, all vacancies are offered internally first. Most transfers and promotions are viewed as opportunities for staff to grow. If an employee wants to, the training and development activities are available—as are the vacancies—to make it happen. The ability to move up into leadership positions is touted as a benefit of working at FCPL when recruiting. It has been a successful marketing tool.

A TOOL: RESPONSIBILITY CHARTING

An important tool Fresno began using some years ago that has served to develop leaders is responsibility charting. Bosch Cobb recommends this tool—long used by organisation development practitioners to help clarify roles and responsibilities— to managers and supervisors for major or complex projects throughout the library. She has found it to be very useful in clarifying who is responsible for what and to what degree. Outcomes of using this tool have been quicker goal attainment, increased accountability of staff, less time wasted in meetings, less duplication of effort, and staff who are clear about responsibilities. For each project all tasks and decisions to be made are listed along the vertical axis and key stakeholders are listed horizontally. Key stakeholders are anyone touched by the project.

In each box one of the following codes should be entered:

- A (approve),
- R (responsible),
- C (consulted),
- I (informed),
- DK (don't know, and need to determine),
- Blank (no relationship to task).

There are several tips useful to completing the chart:

- Define each task and the people involved by both name and title; be very clear.
- Assign one "R" for each task; only one person can be responsible.
- The person assigned the "R" role must understand and accept the conditions of performance on the task, including accountability for budget, time frame, completion dates, and milestones.
- Only the "R" person and the "Cs" need to meet with regard to the task.

WHERE IS FCPL NOW

Recently the California Library Association and the Fresno County Public Library updated their competencies to include "develop political savvy and awareness," that is, be able to identify and enlist the support of strategic partners to complement strengths and weaknesses of the organisation and to obtain key resources and assistance to support the achievement of mutual goals.

To gain knowledge in this arena as well as to promote big-picture thinking, a variety of new experiences were suggested. These include attending Fresno and Clovis business conferences, board of supervisor and city council meetings, the State of the County breakfast, and the California Library Association's legislative day; in-house training on how to get items on the board of supervisor's agenda and on the best and worst experiences in the political sphere; attendance at San Joaquin Valley Library System committee meetings as an orientation to local library governing; obtaining experience with elements of urban planning; attending Friends of the Library board, council, and oversight committee meetings; and visiting branches and obtaining an overview of service areas and goals. I ended my conversations with Bosch Cobb and Turner with two questions: "Is it working?" and "Given budget cuts and hiring freezes, will you continue succession planning and staff development?" Bosch Cobb provided positive answers to both.

Many employees (seventeen) have been promoted, and vacancies are successfully filled rather quickly without having to worry about new employees learning their staff, culture, organisation, county, software, and so forth. Newly promoted employees are ready to go on day one. "We will continue carrying some things forward that are time tested and make changes as well," Bosch Cobb said. The programme is reviewed and updated every twelve to eighteen months, to ensure that it is relevant and meeting the library's needs. Examples of recent changes are the opportunities to increase political awareness and savvy and a move towards e-learning. Continue? "Yes," said Bosch Cobb. "You can't stop. If we are going to move ahead, there is always a need to engage in staff development."

JOHNSON COUNTY LIBRARY

Johnson County Library (JCL) is a busy metropolitan library, as of 2009 serving 370,000 residents via thirteen facilities, supported by 365 employees. For some years, JCL administrators experienced a shortage of qualified candidates for midlevel and senior management positions. Recognising in addition impending retirements from baby boomers and projections for fewer new graduates from MLS programmes, the library decided to develop an internal leadership development programme to grow its own leaders and create its own recruitment pool. Then deputy and now library director Donna Lauffer and her leadership team identified the need on two levels.

First, there was a need for leadership at every level in making decisions and leading projects to make the library more stable and simultaneously more nimble.

In addition, managers and senior leaders interested in advancement needed to build skills in creating, leading, and managing system wide projects. The library aspired to change—both individual and organisational change—resulting in a culture of leadership development that naturally generated leaders and succession rather than a series of programmes or initiatives.

Here is how the programme was described in a nomination for the National Association of Counties Achievement Award *it won* in 2009 (prepared by Pat Hassan and modified). The library created a leadership development steering committee that conceived a two-tiered, two-year programme to address the two levels of need, utilising consultants only for the design of the Tier 2 curriculum. Piloting Tier 1 in 2007 and Tier 2 in 2008 was a learning experience that would guide Cycle 2, which began with the second Tier 1 group in January 2009.

FIRST CYCLE, TIER 1

After nearly two years of planning that included obtaining partial funding, partners, and a curriculum design, the leadership development steering committee launched Tier 1 in January 2007.

Tier 1 was open to all staff, and its twenty-seven participants included a cross section of staff:

- Pages,
- Clerks,
- Paraprofessional and professional librarians,
- Supervisors, and
- Managers.

Tier 1 focused on developing behaviours rather than technical skills. Seven identified behavioural competencies served as the basis for all learning: personal accountability, listening and responding, teamwork and cooperation, initiative, flexibility, customer service orientation, and genuineness. (These same behaviours had been identified in prior years as behavioural competencies that supported the library's values, but because the steering committee members felt that these were not extensive enough for full leadership development, Tier 2 was required.)

Over eleven months, each participant was expected to spend 240 hours in four components:

1. Classroom learning including four-hour monthly sessions about library governance, public governance, and the behavioural competencies.
2. Independent study initiated with a 360-degree feedback evaluation on the seven behavioural competencies, developing an individual development plan, followed by evaluations.

3. Project teamwork (using a Project Runway format but without voting anyone off the show) based on real library needs from the strategic plan, utilising a budget and parameters within which to work.
4. Mentoring by the leadership development steering committee, whose members were trained by external specialists.

Because the partial funding obtained was dedicated to Tier 2, no paid instructors could be used. Instead, former staff development coordinator Tiffany Hentschel and other library managers taught sessions. University of Missouri–Columbia professors and public administration budget experts provided some in-kind support. In addition, the library could not afford to hire substitutes to cover off-desk time that participants spent in the programme. Almost immediately, time constraints forced changes to the programme. The first casualty was individual development plans, in favour of the project teamwork that required more immediate attention, team interaction, and revolving deadlines—in addition to tangible results. Lack of off-desk time and uneven support by some managers were added factors.

Mentoring was also uneven, working well with some assigned pairs but not with others. The project teams, however, provided high-impact change to the library and the highest sense of satisfaction among participants. One of the projects, the "Art in the Stacks" public exhibits programme, received a new name, logo, and contact list.

FIRST CYCLE, TIER 2

To design the curriculum for Tier 2, the library hired Paula Singer and Christi A. Olson as consultants. The intention was that the first Tier 2 graduates would teach Tier 2 in ensuing years, with no further use of consultants.

The consultants envisioned that Tier 2 participants would develop helpful and relevant conceptual frameworks, build leadership skills, and learn how to focus on achieving results for strategic initiatives and complex projects. Tier 2 focused on four key leadership competencies: leads change, influences people, achieves results, and fosters communications..

The consultants designed a programme consisting of eight modules, weekly online sessions, and three consultant-led face-to-face workshops. The three workshops focused on problem diagnosis and resolution, skills development, and group learning. Steering committee members led all other coursework. In addition, participants were expected to spend 1.5 hours per week on reading and written assignments. Tier 2 also utilised self- assessments and individual development plans. Tier 2 goals included increasing leadership skills in complex project management, organising and managing system wide meetings, resolving problems in a group setting, and facilitating public and community forums. Participants also learned to adapt to and manage change at all levels of organisations. As with Tier 1, the Tier 2 curriculum had to be adjusted midway.

By May, the steering committee had dropped individual written assignments and journaling in favour of concentrating on two chief vehicles for learning:

1. Monthly breakfast discussions (moderated in turn by steering committee members) of concepts in consultant-identified management/leadership books; and
2. Action learning team projects that addressed strategic goals.

Each team was given background, a budget, and parameters with which to work intensively over ten months to produce recommendations for solutions to specific issues on materials handling, internal communication, organisational culture, and a new way of thinking. These were already on the library's work agenda, and Tier 2 participants invited other staff members to assist them in intensive investigation and problem solving.

Criteria of success:

- Create a culture of *ad hoc* work teams that come to life and bring everyone's best work forward.
- Bring ideas into the organisation and have a "spirit of innovation" on a daily basis.
- Stop saying and acting "You can't do that" and "It's always been done that way."
- Be forward thinking, carry a forward-looking attitude.
- New leaders emerge and are encouraged and mentored.
- Participants develop or hone key competencies required for successful change and growth of themselves and JCL.

Programme goals:

- Prepare people for library leadership in a complex environment.
- Engage more people in the organisation to work actively on strategic initiatives and community needs.
- Fill the identified leadership gap.
- Foster better communication among a broader group of leaders.
- Create management depth and opportunities to practice skills.
- Increase skills in complex project management, organising and managing system wide meetings, resolving problems in a group setting, and facilitating public and community forums.
- Adapt to and manage change at all levels of organisation.

The first Tier 2's thirteen graduates included five senior managers, two members of the leadership development steering committee, and six Tier 1 graduates. Tier 2 concluded with a celebratory luncheon at which library board members heard presentations on the team projects.

SECOND CYCLE, TIER 1

As the second two-year cycle began in January 2009, the steering committee made the following adjustments to the existing Tier 1 plan, based on input from the first Tier 1 class and initial feedback from participants in the second Tier 1:

- All work time for Tier 1 was scheduled in advance and relayed to both participants and their supervisors; this helped supervisors understand the commitment up front and plan schedules.
- The number of projects was decreased.
- Reading materials for upcoming lectures are to be provided in advance.
- All presenters will incorporate more interaction into presentations.
- More field trips will be part of the agenda. Mentoring will be retained as part of the programme.

RESULTS/SUCCESS OF THE PROGRAMME

The retirement crunch did hit the Johnson County Library in 2007 with eleven retirements, in addition to normal turnover, and Tier 1 resulted almost immediately in movement among staff: seven Tier 1 participants were promoted or transferred during the course of the programme, including three to management positions. Many expressed that they applied for jobs they would not have considered prior to the programme, as even partway through the programme they had gained new confidence and had a better understanding of the organisation.

By the same token, managers began to notice a better appreciation for the complexity of decision-making processes in the library. Four members of Tier 2 have been promoted to date. An unintended consequence of Tier 1 was that the library's biennial staff engagement survey at the end of 2007 reflected improved scores of more than 7 per cent in two areas—satisfaction, loyalty, and growth and development.

TIER 2

The Tier 2 pilot included members of the steering committee, members of the leadership team, and several others. It was a tumultuous time. The library director retired, the staff development coordinator resigned to take a promotion with the county, and the committee chair resigned. Time was limited, workloads high, and reflection less valued by participants than the consultants. With one exception, all participants felt that the correct goals for success were identified. Regarding programme success, participants' evaluations revealed that 83 per cent felt that the programme resulted in creating an organisational culture of *ad hoc* work teams that bring everyone's best work forward; 66 per cent felt that new ideas were brought into the organisation with a "spirit of organisation" on a daily basis; 85 per cent felt that they were empowered to find a new way of doing things; 83 per cent felt that they were free to be forward thinking; 59 per cent felt that there was better integration across projects; 67 per cent felt that new leaders emerged from the process; and 67 per cent felt that they developed or honed key competencies for successful change and continued personal and organisational growth.

Regarding overall effectiveness of Tier 2, 83 per cent of participants felt that they had increased their leadership skills, 75 per cent felt that their new knowledge would be valuable in performing their current jobs, and 75 per cent felt that what they learned would be valuable in new senior positions. After evaluating their experiences with the first cycle of Tier 1 and Tier 2 and their outcomes, library administrators believe the leadership development programme has been extremely beneficial for the organisation as a whole. So important is this effort to the library's long-term success that administrators asked the entire library staff to support the effort by backfilling for frontline participants' time spent in the programme—not for just one year but ongoing since, 2007. The entire organisation has stretched to ensure the success of this programme.

ONLINE COMPUTER LIBRARY CENTER

Based in Dublin, Ohio, the Online Computer Library Center (OCLC) is a non-profit, membership, computer library service and research organisation dedicated to the public purposes of furthering access to the world's information and reducing information costs. More than 71,000 libraries in 112 countries and territories around the world use OCLC services to locate, acquire, catalog, lend, and preserve library materials. We include the OCLC story because most libraries are members, the organisation knows libraries at a deep level, with 1,250 employees OCLC is larger than most library systems, and OCLC is committed to leadership and career development. It also has a formal succession planning programme.

I spent some time talking with George Needham, OCLC vice president, Global and Regional Councils, to learn about that programme. Motivated by the graying of vice presidents and directors, succession planning has been a key initiative of OCLC for almost eleven years, since, president and CEO Robert L. "Jay" Jordan first joined the organisation. Since, that time, the talent management and succession planning programme has evolved and remains a key senior leadership initiative. Top-level commitment to the programme is vital, as is the strong support of HR.

The first iteration of succession planning focused on leadership development, mostly in terms of providing technical business expertise. Sixty or so vice presidents, directors, and others from around the world were invited to attend a programme designed for this purpose by Ohio State University's Center for Leadership Development. Focused on business operations, the programme was dubbed "Business School in a Box." It was a two-week programme, offered one week at a time separated by six months. Topics included how to read spreadsheets and financial reports, mergers and acquisitions, and conducting due diligence. There were also self-assessments designed to identify strengths and weaknesses and build on strengths. In truth, the assessment process did not pass the "smell test," and several participants referred to it as "one step away from voodoo." Many positive outcomes resulted from this programme.

Two participants were later promoted to vice president, the commonality of language increased understanding and effectiveness, and the interaction with professors and OCLC staff from all over the world enhanced cohesion and trust, thus improving business outcomes. Talent management and succession planning is now a far more formal programme and includes many of the steps and processes outlined in this book. Leadership reviews key positions and key contributors in the context of OCLC's strategic plan and human resources needs towards talent utilisation and competency development. It includes a 360-degree feedback assessment for learning how one is perceived and where skills might be missing.

The well-respected Birkman Method has replaced the "near voodoo" assessment tool. Managers, directors, and vice presidents identify employees in management positions on the basis of performance and potential. Managers and above can self-nominate. Anyone wishing to participate in the programme must complete an application, which includes an individual talent development profile of career goals, strengths, and development areas. Development plans are made for and with participants (key talent candidates), who are also invited to attend special training programmes around key leadership competencies with OCLC leadership and participants' managers. A recent programme was "Outcome Thinking— Building Leaders," offered by Impression Management Professionals described as a programme to build on new ways of thinking in order to execute and focus on results as well as on building the plans to achieve them. Offered over two days, the programme series includes Managing Your Message, SMART (strategic mindsets and articulate in real time) Leadership, and Conflict Harmoniser.

MENTORING

Internal, informal mentoring is a strong component of OCLC's succession planning processes. These relationships often cross divisions and are cross-hierarchical, with staff and vice presidents exposed to each other. For example, one of his colleague vice presidents asked Needham to mentor a young creative individual. They meet for lunch once a month and discuss libraries, OCLC culture, management style, and other topics.

Training is provided, including documents and checklists, to help mentors and mentees successfully negotiate and maximize the relationship. In the OCLC culture, anyone can feel free to ask for mentoring. Outcomes of these relationships include familiarity with the talent in the organisation, exposure to difference styles of management and leadership, safe feedback on issues of importance, a perspective on organisational life and politics, and a breakdown of narrow departmental tunnel vision. Needham notes, "I learned at least as much about online community, breaking technology, and blogging from my mentee as he ever learned about libraries from me!"

INDIVIDUAL AND CAREER DEVELOPMENT PLANS

While OCLC has a strong talent management and succession planning programme, it also has a strong focus on individual career development for *all* employees. It trains managers and employees to develop IDPs and expects every employee to have one.

The organisation ensures that this happens by including employee IDPs as a factor on which all managers are evaluated:

- On its web site one can find that OCLC recognises the importance of continuous development and training to ensure employees have the knowledge and tools to perform their job responsibilities at the highest level and to meet the challenges of a demanding library environment in a rapidly changing information age. OCLC encourages employees to develop their skills through the various programmes and development opportunities provided by the organisation, as well as academic offerings through our tuition reimbursement programme.3

The organisation provides development and training opportunities for employees in the areas of individual development planning, management and leadership development, technology training, individual and team assessments and coaching, office automation, quality control, ethics and compliance training, and workforce harassment training. Through Web Junction, it also offers employees online self-paced learning in a variety of genres. Tuition reimbursement (to a maximum of $5,250 per year) is also provided to employees for courses that are relevant to their current position or to one to which the employee might reasonably aspire. OCLC also supports library staff in developing their skills and knowledge through a series of awards and scholarships for new librarians, established professionals, researchers, librarians in developing countries, and ALA Spectrum scholars.

PIERCE COUNTY LIBRARY SYSTEM

The Pierce County Library System (PCLS) is headquartered near Tacoma, Washington. Its seventeen branches, two family bookmobiles, and an Explorers' Kids bookmobile bring people together, enrich lives, and provide children and adults with opportunities to learn. The library is an independent junior taxing district. With a 2009 budget of almost $29 million, it serves 534,000 over 1,600 square miles. Led by executive director Neel Parikh since, 1994, PCLS is funded by a separate property tax levy. County citisens showed their support for the library by reauthorising the library system's levy, to meet the needs of its growing and changing communities—definitely a blessing, and an obligation to the community, that Parikh does not take lightly. PCLS made four levy promises to the community: new materials and faster service, 20 per cent more open hours, additional services for kids and teenagers, and upgraded services and technology for customers by offering more computers with Internet access in libraries for public use and computer classes for adults.

The library's customer focus of giving those who responded positively to the levy, and all members of the communities served, what they want is seen in the following statement of services:

- The Library System's services and resources bring the world of information and imagination to communities. Customers will find helpful, welcoming staff who:
  - Answer questions.
  - Help find good books to read.
  - Assist with using the Library's many resources, including books, magazines, music, movies, audio books, computers and online resources.
- The Library strives to grow and change along with the needs of its customers and constantly reevaluates what and how it offers services.

Parikh and the board of trustees knew that succession planning and the development of leaders would be critical if the system was to grow and change along with the needs of its customers. The board, comprising business executives, requested that a succession plan be developed. The request was supported by PCLS's then new HR director, Holly Gorski, who remarked, "Tumbleweeds will be blowing through this place if we don't do something!" After much study and dialogue, in 2005 Parikh and her executive team decided not to take the route of determining who was going to retire and identifying succession for particular positions. Instead, like others, they chose a multi-pronged approach to develop all staff, improve leadership throughout the organisation, and create a learning organisation. An early step was to evaluate the employee pool to determine who and what percentage of employees could potentially retire within the next ten years (assuming a retirement age of 65).

Their analysis led to identifying three different categories of employees:

1. Top-level leadership: Executive team and leadership team (department heads and managing librarians).
2. Specialty positions: Individuals who do not come from the library profession for whom the library would expect to recruit replacements outside the organisation. Generally for individuals who lead these departments, PCLS would not expect their replacement to come from within the library.
3. Library professional or clerical: Individuals who develop expertise working in the system and would potentially be eligible for higher-level positions within the organisation. This category divides between

MLS librarian career-track and paraprofessional supervisory and specialist positions.

In 2009, Parikh shared the following analysis with the PCLS board:

- We have many positions in the organisation for which we have no trouble recruiting replacements (*e.g.*, library pages, branch assistants, custodians). Some of them may become supervisors or become librarians. I will describe the situation in various tiers.
- Executive Leadership Roles: There are 24 Department Heads and top-level administrators. 37.5 per cent will be eligible to retire in the next 10 years. However, looking more closely at the number, you see a different picture. Of the Executive Team, only 1 out of 6 will be eligible to retire, or 16 per cent. The major impact on the organisation would be the retirement of professional librarians in leadership roles. It is important to note that the library system is becoming nationally known for innovative services. It is likely that high-level positions that become vacant will also attract national attention for applicants. PCLS ideally will look for a balance of internal and external.
- Mid-level Supervisors and Specialists: Of 58 employees 43 per cent will be eligible for retirement in the next 10 years. The majority of that falls in the branch clerical supervisory role. This area is a target for attention for developing leadership skills or leadership opportunities for individuals in the organisations to move into these positions. We are also looking closely at these positions because of the need to expand the number of opportunities for librarians to develop supervisory experience.
- The analysis covers 82 individuals or approximately 23 per cent of the employees in the library. The other 277 employees are generally entry-level positions (such as pages, branch assistants, librarians) or specialty positions (such as Finance Department, custodians, facilities maintenance, graphic designers). There are high retirement rates in some of those categories, but it also easy to recruit for those positions. For instance, nearly half of the page positions are eligible for retirement.
- We have no problem recruiting for this position. For example, earlier this year over 100 people applied for a single part-time page vacancy. These individuals are an extremely important core to the learning organisation and we will pay attention to their learning and growth, building potential for leadership roles.

In another memo to the board, Parikh summarises the library's approach to succession planning in the areas of hiring, nurture/growth, and creating opportunities to lead.

All, she wrote, "are an important part of assuring that we are growing people and 'potential successors'":

- *Hiring—Get the Right People on the Bus:* Recruit and hire high potential talent and ensure that we are hiring people that share the library's vision and with potential to grow and contribute to the library. A key element is regular evaluation of the organisational structure and job descriptions to ensure the library can meet future goals. This includes recruiting talented new graduates from library school or individuals from libraries across the country, in addition to talent in professions. As PCLS gains a national reputation, we are able to attract talent nationwide.
- *Nurture/Growth:* Create an environment that fosters and supports learning and growth. We must offer opportunities to learn and actively support individual growth. This includes not only formal training within the library or outside, but also creating an environment that encourages experimentation, risk taking and decision-making. This is the core philosophy that led to the creation of the "Learning Organisation" and the Learning Department.
- *Create Opportunities to Lead:* This element includes not only the opportunity to lead projects, but also ensuring that our organisational structure allows individuals to develop leadership skills in preparation for higher level positions. This also means evaluating our organisational structure to ensure that it supports future goals and creating career-ladder positions that would lead to positions of increased responsibility.

Parikh is definitely taking a systems approach to succession planning. Several projects were begun to support the succession planning initiative. She knew that a culture change was required to create a succession plan, leaders at all levels, and a truly customer-focused library. One leverage point was through defining leadership, and leadership behaviours, at PCLS. The original list of leadership descriptors was drafted by Parikh and deputy director Georgia Lomax and vetted by the executive team, then introduced to the leadership team (which includes all branch managers and department heads). As part of the rollout and training, managers learned to act and then tell what leadership descriptors they were using.

They now ask, and ask themselves, these same questions. In a series of meetings in each branch and five at the main library, Parikh and Lomax introduced them to all staff. The final list of leadership descriptors is found. "All staff need to be leaders," was the message Parikh sent. Staff responded to one question: "How can we help you become a leader at PCLS?" The responses led to training, coaching, and I2P2, an idea incubator project. Still in pilot stages, I2P2 is designed to encourage ideas and risk taking as well as incubate ideas of potential services and programmes in a safe environment. As in numerous libraries and other organisations, too many employees felt inhibited about putting ideas forward. Parikh and the executive team knew that, for the library to develop a strong culture of customer focus, all ideas would be needed and all staff would need to be accountable.

The leadership descriptors were further operationalised by core skills and qualities required of all staff members along with behavioural dos and don'ts for each. The nine skills/qualities identified are customer focus, teamwork, professional integrity, leadership, communication, problem solving, change and learning, positive attitude, and diversity. They had started with competencies, but that just did not work for them. The dos and don'ts were simply more effective in this culture.

In rolling out the skills and qualities, HR director Holly Gorski wrote:

- These are the skills and qualities all of us need in order to work together and provide outstanding library service, now and in the future. We are currently working to change the Library System's hiring process to ensure new employees are selected based on these attributes. In 2009 we will be changing the performance appraisals for all positions to focus on these as well.

The learning culture being fostered by PCLS relies heavily on coaching, modeling behaviour, and setting expectations. Training is based on an 80:20 model, with only 20 per cent classroom based. Much of the rest is in-the-moment, just-in-time training and coaching. The newly created Learning Team developed "Foundations of the PCLS Learning Organisation". This document articulates the critical elements for PCLS to be a successful learning organisation. The team also used this document to develop a work plan with strategies for each of the items listed.

Staff members are retooling their perspectives, looking beyond their immediate actions and behaviours to what the implications of their behaviour are regarding internal and external customers alike. Employees are constantly asked, and ask each other, "What is the customer perspective on this action or this policy?" A recent illustration is going beyond making a simple change pertaining to e-mail on the server (good internal customer service) to assessing the implications for staff members working at home or away from the office (great leadership and customer-focused behaviour). I asked Parikh how she would know she was successful.

She responded by saying that there would be leaders ready to fill vacancies, all employees would be taking on the role of leader (at their appropriate level), things would be happening and getting done, expectations would be set, and staff would be stepping up with ideas as well as taking responsibility for their decisions and behaviours. Staff would be asking the right questions, retooling their thinking, constantly modeling customer focus. Staff would be living the leadership descriptors. PCLS is spending a lot of time and money creating a culture and a legacy of staff ready to move into new, different, and higher-level positions. In some ways it is the hard way to create a succession plan; in others, it is the only way. I asked Parikh about the time and money, especially in this economy. With further developmental plans tied to succession planning, I was curious: was she going to continue this effort? At their current level of intensity? "Yes," she said, "It's essential: we are investing in our future. Staff salaries and benefits comprise 70 per cent of the library's budget. We must keep developing staff so they are ready, willing, and able to provide customer-focused service—especially when this generation retires." With some realism and a smile she continued, "We are ballot based, as an independent taxing authority—if we are not relevant, we are toast!"

QUEENS BOROUGH PUBLIC LIBRARY

Queens Borough (N.Y.) Public Library (QBPL), *Library Journal*'s 2009 Library of the Year, serves 2.2 million people from sixty-two locations plus seven adult learning centers and two family literacy centers. It circulates the highest number of books and other library materials in the country. The library's budget is $127.5 million. In fiscal year 2009, QBPL circulated 23 million items, opened its doors to 16 million people, and offered 30,000 programmes. It has 6.7 million items in its collections and supports 827,500 active borrowers. Like the County of Los Angeles Public Library, it is a large and diverse library system with many needs, including that for a strong cadre of potential managers and leaders. Succession planning at QBPL, though not formal, is purposeful. What follows are several initiatives described by Tom Galante, CEO and library director.

SUCCESSION PLANNING FOR COMMUNITY BRANCH MANAGERS: MONEY AND EDUCATION

The library recently made some organisational changes to facilitate mid-management development and succession planning. It took money. Many of the forty assistant community branch manager positions were open. Senior librarians did not want to promote into the position, for there was little salary incentive to do so. To fill the vacancies, the library added $3,000 to the salary. That broke the ice. The assistant manager positions are now filled. But that was not enough to prepare for the future. Assistant community branch manager is a key feeder position in the community library system, so the need to provide learning and development opportunities for the incumbents was clear. The library contracted with a library school that created and facilitated a management certification programme for twenty-five employees. Many were assistant branch managers. The curriculum included the topics of management, budget and finance, technology management, human resource management, building management, and general administration.

A course with a rigourous curriculum, it was offered on-site, once a week for six months. Homework was required. After completion of five courses over three years, all participants graduated. "The outcome," said Galante, "has been great. These employees, current and prospective library managers, have been networking, sharing their experiences, and learning from each other. They have begun peer coaching and all have a broader view of the organisation.... And," he adds proudly, "there have already been a number of promotions."

DUAL CAREER LADDERS

To support retention of professional librarians, including its library managers, QBPL restructured its compensation structure, including new positions, enhancing its already existing dual career ladders for librarians and managers. To the positions of senior librarian, supervising librarian, and principal librarian a second level was added. For senior librarian positions, a third level was added to support promotions into select assistant manager positions. (The move from Librarian I to Librarian II is relatively automatic.) In both ladders, after six months of satisfactory performance, jobholders are automatically moved to the next level and receive a salary increase.

SUCCESSION PLANNING AT THE SENIOR LEVEL

The library has taken a similar approach to creating a pipeline for system wide management positions. Because the size of the system justifies it, QBPL has seven associate and assistant director positions reporting to public service department heads (directors). Four of those positions are responsible for supervising community library managers. In addition, various support departments include an assistant director position. All in these positions lead major organisational initiatives as part of their development as senior leaders. All are observed, supported, and developed to be able, at a minimum, to serve in an interim capacity in the event of a department head vacancy.

KNOWLEDGE MANAGEMENT AND CAPITALISING ON RETIREES

Galante is concerned about losing good people to early (or regular) retirement. To date, knowledge transfer planning has been minimal. To help the system buy some time, and to appeal to those retiring and looking for more flexibility and free time, two policy changes were made. First, QBPL now provides an opportunity for those interested in retiring to work part-time. Second, the library is offering retirees the ability to work at a lower-level position yet keep their seniority when setting the pay rate. For example, if the individual was paid at fifteen-year experience in the salary range of the job she is leaving, her new salary remains at the fifteen-year salary range of the new position. This option has proven attractive to retirees who might have otherwise left the system without transferring their knowledge, mentoring new staff, or supporting programmes.

TRANSFERS AND JOB ROTATION

Similar to other libraries, QBPL has been rotating staff into different community branches and central. With over seventy locations, there are many opportunities for job transfer. Because the demographics of this system vary widely, staff transferring often find themselves in a very different environment serving a different community and customer. "This provides a broader view and creates stronger, flexible, customer-oriented staff." For union-represented positions, the labour agreement provides for internal transfers for similar positions based on seniority if QBPL-specified job requirements are met; for union and non-union supervisory and management positions, interviewing is done to select the best candidate from external and internal applicants. Rotations and transfers extend to the top of the library system as well. In addition to the COO, whose responsibilities include all public services, a dozen department heads report directly to him. With a few exceptions, half of them trade jobs every year.

ON THE LOOKOUT

Galante acknowledged that he is always recruiting, always on the lookout for talent. He knows that not all positions can, or should, be filled from within. He has been networking and searching for a new wave of managers: creative individuals who can support the new service model of delivering to customers what they want and need. He also wants to recruit leaders who can deal with City Hall—not a typical competency, or desire, of many senior library managers.

SANTA CLARA COUNTY LIBRARY

Succession planning at Santa Clara County Library (SCCL) starts at the point of hiring, where a solid job description reflecting the desired skill set and competencies propels the library towards its strategic BHAG (big hairy audacious goal): "Building upon our reputation for service excellence, the Santa Clara County Library will have the highest percentage of library service area cardholders in the nation." The three specific areas the library will focus on in the next five years are convenience, public awareness and marketing, and information literacy. So how does Cervantes find and develop the leadership that will continually propel the library towards meeting its BHAG? She engages in two distinct processes, one external and the other internal.

EXTERNAL VIEW

One way to locate leadership is by investing years actively watching, waiting, and creating a good reputation for the library. Cervantes keeps her eyes and ears open for the up-and-comers in the library community. She goes out of her way to meet them when their paths cross, reads the articles they write, and watches them present at conferences. Cervantes invests her time so she has a front-row seat as talent rises. When the library's deputy county librarian retired last year, and when several community librarians (managers) retired, several librarians nationwide were invited to participate in the county's recruitment process.

INTERNAL FOCUS

Cervantes's most important and intense focus is internal. SCCL really works developing internal staff. "This library system," she said, "seeks to prepare staff for their next job and provides the opportunity to develop leadership within their current job."

Job Rotation

Job rotation is in its first iteration at SCCL. It is designed to help staff acquire big-picture thinking and deliver district wide service while supporting staff to grow, stretch, and explore. One facet of job rotation is moving community library staff into other community libraries and into headquarters jobs as well as ensuring that employees assigned to headquarters have experiences in community libraries. At another level, the library is trying out the rotation of three senior management positions among the incumbents for twelve-month periods: system wide circulation manager, reference librarian (which includes 24/7 virtual reference and assisting with collection development), and services managers (adult, youth).

An opportunity arose when a community librarian took medical leave. To fill the gap, the library interviewed qualified managers to take a temporary assignment at the largest and busiest library in the system (2.5 million annual circulation). This resulted in an experienced community librarian from a much smaller library having the opportunity to take on new challenges, learn, and grow. Consequently, a programme librarian (manager) became the acting community librarian, and a librarian became a programme librarian (adult or youth services manager) for the same period of time.

Cervantes shares two success stories. One shining star in the organisation stepped forward and volunteered on an early version of the library's web page redesign. This star, Allison Parham, is now an electronic resources librarian and leading a formal web redesign project for the library. Paul Sims, formerly an SCCL librarian, is now the technical services manager for Mountain View Public Library. ("Sometimes our succession planning benefits other libraries!") Sims graduated from the San Jose State University MLIS programme and went on to become an adjunct faculty member.

Building on his enthusiasm for the SJSU/MLIS programme, Sims asked if he could offer an orientation to potential students from SCCL staff ranks. He developed the presentation, including PowerPoint slides, and promoted the workshop to recent graduates, current MLIS students, and potential librarians.

Both Cervantes and Sarah Flowers (former deputy county librarian) were invited to speak about their own career paths and the SCCL opportunities afforded to MLIS graduates. At least two of the dozen or so who attended this workshop enrolled in the SJSU/MLIS programme, and one or more completed their undergraduate degree requirements with Sims's encouragement. "Succession planning," said Cervantes, "can be viral."

Development beyond Boundaries

This library system goes beyond its own boundaries to develop staff. Staff members at all levels are encouraged to become involved and engaged with the California Library Association, ALA, PLA, and the Urban Libraries Council (and pays institutional membership dues and conference attendance fees). This ensures that the library's name is out there, which results in attracting high-quality candidates when vacancies occur. Of course, library staff and the library gain as well. Involved employees learn from their efforts with CLA and other professional associations, develop technical and leadership skills, and build networks. Because one of its goals is to be involved with the cities and county it serves, SCCL also encourages service on local chambers of commerce, the arts and culture, non-profits, and other key constituent communities.

The library pays the dues of managers and supports involvement and leadership opportunities in local volunteer organisations for all staff. One manager who stands out to Cervantes is Rosanne Macek, Morgan Hill community librarian. Macek joined the SCCL staff as a children's programme librarian in 2001, became community librarian in 2002, completed the Leadership Morgan Hill programme sponsored by the Morgan Hill Rotary Club, and is now working on a master's degree in public administration using the library's tuition reimbursement programme. SCCL has been working actively on succession planning since, 2005. At the time it was facing several retirements among key library managers.

Earlier, deputy county librarian Julie Farnsworth had created a leadership training programme for potential leaders and invited employees to self-identify. Participants in the leadership programme completed nine classes covering all aspects of management and leadership in the SCCL system. More than fifty emerging leaders completed the programme during two series of classes. SCCL places a premium on developing leaders internally and wisely also pays attention to future leaders nationwide. Cervantes showed us the importance of having a variety of smaller, targeted leadership development programmes in addition to formal, large programmes.

SNO-ISLE LIBRARIES

Located in the north Puget Sound region of Washington State, Sno-Isle Libraries, with twenty-one locations in Snohomish County and Island County, serves as a community doorway to reading, resources, and lifelong learning and a center for people, ideas, and culture. Jonalyn Woolf-Ivory is the library director. Pat Olafson, HR director, explained some of the library's efforts in succession planning. Olafson and her colleagues have been thinking quite a bit about succession planning in recent years. Familiar with the literature on the graying of the library workforce, and looking (literally) at the members of the Sno-Isle workforce, they decided to identify potential vacancies and to develop a backup plan towards ensuring stability and continuity in providing excellent library service to the communities served.

The board of trustees was also interested in having bench strength for senior positions in the organisation. The first step was to identify key jobs. Olafson then matched the key positions with the people in them to ascertain the level of risk of retirement each one might be in—that is, she looked at data on each individual holding these jobs to get a deeper understanding of their age and service and a picture of when retirements might take place. She created a schema of employees: at immediate risk (IR), at risk (AR), and at low risk (LR) for retirement. Olafson defined these categories in concrete terms based on the retirement eligibility provisions of the pension plans.

Those in IR are 60 years of age and above today with an anticipated (for the purpose of this exercise) retirement date in the next five years. AR staff in key positions are ages 55–59 or age 50 with at least ten years of service. It is anticipated that these individuals will move into the IR category in the next five years. LR employees do not fall into either of the other categories by age or experience. Another organisation's definitions might differ depending on retirement plan provisions covering its employees. Olafson then linked those in key positions to their risk of retirement. Among those in key positions, she found four IR and three AR staff members holding key positions. Olafson mentioned some examples, starting with the library director, and included herself.

The director, at age 55, has twenty-nine years of pension service credits. She is viewed as AR. Olafson, the HR director, needed to code her own position as IR. At age 63 with more than fifteen years of pension service credits, she is eligible to retire within five years. Over the years, with encouragement from the board, positions have been installed that not only filled a workload need but also were intended as immediate temporary backup in case of a vacancy in some management positions. For example, several of the larger Sno-Isle community libraries have an assistant managing librarian position, and there is an assistant manager in collection development.

Incumbents in these positions could step in until a replacement is hired when someone in a key position and IR retires earlier than anticipated. Library leadership took this approach further and realised that some of those designated as "backup until filled" might not take (or even want) the vacant key position or might not be ready to take on the full responsibility long term when the time comes. With encouragement from the board to develop a deeper bench and to work towards "growing their own," Sno- Isle identified "developmental positions" (designated "Dev" on the chart; defined as a position, not a person) that could be a step towards a key position. Here Olafson again looked at service and age, this time for individuals currently holding positions categorised as developmental to determine who might retire and create an opening in one of those jobs. They too were coded as IR, AR, and LR.

This analysis indicated that several developmental positions could be open in the next few years due to retirements. This provided a list of potential developmental opportunities. In addition, Sno-Isle has experimented with creating one developmental position to broaden the experience of those who may be interested in library administration. The facilities manager job was recently created (as a temporary position, for two years only) to provide developmental work experience in facilities management and capital facilities development. The incumbent is acquiring a great deal of experience and exposure working on special assignments such as branch renovation projects and creating a preventive maintenance plan for every building.

She is now the key contact for building issues in each branch. In addition, she attends community and board meetings and meets regularly with the library director. Previously she was a manager of a large building and will have the opportunity to return to this position at the end of two years. Of course, by allowing staff to take a temporary job and return to their original job, Sno-Isle created a whole string of temporary positions, creating developmental opportunities for many across the system. At the end of two years the library leadership, with input from the incumbent, will decide whether to retain the facilities job as a temporary developmental position or make it a regular assignment.

Along with creating development opportunities in a variety of jobs, Karri Matau, director of strategic initiatives, is charged with creating a leadership development programme for the organisation. This programme, which will support succession planning efforts, is still in developmental stages. Many—if not most—libraries find themselves in difficult financial straits because of the recession. Thinking about this, I asked Olafson a question for which she had an interesting and clear answer. "Pat," I asked, "in the beginning of this conversation, you talked about the budget constraints facing Sno-Isle Libraries. You mentioned the potential of a hiring freeze.

How much leadership development and succession planning do you plan to continue in these tough times?" Olafson's answer was not one I often hear. "We know we need to have leadership development initiatives and succession planning in process even when times are bleak. Strong, skilled employees are a key ingredient to facing tough times and to carrying out our strategic plan.

The library district cannot afford to put leadership development on the back burner." Sno-Isle library leadership has made a choice—one that has them working diligently to ensure that knowledge is transferred as long-term employees get ready to move into the next phase of their lives and younger members of the workforce get ready to take the baton and bring the library into the future.

LEADERSHIP

During the early nineteenth century, Wellington's and Napoleon's observations made sense. With the onset of battle, communications became muddled, artillery was immobilised, and a commander's ability to control his forces was limited. Consequently, the leadership of a single general could prove decisive in battle by maintaining clarity of command and control. We are now at a totally different stage of warfare. This not to say that the fog of war has completely lifted, but visibility and synchronised actions, and the speed, precision, and lethality of response is beyond comparison to anything that has preceded it. The battlefield success of the doctrine and technology of Network Centric Warfare was not based upon a single brilliant plan, or a single individual or group, but rather was a property of the network, both technologically and organisationally. As Operation Iraqi Freedom so vividly illustrated, battle plans can now be changed very rapidly, affecting all aspects of operations—strategy, tactics, logistics and PSYOPs, operations, kinetics, and all types of forces.

The competencies that make NCW a success are network properties; they are no longer solely the province of charismatic leaders or chance, but the result of diverse competencies and a new understanding of the role and growth of network leadership, and how it is learned and rewarded.

EARLY LEADERSHIP

Leadership among Greek warriors was based upon "a first among equals" principle. Such leadership was a product of a culture of equality and mutual accountability. In a very tangible sense, cultures are networks of social relationships. Military cultures, especially in battlefield situations, have highly articulated roles and codes of conduct and mutual accountability.

Although an individual may gain prominence and status apart from a group, it is often not the result of individual achievement, but how the individual exemplifies certain traits that represent the best traits of that group, such as sacrifice, decisiveness, courage, initiative, and prowess. In fact, to attribute successes to the individual that derive from the group undermines a core principle of true leadership: the group comes before the individual.

In the following stanzas taken from Alfred Lord Tennyson's ode to Wellington, many of the qualities that continue to make leaders great are captured:

- ...Mourn for the man of amplest influence, Yet clearest of ambitious crime, *our greatest yet with least pretence,* Great in council and great in war, Foremost captain of his time, *rich in saving common-sence* And, as the greatest only are, In his *simp licity sublime...*
- . . . *Who never sold the truth to serve the hour,* Nor palter'd with Eternal God for power; Who let the turbid streams of rumor flow Thro' either babbling world of high and low; Whose life was work, whose language rife *with rugged maximus hewn from life;* Who never spoke against a foe; Whose cighty winters freeze with one rebuke All great self-seekers trampling on the right. *Truth-teller was our England's Alfred named;* Truth-lover was our English Duke; Whatever record leap to light He never shall be shamed...

By embodying the best qualities of a group, a military leader does not try to elevate himself above his peers, but brings Honour and distinction to them, be they his company, brigade, division, or service. These qualities of "simplicity sublime" and "truth-teller" are parts of the best of military culture. They are hard to transfer from the field of battle into bureaucratic and administrative assignments, where often different kinds of codes of conduct are rewarded. As noted earlier, small networks of 150-200 individuals can still be coordinated by face-to-face relationships and personal codes of Honour and accountability.

At such a scale, combat relationships are more transparent and accountable, and hence, not so easily "gamed" and "politicised" as in hierarchical, formal organisations. It is not surprising that many who succeed on the battlefield fail to adjust to the rules of a bureaucratic organisation, whose codes of success are often at variance with those of the battlefield group.

In bureaucratic organisations, successful leadership can entail the subordination of the interests of the group to the promotion of the individual, as visibility to outside parties is associated with an individual leader who is *personally* credited with a certain policy or success. Under such circumstances, the leader in bureaucratic groups becomes a marker, a kind of shorthand, for the success or failure of an issue, policy, or campaign—not the exemplar of the group.

This kind of leadership can entail taking much of the credit and little of the blame, thereby undermining the very principles of transparency and accountability upon which effective peer networks depend. The systemic failure of corporate leadership and governance in the United States over the last 10 years can be partly attributed to a bureaucratic culture wherein a company's success was almost totally attributed to the skills of the CEO and senior management.

This was reflected in senior executive compensation packages that ballooned to 301 times the average worker's pay package. Yet when the downturn came, and even widespread fraudulent practices were revealed, very few corporate leaders were held accountable, and shareholders and employees assumed the bulk of the losses. These failures were neither personality - nor individually-based, but were systemic in terms of how leaders were selected, cultivated, rewarded, and held accountable.

The systemic subversion of governance leadership roles needed to achieve independence, truth telling, and transparency has been its own kind of perverse "network effect." This chapter's treatment of leadership is not founded upon any "great man" leadership model.

This is not to say that individual qualities are not important, but rather that sustainable and replicable qualities of leadership are treated here as a network property, made possible by the combination of the character of the social network and the individuals themselves. Moreover, it will be argued that there are several different types of leadership roles and the relative importance and combination of these roles depends upon the circumstances and structure of the organisational networks involved.

THE CORE OF LEADERSHIP

Leadership is the art of engaging the hearts and minds of ordinary people to achieve extraordinary results. This Isn't the Company I Joined, I've been interviewing gifted leaders from a wide range of industries. Each has his or her unique corporate responsibilities to carry out. Each has to deal with widely different competitive pressures, customer demands, marketing strategies, stockholder expectations, and Workforce requirements.

Each represents an organisation that is affected in specific ways by the new global economy, the IT revolution, the disappearance of stable currency values worldwide, and the collapse of the old Industrial business paradigm as an organising model for their companies. But all share one thing in common: an apparently innate set of emotional and intellectual qualities that make up what I call the Core of Leadership.

The components of that core are:

- Vision.
- Integrity.
- Trust.
- Values.
- Vulnerability.
- Motivation.

Together they produce what we all instantly recognise as leaders. How they do it is easier to note in practice than it is to define in principle. Because we aren't just talking about special skills or strategies these people exercise, we're talking about individual character. Like the force of gravity or the lump of uranium in a nuclear generator, the leadership core works invisibly. And like any living system, it sometimes works intuitively and mysteriously. But its positive effects upon others can be readily observed, and those observations, in turn, can be put to immediate use by anyone charged with leading fellow employees at any level of an organisation.

LEADERSHIP AS VISION

In contrast to control-minded authority of the past, today's leaders must exercise power through a shared purpose and vision. An organisational vision is not the same as long-range or even strategic planning. Planning is a linear process; progression Towards a goal. Vision is more holistic — a sense of direction that combines a good business strategy with a comprehensive organisational purpose that declares its own importance.

A vision describes a business as it could become over the long term and outlines a feasible way of achieving this goal. To transform an organisation, leaders must adopt and communicate a vision of the future that impels people beyond the boundaries and limits of the past. Leaders who articulate such visions aren't mystics, but broad-based thinkers who are willing to take risks. Visionary leaders don't have to be brilliant, highly innovative, or incredibly charismatic. But they do have to be intently focused on what it is they are trying to achieve. Fred Smith, ounder and Chief Executive Officer of Federal Express, put it in these very practical terms: "If there is any indication that the leader is not totally committed to achieving the vision, then all the sweet talk in the world will not get people to support it."

LEADERSHIP AS INTEGRITY

A leader must be seen to stand for something, must act from deep-seated principles, and must rely on strong personal beliefs. Leading with integrity implies a willingness to embody the attitudes and Behaviours you want to see in employees. Steve Wikstrom is the Co-Chief Executive Officer of Reell Precision Manufacturing Corporation, a $35 million company that produces wrap spring clutches and constant torque hinges for foreign and domestic customers. "In our company we try to create relationships that allows us to 'call' one another on Behaviour that doesn't represent our values.

A recent example occurred during the development of our latest strategic plan. Every year we get the top dozen leaders together once a week, for six to eight weeks. At the end of each of the weekly sessions, we have 'homework' assignments to prepare for the next meeting. At the beginning of one session, a participant told us that at the last meeting he had offered to send us information that we had agreed to review and return with our comments. He went on to say that of the twelve messages he sent out, only three responses had been received. He then asked all of us what we were going to do about this issue of 'irresponsibility.' The meeting stopped and we discussed how to better Honour

our commitments. Right at the top of the organisation's leadership, we are aware of the need to mirror whatever Behaviour we expect to receive in kind."

LEADERSHIP AS TRUST

Until recently, managers' primary function has been supervision — telling employees what to do and measuring how well they did it. But the new breed of knowledge workers increasingly don't want or need to be micro-managed. They need to be set free in the sphere of their own authority. They need to be trusted. Trust is an attitude of confidence in another person, a positive set of expectations about that person's competencies and character. The powerful influence of one person's expectation on another's Behaviour is known as the "Pygmalion Effect." Eliza Doolittle explains it in George Bernard Shaw's play Pygmalion: "You see, really and truly, apart from the things anyone can pick up, the difference between a lady and a flower girl is not how she behaves but how she's treated. I shall always be a flower girl to Professor Higgins because he always treats me as a flower girl and always will; but I know I can be a lady to you because you always treat me as a lady and always will." The difference between leaders who complain about the lack of responsibility in today's employees and those who speak with pride of the creative contribution and dedication of their staff may lie in the realm of management's expectation.

LEADERSHIP AS VULNERABILITY

Recognition of the potential of the Workforce for contributing solutions to organisational problems has increased while the infallibility of leaders and the certainty of management tasks have declined. The unquestioned authority of leaders in the corporation of the past has been replaced by the need to acknowledge the expertise of those below, and to enlist employees as true partners. Moving from a model in which leadership made all the decisions and knew all the answers to an organisational environment of openness, candor, and empowerment takes a willingness by leaders to become and remain highly vulnerable. There has never been a time in which our organisations have experienced more uncertainty and chaos. It may sound ironic, but the corporate leader who can say to his or her employees, "Sure, I'm scared too," will have done more for company morale with that single admission than a dozen phony pep talks ever could. Why? Because, as Sue Swenson, president of Leap Wireless, observes: "When leaders are perceived as human and vulnerable, employees identify with those attributes and begin to see the potential for success and leadership in themselves."

LEADERSHIP AS VALUES

Webster defines value as "a principle, standard or quality considered inherently worthwhile or desirable." The root is the Latin valor, which means strength. Values are a source of strength for an enterprise or an individual. As leadership strategy moves from coercion to cooperation, the key to bonding people to the goals of the organisation automatically becomes the intangibles — relationships, commitments and shared values.

Founding President and Chief Operating Officer of Ritz-Carlton Hotels, "Values are the heart and soul of our organisation. It is not enough for people just to fill functions. They have to know what we are all about." Leaders must stay focused on values and keep them energised — which is the hardest part.

For that, you need to find processes that renew and revitalise values. One process that Ritz-Carlton uses is called the "Line Up." Fifteen minutes before shift begins every day, the leader of the line up goes through the basics of that day. Employees of R-C all over the world are reminded of the same "value of the day," as prepared by the corporate office. Added to that is a "teaching" — an issue brought to our awareness, based on customer-service input, and then some comments about the daily value that are customised to the individual hotel.

LEADERSHIP AS MOTIVATION

The secret to being a great motivator is realising that motivation isn't something that can be forced or ordered. Motivation is an intrinsic capacity of human beings that can be tapped, nurtured, and developed — but never coerced. In essence, all motivation is self-motivation.

It manifests when leaders hold a compelling vision of the future, have a strong personal desire to realise the vision, and possess the ability to engage people's individual motivation in the common cause of that vision so that a true interconnection emerges. Motivational leaders inspire exceptional levels of commitment and performance. Prior to forming his own public relations firm, Bob Dilenschneider served as president and CEO of Hill and Knowlton.

He talked with me about his most memorable boss: "Barney Clarke, the CEO of Columbia Gas Systems, was brilliant — a genius who thought way outside the box. Although I suspect he had the answers all the time, he spent hours talking with us, involving us and making us feel as if we were an integral part of a huge change — as if we were making history.

And he got so much out of all of us. We'd work 'round the clock. Working with Barney was exciting, exhausting, incredibly intense, and absolutely thrilling!"

THE RELATIONSHIP BETWEEN LEADERSHIP AND INFLUENCE

What is the relationship between leadership and influence? Is leadership always influence and is influence always leadership? To say that leadership always entails influence is like saying that all snow is white. It's true but the inference doesn't work the other way. That is, not all white things are snow. Similarly, although all leadership is influence, there are lots of types of influence that don't count as leadership.

Here are a few examples:

- Intimidating or forcing someone to do something.
- Bribing someone to do your bidding.
- Paying for things you want someone to do for you.
- Teaching a student to behave better in a classroom.
- Encouraging your children to eat their vegetables.

The last two examples are not leadership because they have nothing to do with a group striving to achieve a goal. Teaching students and encouraging children to eat vegetables is for their own interest, not for the good of a larger group. Similarly, salespeople may be very influential but their influence is self-interested. The salesperson and the customer do not constitute a group.

FORMAL AUTHORITY AND LEADERSHIP INFLUENCE

Suppose you are the boss and you decide to ramp up production by 50 per cent, requiring everyone to work faster and longer hours without overtime. Is this leadership? No, it may be influence but it is not leadership because the employees had no choice.

To say that leadership is informal influence means that followers have a free choice to follow or not. What are some prime examples of true leadership influence? One of the most familiar is Martin Luther King's demonstrations against segregation on buses which led the U.S., Supreme Court to outlaw this practice. King had no formal authority or other power to move the U.S., government.

This is the real meaning of leadership. Another example of genuine leadership influence was the Sony employee who influenced management to adopt his idea for PlayStation despite their feeling that Sony wasn't into making toys. Whenever you convince your colleagues or your boss to adopt a new idea, you have shown them leadership. Or, you might simply set a good example for others and, if they follow, you have shown leadership. Market leading businesses influence their competitors to change course, another example of real leadership. When executives make decisions that take their teams in new directions, they are taking managerial actions, NOT showing leadership because employees have no choice. To count as leadership, influence must be informal and followers must get on board completely of their own free will. Leadership is also a group phenomenon and is aimed at serving some unselfish purpose, something to improve the group's effectiveness. For this reason, even if your children willingly follow your plea to eat their vegetables, you haven't shown leadership because you and your kids are not a group working Towards a common goal.

INFORMAL LEADERSHIP AND INFLUENCE

We often distinguish between formal and informal leadership. The only difference between these concepts is that the informal leader takes charge informally. The formal leader has been given formal authority to govern the group while the informal leader is granted this role by the group itself. The informal leader has personal power - charisma, knowledge or some form of expertise that the group values. It is vital to recognise that the conventional concept of informal leadership is not the same thing as saying that all leadership influence is informal. The conventional concept, formal or informal, is all about being in charge of the group. The claim made here is that real leadership is independent of position, as it was in the case of Martin Luther King. He was not an informal leader in the conventional sense - the Supreme Court didn't recognise him as their informal leader.

As another example, a technical geek might influence his peers to adopt a new piece of software. He has influenced them informally. However, this geek might be so disinclined to manage the group that they might never view him as their informal leader - someone who they would turn to for help in organising their day to day work, who they would look to for advice and the resolution of conflict. The geek's informal leadership is a one-off act, not an ongoing role. His influence is informal but he is not what we normally call an informal leader because he has no interest or ability to take charge of the group in a managerial sense. So what? By reformulating the meaning of leadership, I am saying that the old distinction between formal and informal leadership is outdated. There is really only formal and informal management because all leadership is informal where this term refers to willingly following someone's lead NOT to informally taking charge of the group.

6

The Human Relationists and The Behaviourists

INTRODUCTION

"Human Resource" is regarded as the most important resource for the advancement of the nation. If it is not properly developed, it cannot be put to proper use. Human force is the basic raw material for the development of an advanced nation. Peter Drucker "The most valuable asset of a 21st century institution will be its knowledge workers and their productivity. In an organization staff development and staff training are parts of the bigger concept of human resource development (HRD). The HRD encompasses the broad set of activities that improve the performance of the individual and teams of an organization. The HRD is considered as the most vital link of the library. The HRD involves both management and operative functions. Operative functions include procurement, development, compensation, integration and maintenance of personnel.

It is the most powerful tool for any organization's success and the training of employees is regarded as one of the most important functions of effective resource management. In order to obtain a competitive edge in providing the best services to the customer, training which will develop a well-trained workforce is vital to render efficient and effective services in modern library and Information centers. Further, libraries require appointing staff, which possess IT skills so that they are in a position to perform a wide range of functions. This particular chapter has been brought out to get a view of human factor, which is one of the most complicated aspects of any system. Yet, it's the one that gets the least attention, is least discussed, the least researched, and perhaps the least understood.

METHODOLOGY

Questionnaire method and on the spot interview was conducted for collecting the data. The target group comprises almost all the staff of each and every library. Altogether a total of 160 questionnaires were distributed among the three types of libraries of which 118 were collected. The Age group of the respondent was divided into three categories *viz.*, 31-40, 41-50, 51-58 and 58 and above respectively. It was found that the majority of the staff was in the age group of 41-50 followed by those in 51-60, 31-40 and 60 above. Sexwise, the ratio of male and female was found to be 66.94 male to 33.05 female.

TRAINING PROGRAMME FOR STAFF

Effective training programme for the library staff is a must to acquire authentic meaning of a library. There are different methods of training, which can be adopted by an organization.

Some are:

- Sending staff for relevant courses and seminars.
- Library professionals must regularly read literature not only in their field of specialization but also allied fields especially on IT.
- Job learning training can be carried out at work place itself.
- Information literacy programme within the libraries.
- Network literacy programme.
- Computer literacy programme.
- UGC sponsored programme.
- Staff must be trained to install software and tackle simple technical problems.
- Training must be given to familiarize with some Operating Systems (OS) such as MS DOS, MS WORD, MS EXCEL, MS POWERPOINT, etc.
- Knowledge of e-mail technology must be given.
- Training in data organization, structuring and presentation of contents must be given to library professionals.

STATUS OF AUTOMATION

Sl. No.	Category	No. of Libraries not Automated at All	No. of Libraries Partially Automated	No. of Libraries Fully Automated	Total
1	Public		2	-	2
2	Special	5	4	-	9
3	Academic	12	6	-	18
	Total	17	12	–	29

From the data collected, it was brought to light that most of the libraries were partially automated doing minimal of jobs or sometimes just for namesake. Not even a single library was found to be fully automated. Out of 29 libraries, 12 were partially automated and the rest was far from the idea of automation for the next 5-10 years.

TRAINING RECEIVED BY STAFF REGARDING APPLICATION OF IT

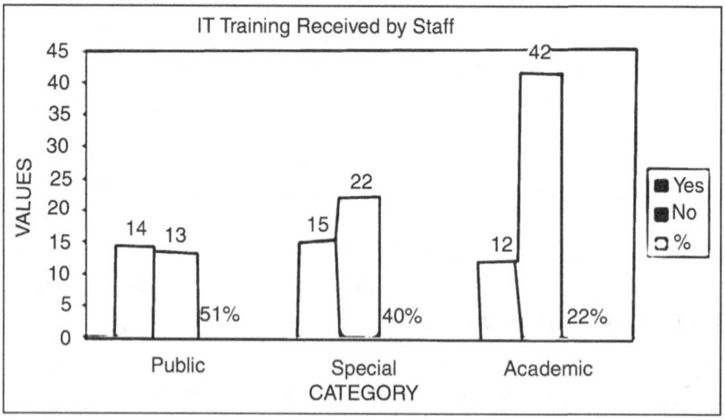

Since, we found that the status of automation in libraries was very poor. Hence, the training received by library personnel was also naturally very few. It is clear that only 34.74% received training in one way or the other through orientation, conferences, seminars held in the state as well as in other parts of country outside Manipur.

This reflects the sad picture of the functioning of all the Government institute libraries of Manipur. A strong library Movement is the need of the hour to propagate the importance of library to the society by those person who is in these fields.

NECESSITY OF IT TRAINING

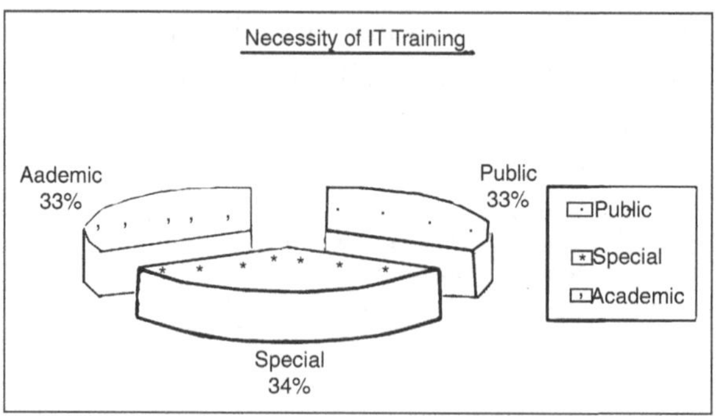

Regarding the advancement in Information Technology and its application in libraries, majority of the respondent accounting for 90.67% agreed to the necessity of training in application of IT in their libraries. A mere 9% or so did not respond to it for they were just office bearers, helpers etc. Not only majority of the respondent agreed to the importance of IT training, but they all voice the same opinion of automating their libraries at the earliest possible time to provide efficient and effective services to the readers.

The table reveals that maximum respondents were of the opinion that the main factor which affects application of IT of the libraries is equipments to a great extent, followed by finance, training of library professionals, motivation and support from the authority.

Table 7.1 Factors which Effects the IT Application in Libraries.

Sl. No.	Reasons	Great Extent	Small Extent	Not at all	Total
1	Equipments	111	7	-	118
2	Finance	97	21	-	118
3	Motivation	20	40	58	118
4	Support from Authority	18	19	81	118
5	Training	110	8	–	118

FINDINGS

The finding of the data analysis can be summarized as follows:

- All of the libraries surveyed where financed and managed under the state government.
- The rate of computer literacy among the library professionals was very poor nearly 65% of the staff was computer illiterate.
- Almost all the libraries do not follow any staffing pattern.
- Out of the 29 libraries under the study only 12 were partially computerized with no standard library softwares.
- The scope of continuing education, training of the professionals was very limited.

Problems of IT Application in the Libraries

The step motherly treatment by the colleges authority as well as the government towards the development of libraries is one of the main problems plaguing the state.

- Lack of funds.
- Lack of innovation and professional ethics amongst the Library professionals.
- Lack of qualified staff.
- High cost of IT infrastructures.
- Library professionals lack knowledge and training in IT application.

SUGGESTIONS

- The professionals should be provided with required motivators such as monetary gain, working conditions, authority in decision-making, personal growth and development, self-esteem etc. to upgrade their skills in the ever-changing digital environment.

- Selection and recruitment of library professionals should be more stringent and the skill and qualification required should be consistent with the nature of the jobs to be performed.
- The main hurdle from the study towards digitization of the libraries was the finance. Here as a suggestion we would like INFLIBNET or any such organization/agencies to provide financial assistance or minimum hardware and software which at present are being provided to Universities all over India.
- Professionals should be encouraged to participate in training programmes, seminars, conference etc to keep abreast of the latest trends in the field of their studies.
- The professionals should also try to develop their skills and competencies in a changing library situation.

SKILLS FOR LIBRARY AND INFORMATION PROFESSIONALS WORKING IN WEB-BASED LIBRARY

The Due to the tremendous growth and continuous development of technology, the role of library becomes more responsive in making the users techno-savvy. Technological developments have affected not only the formats and sources of the information, but also how and where to provide library services. Libraries and their resources have partially moved to the virtual world of the Internet. As a result, library users can access the resources from outside the physical library. In an effort to reach users accessing the library via their computers, many libraries and library consortia are extending their services to include virtual reference.

Technology now allows users to submit their queries to the library at any time from any place in the world. Web Based Services, Digital Library Services, Internet Library Services and Electronic Library Services are terms with similar meanings. As more libraries move towards providing services in a digital environment, the improved access to remote library collections is making the use of electronic information resources more realistic and more attractive.

Traditional online services had transformed themselves into internet-based online services using web-based technologies. From traditional online services to today, four generations of information retrieval tools have passed that assist users in searching the World Wide Web.

The first generation of information retrieval tools was designed for use with bibliographic databases. The first generation provided access to references to the end documents rather than to the documents themselves, and indexing and searching were thus applied to document surrogates, such as titles or abstracts. These tools require considerable human efforts to collect, arrange, code, and annotate the various resources. A primary benefit of the first generation of tools is providing users with easy browsing capabilities. The second generation of tools attempts to collect and index resources as an automated function. Automatic collection and indexing reduces the amount of human effort. The ability to search through massive amounts of information and locate the desired information for the user is the primary benefit of the second generation of tools. The third generation deals with World Wide Web Meta search engines, such as Harvester and Meta crawler.

The fourth generation involves new ideas such as search agent technology currently being developed to search for information on the web. Web-based search engines are as a means of finding relevant pages on the Internet. Different search engines, directory, meta-search engines, gateways, subject portals, electronic journals and on line databases each type could be used in a different way, from simple keyword searching up to peer reviewed web sites.

WHAT IS WEB BASED LIBRARY SERVICE

A digital Library service manages and develops electronic services, the library web sites and library staff. It can be defined broadly as 'an information access service in which users ask questions via electronic means, *e.g.*, e-mail or web forms'.

WHY WEB BASED LIBRARY SERVICE

Library service on the internet requires many of the same qualities as traditional references: accuracy, promptness, courtesy, an understanding of the information need. It provides users with the convenience of accessing information in their own time, saving them traveling cost and time and new options for answering reference questions.

The provision of these services is not constrained by the traditional opening hours but can be offered on a 24-hour, seven-days-a-week basis known as 24/7. And while there may be a disadvantage in not having a face-to face encounter, there are many advantages to this new medium and the greatest advantage is that many more users can be helped by using electronic library services. Advantages and disadvantages of electronic access over printed form access are showed in table.

Web based services are established due to the following reasons.

- Ensuring the needs of users and the accessible information sources are suitable matched at all times.
- Delivering those information sources to the user in a timely and appropriate fashion.
- Ensuring the information provided is high quality, accurate and appropriate.
- Assisting the user in interpreting the materials, if necessary.
- Promoting user awareness of new services and information sources as they develop.

- Providing users with individualised guidance and support as they build their information search and application skills.

Table. Advantages and Disavantages of Printed from over Electronic Access.

S.N Advantages of Print Form	Electronic Form
1. Format is tested and standardised development	Format is in the early stages of
2. Easy for users to use	Requires some training for users to use
3. No special equipment needed	Special equipment required (hardware, software, printers, etc.)
4. Easy to locate (if shelved properly) problems, internet connection	Access is currently unreliable (URL problems, etc.)
5. Use is limited only to copyright laws licensing	Use is limited by copyright laws and agreements
6. Archiving is effective and permanent	Archiving is "up in the air"

Table. Advantages and Disadvantages of Printed Form over Electronic Access.

	Disadvantages of Print Form	Electronic Form
1.	Operating costs are considerable (ordering, cataloging, claiming, and binding)	Operating costs are minimal (no cataloging, binding, or claiming)
2.	Requires shelving	No shelving required
3.	Often mutilated, stolen, or misshelved	Cannot be mutilated, stolen, or misshelved
4.	Requires extensive storage space space	Saves considerable storage
5.	Allows only one user at a time	Allows for multiple users with simultaneous access
6.	Slow delivery via "snail mail"	Immediate receipt of issue
7.	Issues are easily lost in the mail or missing	No more missing issues
8	Slow publication	Fast publication

DIFFERENT RESOURCES FOR WEB BASED LIBRARY SERVICES

Today, users may have access a variety of textual information resources. There are different kinds of webbased reference resources and services for accessing information from libraries such as OPAC, Gateways, Portals, Subject Portals, Electronic Journals, Online Databases, Subject Directories and Search Engines.

These resources overlap considerably in the type of information they cover, and sometimes it is difficult to distinguish between some of them.

A library should have a good collection of these resources like selected Web links, subscription resources, and library materials in well-organised pages for serving better services to their users. Many libraries and organisations are providing digital reference service through collaborative services. Existing library consortia are adding digital reference to current shared services, and networks of libraries. Some regional library consortia are offering member libraries the opportunity to share reference questions with each other using the Internet and other technologies.

OPAC

OPAS's - On Line Public Access Catalogues, form an important part of many digital library's collections. It allows users to search for the bibliographic records contained within a library's collections. Now days, some OPAC also provide access to electronic resources and databases, in addition to the traditional bibliographic records.

GATEWAYS

A gateway is defined as a facility that allows easier access to network based resources in a given subject area. Gateways provide a simple search facility and a much-enhanced service through a resource database and indexes, which can be searched through a web based interface. Information provided by gateways is catalogued by hand. Gateways cover a wide range of subjects, through some areas, such as music and religious studies, currently lack subject gateways.

Some well-known gateways are as follows:

- Internet Public Library (IPL),
- Bulletin Board for Libraries (BUBL),
- National Information Services and Systems (NISS),

PORTALS

In the library community, portals may be defined as an amalgamation of services to the users where the amalgamation is achieved through seamless integration of existing services by using binding agents such as customisation and authentication services, search protocols such as Z39.50, loan protocols such as ISO10161, and e-commerce. The result is a personalised service which allows the individual to access the rich content of both print-based and electronic systems. Portals are either commercial or free web facilities that offer information services to a specific audience. The facilities include web search to communication to e-mail to news, etc.

There are three kinds of portals; Consumer (or horizontal), Vertical and Enterprise.

1. Consumer portals are aimed at consumer audiences and offer free e-mail, games, chat, etc. Examples are Yahoo!, MSN and AOL.
2. Vertical portals, target a specified audience, such as a particular industry, and offer many of the consumer portal features. Example includes VerticalNet.
3. Enterprise portals on the other hand are similar to consumer portals, but they are offered only to corporations or similar organisations. Examples include Epicentric and Corporate Yahoo! These portals can be best understood as electronic pathfinders for users, pulling together

in one place in a web site selected links to subjects or interest-oriented resources located on the WWW.

SUBJECT PORTALS

Web Search Engines had been developed initially by computer scientists, by borrowing techniques from information retrieval search such as best match searching and relevance ranking. Information professional are increasing bringing their skills to help organise the growing wealth of Internet resources. A good example of their influence is the development of subject-specific web search engines known as subject portals, where evaluation of material covered is a major concern.

Two prime UK subject portals are SOSIG Social Science Information Gateway, covering social science resources and OMNI Organising medical networked information covering medical resources. Subject portal sites can be very helpful, but they should be used with care.

Users should bear the following points in their mind:

- The aim of the subject portal is to list and review the most important sites on the web relevant to that subject. The sites are usually constantly peer-reviewed to ensure that the site is relevant and up to date.
- New sites are appearing all the time. Relying on a subject portal site to find everything users require may mean that they miss an important site that has recently appeared and has not yet been reviewed by the producers of the particular subject portal.
- A subject portal is a one stop shop for information on the topic it covers. Users don't have to carry out extensive Internet searches in order to find the information require. They can simply go to the required subject portal site.
- Subject portals save users having to have long lists of bookmarks (saved addresses of web pages), which are often, cumbersome and time consuming to arrange and keep up to date. However, if users do prefer to use bookmarks they can arrange them in an order to suit the way they work and not have an order forced on them by the subject portal.
- A subject portal site is only as good as the reviewers who peer-review the site listed. The reviewers need to have a policy of keeping the portal sites up to date and of constantly reviewing the sites they list, to make sure that they are still relevant and still contain good, timely information.
- A subject portal may be available to everyone who needs to use it to only certain groups of users. A good portal should be publicly available to anyone who needs it.

ELECTRONIC JOURNALS

Electronic journals form a large part of the collection of a library for providing web based services. Today many journals are available electronically - some are full text and some contain only bibliographic information with abstract. Major advantage of electronic journals is that they are constantly updated and easy to access but disadvantage is that breaching of copyright law is very easy. They are available as bitmaps, PostScript, PDF, ASCII, SGML and HTML. Library services may be delivering to users on CDRom, through e-mail or through web. Some international societies and associations have developed their own digital libraries through which users can get access to all their publications. Services are available to the members of society or associations through subscription.

ONLINE DATABASES

These are large collections of machine-readable data that are maintained by commercial agencies and are accessed through communication lines. Many libraries subscribe to them for easy access and use of current information. The disadvantage is that only bibliographic data is presented and not full text. The information cannot be accessed when the system is down for any reason. Examples Ei Compendex, SciFinder Scholar, Web of Science, Current Contents, etc.

SEARCH ENGINES

Search Engines are huge databases of web page files that have been assembled automatically by machines where as the subject directories are human-compiled and maintained. Search engine indexes every page of a web site and subject directories linked only homepages. Search Engine is the popular term for an information retrieval (IR) system. A search engine is computer software that searches a collection of electronic materials to retrieve citations, documents, or information that matches or answers a user's query. The retrieved materials may be text documents, facts that have been extracted from text, images, or sounds.

A query is a question phrased so that it can be interpreted properly by search engine. Depending on the type of software, it may be a collection of commands, a statement in either full or partial sentences, one or more keywords, or in the case of non-text searching, an image or sequence of sounds to be matched.

SUBJECT DIRECTORIES

Subject directories differ from search engines in that search engines are populated by robots that finds and index sites whereas humans making editorial decisions that populate subject directories. Subject directories are basically index home pages of sites and can be classified as general, academic, commercial or portal. Among the well known subject directories are the Argus Clearinghouse and Yahoo. Strengths include relevance, effectiveness and relative high quality of content. Weaknesses are that they lack depth in their coverage of the subjects.

NEW WEB BASED LIBRARY SERVICES

VIRTUAL LIBRARY TOURS

Web sites of libraries provides virtual library guide to the physical facilities including collections, services and infrastructure available in the library. The combination of library maps and floor plans, library departments and photographic views are used for the tour. Virtual library tours are also using new technologies such as QuickTime movies etc and are beginning to replace image maps on main campus Web sites.

ASK-A-LIBRARIAN

Ask-A-Librarian services are Internet-based question and answer service that connects users with individuals who possess specialised subject knowledge and skill in conducting precision searches. Most "Ask-a-Librarians" services have a web-based question submission form or an e-mail address or both. Users are invited to submit their queries by using web forms or through e-mail. Once a query is read by a service, it is assigned to an individual expert for answering. An expert responds to the query with factual information and or a list of information resources. The response is either sent to the user's e-mail account or is posted on the web so that the user can access it after a certain period of time.

Many services have informative web sites that include archives of questions and answers and a set of FAQs. Users are usually encouraged to browse archives and FAQs before submitting a question in case sufficient information already exists.

REAL TIME SERVICES

A new and exciting method of digital reference service that libraries are attempting to provide more and more now is live reference. These are real-time, interactive reference services in which the users can talk to a real, live reference librarian at any time, from anywhere in the world. User and librarian can interact using chat technologies, and unlike with e-mail reference the librarian can perform a reference interview of sorts by asking the users to elaborate or clarify if needed before proceeding to answer the question. The librarian can perform Internet searches and push web sites onto the user's browser, and can receive immediate feedback from the users as to whether their question have been answered to satisfaction.

BULLETIN BOARDS

A bulletin board is an electronic communications forum that hosts posted messages and articles connected to a common subject or theme or interest. It allows users to call in and either leaves or retrieves messages. The messages may be directed to all users of the bulletin board or only to particular users. But all messages can be read by all users. Several libraries are using bulletin boards for their web-based library services.

The bulletin board system is also used as an interactive interface to invite suggestions on activities and services of a library. It can also be used as an interface to distribute library services.

WEB-BASED USER EDUCATION

Web guides and teaching tools are found everywhere on the Web because they are easily updated, accessed, and printed on demand. The web-based user education provides a high degree of interactivity and flexibility to the users. The library web sites can use web-based user education for imparting training to users in teaching the basic library skills along with glossary of library terms, using Library OPAC, locating books, magazines, biographical data and other library materials, understanding how to navigate the libraries web site and how to select the most relevant database, instructions for searching CD ROM and guidance in locating web-based databases and other electronic resources and instructions on subject searching training, using Boolean operators and searching internet resources through search engines.

WEB FORMS

Library web sites have some web forms for suggestions and comments on the Library Services. Different types of Web Forms are available on web that may be an Indent form for acquiring some publications, interlibrary loan request form for document delivery, Ask-a-Librarian forms, on line reservation form or user survey form, etc.

INDIAN SCENARIO

The Indian libraries also have realised to give web based services to users and they have recognised that working together can accomplish for more than they can do individually. Many Indian libraries in India are not geared up for accessing e-journals due to various reasons including user ignorance, infrastructure and initial funds. The library and information networks in India were initiated in early eighties. The growth during this period can be linked to some of the policies that Government of India pursued. Some institutions like CSIR, ISRO, DRDO, DAE, ICAR, SIRNET, NICNET, NISSAT, INFLIBNET, MHRD and IIM libraries are actively working continuously to improve the present situation.

They spend annually a huge amount of money towards library acquisition, especially towards journals, e-journals and e-databases. Some initiative include, Indian Institute of Management for accessing bibliographic databases, CSIR laboratories for Science Direct, FORSA for accessing Astronomy and Astrophysics journals, Hyderabad Knowledge park members of J-gate, INFLIBNET (UGC–INFONET) initiative for full text and databases like BIOSIS and CAS and INDEST for a host of full text sources and few bibliographic databases for the benefit of IITs, IISc, NITs and Engineering colleges. In India, library consortia are emerging as one of the important service to users. The Indian consortiums will help the library to provide better services to the users by investing meagre amount.

To expand the access for more number of e-journals, e-books and other resources, we have to develop the digital library infrastructure as a platform for e-learning.

THE FUTURE OF WEB BASED SERVICES

Library Web services will continue to spread out, offering more full-text electronic journals and indexes that do not now include full text will begin to do so, or link to external resources. Bibliographic access to full-text periodicals either through cataloging, databases, or vendors will be in improved form. There will be more Web forms for user feedback, and perhaps a virtual librarian who interacts in real time chat or video conferencing. More Document delivery services to distance education or users and Savings on Interlibrary Loan and user convenience are incentives.

Information resources through creative consortia purchasing will be popular. A well-developed user education modules or tutorials, especially to support independent exploration of library and Web resources. Somebody will have to figure out how to keep Word users from saving print documents as XML, without thinking in terms of Web, not print, space. XML will be embraced as a way to control page appearance and behaviour, but it will take a while for people to figure out how to use it well and there will be trends we haven't thought of yet...

WEB PUBLISHING: GETTING STARTED

WEB PUBLISHING

The Oracle's Hyperion® Data Relationship Management Web Publishing module provides an auxiliary means of accessing Data Relationship Management system functionality.

This application provides the following capabilities through a Web browser interface:

- Viewing hierarchies and node properties.
- Running exports.

- Printing hierarchy trees.
- Searching for nodes in a given hierarchy.

Data Relationship Management Web Publishing connects to the Data Relationship Management application server, but operates in a read-only mode. Various requests can be made using HTTP to either retrieve information or execute a command such as running exports or reloading from the database. Figure provides a top-level view of Data Relationship Management Web Publishing in relation to the Data Relationship Management architecture. Web Publishing can be run on its own server or hosted on the Data Relationship Management multi-tier Web Server or the primary application server.

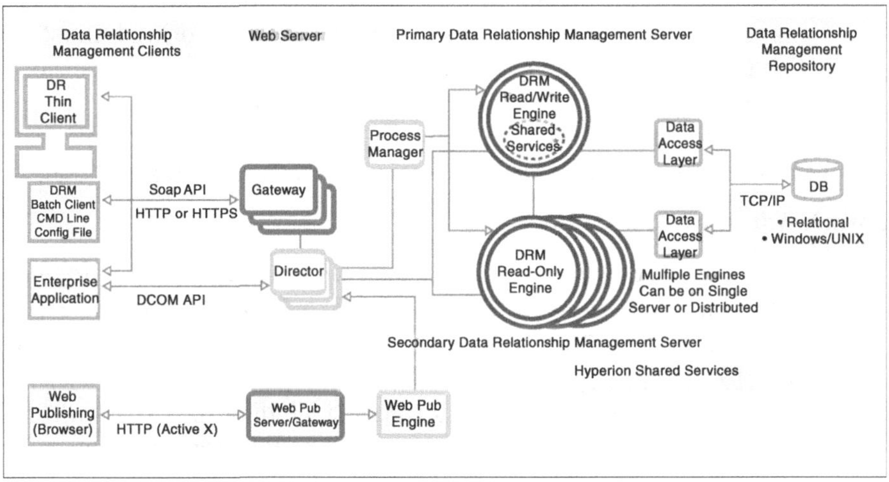

Fig. Data Relationship Management Web Publishing Architecture.

SYSTEM REQUIREMENTS

The following topics describe the Data Relationship Management Web Publishing system requirements for the Web server and the client computers.

Web Server Requirements:

- Windows 2000 Server or Windows Server 2003.
- Internet Information Services (IIS) version 5 or later.
- Microsoft Data Access Components (MDAC) 2.7 or later (required only for MS SQL.)

Client Computer Requirements:

- Windows 2000 or later (ME, 2000, XP, Server 2003)
- Internet Explorer version 5 or later.

INSTALLING, CONFIGURING, AND UNINSTALLING

PRE-INSTALLATION TASKS

The following topics describe tasks that must be performed before you can install and use Data Relationship Management Web Publishing.

System Administrator Tasks

Your Data Relationship Management system administrator must complete the following tasks before you can install and use Data Relationship Management Web Publishing:

- Ensure that the Data Relationship Management system Release 9.3 is currently installed and operational.
- Create a new Data Relationship Management user name specifically for accessing Data Relationship Management Web Publishing (for example: mdm_Web). Assign the desired access rights to the user.
- Since the engine needs access to all paths that might be used for exports, provide a list of these paths to the network administrator. The system preference WebExDir controls the directory root for file storage location on the Web Publishing server.
- Configure the appropriate Data Relationship Management system preferences related to Data Relationship Management Web Publishing.

Network Administrator Tasks

Your network administrator must complete the following tasks before you can install and use Data Relationship Management Web Publishing:

- Create a new network user/application id that the Engine can use to login to the system.
- This id should have full access rights (including file creation) to any network shares that are designated for Data Relationship Management exports.
- Verify that IE browser policies allow for the use of digitally-signed ActiveX controls.
- While most Data Relationship Management Web Publishing implementations provide for browser access, some may be used strictly for automating exports. Configuring the browser can be skipped if interactive access is not desired.

General Tasks

In addition to system administrator and network administrator tasks described in the preceding topics, the following tasks must be performed before you can install and use Data Relationship Management Web Publishing:

- You must manually uninstall prior versions of Data Relationship Management Web Publishing before installing Data Relationship Management Web Publishing Release 9.3.
- Ensure that the intended host machine(s) meet or exceed the minimum system requirements defined in this document.
- Ensure that the user performing the installation has administrative rights to the Web server machine.

- Ensure that the Data Relationship Management Web Publishing release package is available.

INSTALLING DATA RELATIONSHIP MANAGEMENT WEB PUBLISHING

To install Data Relationship Management Web Publishing:

- Do one of these tasks:
  - If you have a Data Relationship Management Web Publishing CD or DVD, insert the CD or DVD into your CD or DVD drive.
  - If you downloaded the Data Relationship Management Web Publishing software from the Download Center:
    a. Navigate to the directory where you downloaded the installation programme.
    b. Select File > Run or Start > Run and enter Drive:\Folder \mdm_web_pub_server_setup.exe, where *Drive* and *Folder* are the installation programme location.
- Review the Welcome box and click Next.
- Read the license agreement, select I AGREE and click Next.
- From Web Publishing Installation Options, do one of the following:
  - Click Next if the computer where you are installing Data Relationship Management Web Publishing is also a Data Relationship Management Web server.
  - Select Ntier Director if Data Relationship Management Web Publishing is being added to a computer that is not a Data Relationship Management Web server or if it is a standalone server, and click Next.
- Click Next to accept the default installation directory, or click Change to select another directory, and click Next.
- Do one of the following:
  - If you are installing Ntier Director, continue with the next step.
  - If you are not installing Ntier Director, continue with step 8.
- Enter the machine name or IP address of the Data Relationship Management primary application server and click Next.
- From Windows COM+ Logon, enter a user name and password for a user who has rights to perform the following actions and click Next:
  - Edit registry settings
  - Read and write to the local file system
  - Launch processes
  - Run as a service
- Click Install.
- Optional: After installation completes, you can select Launch Data Relationship Management Web Publishing Console.
- Click Finish.

MANUALLY CONFIGURING DATA RELATIONSHIP MANAGEMENT WEB PUBLISHING

Configuration must be completed for the following:

- Data Relationship Management Web Publishing Service
- IIS Virtual Directory/Pool Configuration
- Data Relationship Management Web Publishing Engine
- When installing on a stand-alone server: COM+ Director and Process Manager Proxy Components

Configuring Data Relationship Management Web Publishing Service

To configure the service:

- Select Start > Programmes > Administrative Tools > Services.
- Select the Hyperion Data Relationship Management Web Publishing service.
- Right-click the service and select Properties.
- On the General tab, ensure that Startup Type is set to Automatic.
- On the Log On tab, select This Account.
- Enter a username and password for a Windows administrative user..
- Click OK.
- Close the Services dialog box.

Configuring Internet Information Services

For IIS 5.0:

- Select Start > Programmes > Administrative Tools > Internet Services Manager (or Internet Information Services (IIS) Manager).
- Expand to the default Web site.
- Select the mdm_web virtual directory.
- Right-click and select Properties.
- On the Virtual Directory tab, verify the following:
  - The Local Path is pointing to the Data Relationship Management Web directory.
  - The Read option is selected.
  - Execute Permissions is set to Scripts and Executables.
  - The Application Protection is set to High (Isolated). Selecting this option enables you to unload the mdm_web application without restarting IIS.
- On the Directory Security tab, enable and configure anonymous access.
- Click OK.
- Click OK.
- Close the IIS Manager.

For IIS 6.0 or later:

- Select Start > Programmes > Administrative Tools > Internet Services Manager (or Internet Information Services (IIS) Manager).
- Expand to the default Web site.
- Select the mdm_web virtual directory.
- Right-click and select Properties.
- On the Virtual Directory tab, verify the following:
  - The Local Path is pointing to the Data Relationship Management Web directory.
  - The Read option is selected.
  - Execute Permissions is set to Scripts and Executables.
  - Application Pool is WebPool. This setting enables you to unload the mdm_web application without restarting IIS.
- Click OK.
- Select the Web Service Extensions node and select Active Server Pages from the list of Web Service Extensions on the right.
- Verify that the Status column displays the status Allowed.
- Create a new Web service extension named mdm_web_pub_gateway that points to mdm_web_pub_gateway.dll and is set to Allowed.
- Close the IIS Manager.

Verifying System Access

To verify system access:

- At the prompt, select to install the mdm_web_client ActiveX control: This digitally signed control is safe to install. If you are not prompted to install the component, then it may be necessary to adjust the current browser settings to allow download and installation of ActiveX controls.
- Click OK: The Data Relationship Management Web Client page is displayed. No data (versions or hierarchies) is displayed until the service is started at the end of the installation/configuration/ startup process.

Configuring Data Relationship Management Web Publishing Engine

To configure the Web Publishing Engine:

- Select Start > Administrative Tools > Component Services.
- Expand the Component Services node to the DCOM Config folder.
- In the DCOM Config folder, select the mdm_Web_Pub_Engine object, right-click and select Properties.
- For Windows 2000 only: From a command line prompt, type: dcomcnfg.
  - In the list of applications, select the mdm_Web_Pub_Engine object and click Properties.
  - On the General tab, set Authentication Level to None.

- On the Identity tab, select This User and enter the same user and password that were configured for the Data Relationship Management Web Publishing Service.
- On the Security tab, under Launch and Activation Permissions, select Customise and click Edit.
- Add the user that is configured for IIS anonymous access to the mdm_web virtual directory.
- Allow Local Activation for this user.
- Repeat this process for the Access Permissions section, by selecting Customise > Edit, and adding the same user and enabling the Local Access permission.
- Click OK to close the Properties dialog box.

Configuring Director

If you install on a stand-alone server where Director does not already exist, you must configure the COM+ Director component.

To configure the COM+ Director component:

- Select Start > Programmes > Administrative Tools > Component Services.
- Drill down and select the Director component.
- Right-click and select Properties.
- On the Security tab, verify that Enforce Access Checks for this Application is not selected.
- On the Identity tab, verify that the appropriate user is setup and then close the Properties dialog box.
- Drill down to the Components folder of Director.
- Select all components by pressing CTRL-A, then right-click and select Properties.
- Verify that Enable Object Pooling is selected on the Activation tab and then close the Properties dialog box.
- Close the Component Services window.

Configuring Process Manager

If you install on a stand-alone server where Process Manager does not already exist, you must configure the COM+ Process Manager Proxy component.

To configure the COM+ Process Manager Proxy component:

- Select Start > Programmes > Administrative Tools > Component Services.
- Drill down and select the Process Manager component.
- Right-click the component and select Properties.
- On the Activation tab, verify that the remote server is correct.
- Close the Component Services window.

USING THE DATA RELATIONSHIP MANAGEMENT WEB PUBLISHING CONSOLE

The Data Relationship Management Web Publishing Console is designed to allow configuration, control and monitoring of the Web Publishing system. The Server Monitor Page allows the Web Publishing Service to be controlled (Start, Stop, Restart, Force Shutdown) and displays the current status of the service.

In addition there are three tabs for further information:

- System Status.
- Event Log.
- Web Server.

The System Status tab shows some basic operating system information as well as information on COM+ and DCOM (Out of Process) applications. Currently Web Publishing does not use any COM+ so this section is blank.

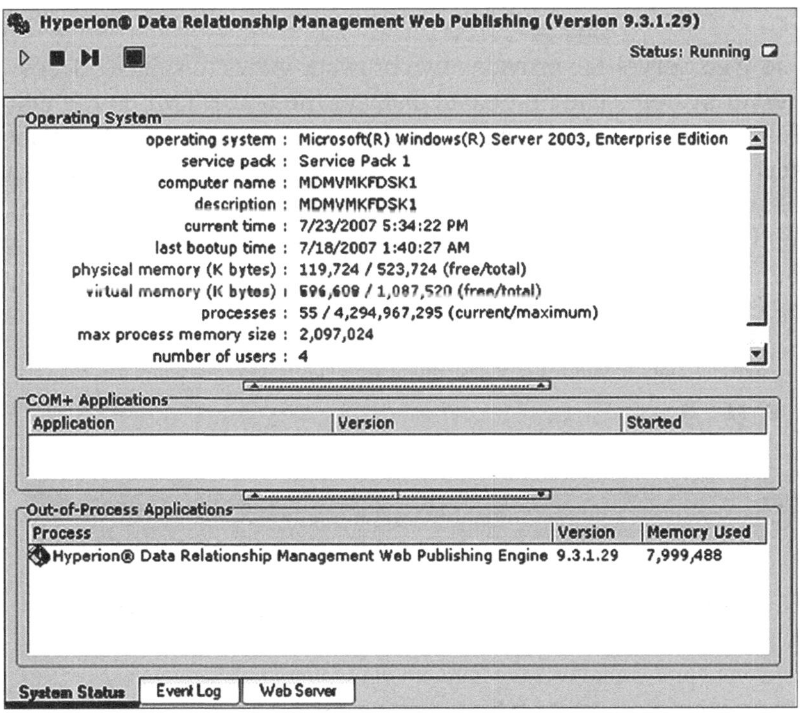

The Event Log tab filters the application event log to show events for the Web Publishing module. Clicking on an event in the top panel shows the detail for the event in the lower panel. Events shown are filtered to include only events after the console was started. To see historical events you can check the Show History and click Refresh. Clear resets the filter time to the current date and time.

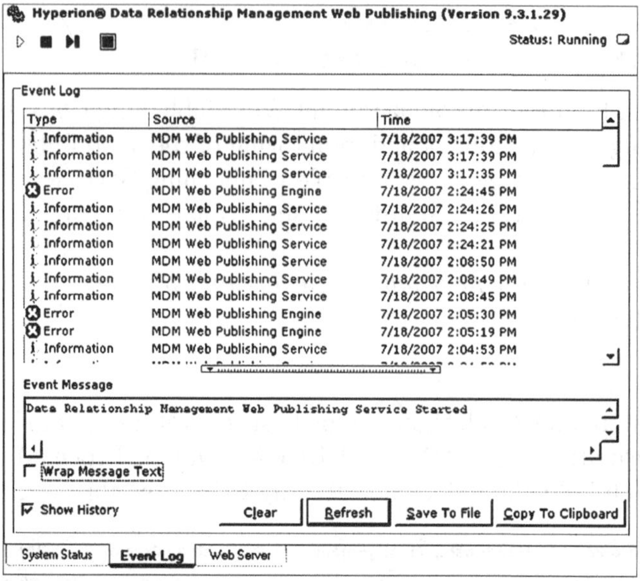

The Web Server tab provides two browser views to validate access to the Web Server system. The first panel displays the test HTML in the mdm_web virtual directory and validates access to the virtual directory for Web Publishing. The second view tests the Web Publishing Gateway to perform the List Versions command. If the system is up and running, the list of versions available for Web Publishing is displayed. When stopping and starting services such as IIS, you may need to refresh these views. To refresh, right-click on the view and select Refresh.

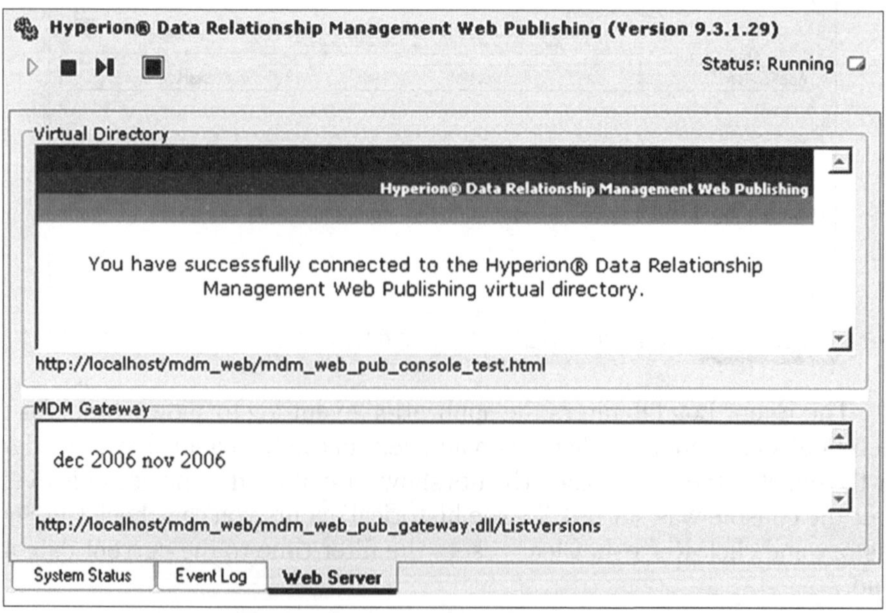

You can set the Data Relationship Management username and password for the Web Publishing module on the Configuration page. This user is the Data Relationship Management user that the Web Publishing engine uses to retrieve the data for display on the Web client. Limiting access to this user allows the Web Publishing to be restricted.

It is important that the user specified for Web Publishing be exempt from session timeout. Thus, the system preference IdleTimeExcludeUsers should be set to include the name of the user for Web Publishing. If this user is not excluded from session timeout, then the Web Publishing service needs to be restarted each time the user session expires.

CONFIGURING DATA RELATIONSHIP MANAGEMENT WEB CLIENT

Data Relationship Management Web provides a specific set of frequently-used Data Relationship Management functionality in a Web browser. This document assumes that the user is already familiar with the overall Data Relationship Management system, including its terminology and feature set. The appearance and behaviour of Data Relationship Management Web Publishing can be configured using both System Preferences and embedded parameters.

ELECTRONIC THESES AND DISSERTATIONS FOR INDIAN UNIVERSITIES: A FRAMEWORK

Even though the electronic publishing and writing offer demanding environment in academic scholarship, the theses and dissertations are still written and published in print and archived in shelves in university libraries where the vast majority gather dust, read by perhaps one or two interested researchers who access them in print with lot of difficulty, often for a fee and most are never consulted at all. Digital libraries of electronic theses and dissertations (ETDs) offer an alternative to this waste of valuable academic scholarship and offer researchers and University Libraries in India opportunities to explore the possibilities electronic publishing trend in academic sector. The emergence of UGC Infonet, the aspiring and dream project of University Grants Commission, which also aims at Content Creation by Indian Academic Sector, will definitely boost this idea.

UGC-INFONET

As technology is becoming a driving force in the contemporary education systems, University Grant Commission has launched an ambitious programme to bring about a qualitative change in the academic infrastructure, especially for higher education. Under this initiative UGC is modernising the University Campuses with State-of-the-art campus wide networks and setting up its own nationwide communication network named UGC-Infonet. UGC-Infonet will be a boon to the higher education systems in several ways to facilitate spread of quality education all over the country. This will function as a tool to distribute education material and journals to the remotest of areas and a resource centre for researchers and scholars for tapping the most up-to-date information. As a main feature of UGC Infonet, a data center with large server capacity is being set up, where content of common interest can be maintained. Each University will have the option of hosting their web site, digital content like ETDs and the E-journals subscribed through INFLIBNET Consortia.

THESES AND DISSERTATIONS IN INDIA

Indian universities play a major role in generation and dissemination of knowledge by conducting research works and producing Ph D theses as a unique genre of information sources. Every year, nearly 8000- 10000 Ph Ds are awarding in India.

The purpose of the thesis is to provide an experience in scholarship, which will be of enduring value to the student in understanding how new knowledge is acquired and communicated within the chosen field. These works contain valuable content, including focused literature reviews and details on research, which are not generally made available elsewhere.

At present there are some lacunas in publication, control and access theses information in India, and some attempts have been made to address them. At the moment, most unpublished theses are hard to get hold of, as they are filed only in the university library where the student has worked. The Indian thesis literature is beset with many problems like Lack of Systematic acquisition, Lack of Access, Uncertain publication practice, Enormous Growth in the number of theses, etc. In western countries, these problems were addressed already and serious attempts have been made to solve them. In North America, less than 5 per cent of all accepted dissertations and masters' theses are initially conceived of and executed as electronic documents.

BENEFITS OF ETD

- Broader exposure of university research through greater accessibility;
- Opportunities to use new forms of creative scholarship through use of interactive elements, multimedia, hyperlinks, etc.;
- Ability to have a hyperlink to the thesis/dissertation on homepages and electronic CVs;
- Professional development experience for research students as they learn the basic skills of scholarly publishing in an electronic format;
- Conservation of paper, library storage space and of library staff time;
- Theses and dissertations more immediately accessible: publication occurs near point of submission rather than three to four months later; and
- The option to have theses or dissertations accessible to any potential reader every day at any time.

ELECTRONIC THESES AND DISSERTATIONS FOR YOUR UNIVERSITY

Format to Create ETD

PDF stands for *Portable Document Format:* Adobe Systems developed the PDF standard and provides the premiere package for creating and manipulating PDF files, Adobe Acrobat. The process of converting to PDF takes instructions that would ordinarily be sent to a specific printer and prepares them to be viewed or printed on any computer with the free Acrobat Reader installed. Postscript is a standard language developed by Adobe Systems, which is used to send instructions to postscript compatible printers. These instructions describe the contents of all text and graphics to be printed, and where on the page each piece of content is to be printed. Ordinarily, these instructions are transferred to a Postscript printer, which interprets them, creates a printed copy based on the instructions, and then discards the instructions.Other file types for image files can be.gif.jpeg, or.tif; for video files.mov.mpg, or.avi; and for audio files.aif.midi.snd.wav, or as CD-DA, CD-ROM/XA, or MPEG-2.

Facilities Required

Researchers need to create their original thesis using a word processor, such as Microsoft Word or WordPerfect and once it is done, then it can be converted to a PDF file, which will retain the original document format (for the purpose of future editing). Conversion into a PDF file is a straightforward process. Libraries and Campus labs have to be equipped with Windows based computers set up to convert theses and dissertations written in Microsoft Word to Adobe Acrobat format. This application will allow us to convert the word processing document to PDF format as well as create bookmarks. Researchers must submit the document on disk, CD, or Zip drive; the conversion machines are not attached to the network. Library staff can provide assistance with using the software to convert files, but cannot assist with document preparation.

SOFTWARE TO MANAGE ETDS

D-Space is a groundbreaking digital library system that captures, stores, indexes, preserves and redistributes the intellectual output of a university's research faculty in digital formats. The future of Etheses and of archiving and searching in general depends on institutions being able to deliver top quality services, with a high degree of interoperability. This means, among other things, that systems must continue to be developed and they must be able to handle many different types of digital object. It is believed that DSpace will fulfill these requirements to a higher degree and will continue to improve in this way in the future.

As an open source system, DSpace is now freely available to other institutions to run as-is, or to modify and extend as they require to meet local needs. From the outset, HP and MIT designed the system to be run by institutions other than MIT, and to support federation among its adopters, in both the technical and the social sense. INFLIBNET believes that it is our responsibility to lead the charge for a realistic assessment of how we can head off an otherwise inevitable loss of academic resources.

Awareness building in Open Archives and Institutional Repositories in Indian academic Institutions will be the main focus of INFLIBNET in coming future. For long-term preservation of our knowledge base and cultures, we have to find out an economical way to save digital content for future generations.

Institutions in India started using variety of open source archiving solutions like Green Stone, E-Print, DSpace etc since 2000. After experimenting all popular solutions, INFLIBNET decided to opt DSpace for its Institutional Repository and archive its publications, conference proceedings, lecture notes, etc. The capability of Dspace to handle multilingual content, even at Metadata level using globally accepted UNICODE standard was the important issue for selecting this solution, especially a country like India with its mullti-lingual dilemma in digital content creation and storage.

It has been installed in test-bed and experimented its capabilities and performance. After all sorts of testing required, Dspace was customised according to our requirements and it was installed on one of the WWW Server on Linux platform. Then we have requested Corporation for National Research Initiatives (CNRI) site for providing *Persistent Identifiers (CNRI Handles)* which promotes interoperability among open archives through Open Archives Initiative Protocol for Metadata Harvesting (OAI-PMH). The Handle System® covers assignment, management, and resolution of these persistent identifiers and are compliant with the IETF's Uniform Resource Name (URN) specification.

ROLE OF THE FACULTY AND REVIEW PROCESS

Faculty will continue to be responsible for upholding the quality of the thesis or dissertation, whether that thesis or dissertation is submitted using electronic formats or through paper. The electronic format can facilitate communication among members of the dissertation committee and the student. Electronic distribution of drafts allows multiple readers to markup and comment within one copy of the work simultaneously, regardless of the readers' physical location, and to see others' comments. It also allows the student to collate the comments of all readers within one document.

For defence, some committees may require that students provide all members of the committee with a paper copy of the ETD before the defence; others may elect to read on-screen or to have committee members take individual responsibility for working from screen or paper they print out themselves. Printed versions of the textual components of an ETD can always be made available to committee members at their request. If non-text elements of the ETD are part of the defence, the committee can consider the most effective way to ensure that all members of the committee have access to non-text elements during the defence. After the committee approves thesis or dissertation, it can be sent to a particular contact person in the library for processing, who will be responsible for processing ETDs by making sure that the file's formatting is correct, the links work, etc. Metadata of ETD can be created and made available for searching and accessing.

ISSUE OF COPYRIGHT

The copyright issue involves two components: Protecting the information/work produced as part of the research programme; and Granting license to University or to any ETD Programme to make the work available for use. This also includes obtaining permission to use parts of the work that have already been published in other sources.

If the material we are quoting or reproducing does not fall under the general guidelines of "fair use" then as suggested, need to get written permission from the copyright owner. Since a dissertation or thesis is published for non-profit educational purposes, the author is permitted limited use of copyrighted material under the guidelines of "fair use." The purpose, amount, nature and effect of the work reproduced determine whether or not one must seek permission from the copyright owner. More information about copyright issues in general.

INDIAN INITIATIVES

As a bibliographical tool to know about theses of awarded Ph Ds, Association of Indian Universities started publishing of Doctoral Bibliographies in all subjects and Theses of the Month column through its weekly publication *University News*. In 1994, INFLIBNET hosted a regularly updated free online union database of Ph D theses submitted to Indian universities. At present it is freely available for searching at INFLIBNET web site and contains around 1,40,000 of unique bibliographical records covering all subjects and all universities. Being the data supplied by the Universities themselves, it is considered as the only authoritative online-tool available to find-out the research out put of Indian Universities.

Recently University of Mysore, in collaboration with NISSAT and Ford Foundation initiated a project called Vidyanithi to host individual full-text thesis from various universities who are willing to become a member of this project. Even though, this project tries to evolve as a national depository for Indian theses, but it is not compulsory for Universities to become a part of this project. All these efforts are, off course, helpful for researchers in locating theses, but in the case of access, still we need remedies.

IN THE END WE CAN SAY

Popularisation of ETDs and its full advantages for faculty, students, and researchers are the foremost attempt to be start of. Brochures, communications, web sites etc conveying this information need to be written, designed, published and disseminated to all affected by this far-reaching change. Workshops and training programmes for both students and faculty need to be developed that cover issues of copyright and choice of access, and that encourage research scholars to carefully consider the ethics of restricting their research from access by the national and international scholarly community. Well-equipped computer labs must be put in place to provide workstations, software, and technical support staff for students writing ETDs. And standards need to be developed for the presentation of dissertation research—standards which facilitate the development of a useful and easily navigable digital collection of works, but which do not unnecessarily constrain the use of software and design considerations graduate students deem essential to their research. Careful consideration of these requirements and their full support will contribute substantially to making this transition smoothly. The potential ETDs have to transform graduate education in ways that benefit both students and the scholarly community depends upon it.

SEARCH TECHNIQUES FOR ACCESSING CD-ROM DATABASES

Due to the development of information technology, information is increasingly recorded in digital format and electronic databases which are continually becoming more complex, information storage and retrieval As the technology obsolete very fast, CD-ROM is also facing problems due to emergence of the DVD. In today's business, education, and government environments the amount of information, data and software being archived and distributed on CD-ROM and DVD-ROM media is overwhelming. For years the medium of choice for storing, archiving and distributing digital content has been the CD-ROM.

As capacity requirements of data intensive applications and databases grow, DVD-ROM, with a capacity potential over 13 times that of CD-ROM, is fast becoming the most popular medium. (CD-ROM media can store up to 700 MB of data). Single-sided, single layer DVD-ROM media can store up to 4.7 GB of data. Doublesided, single layer DVD-ROM media store up to 9.4 GB of data). DVD which is used primarily with movie/ video features will not affect the CD-ROM, but DVD-ROMs will be, which can carry information on both sides of the disc. DVD-ROM will replace the CD-ROM, but that it will take a few years.

As information is increasingly recorded in digital format and electronic databases are continually becoming more complex, information storage and retrieval processes have profoundly changed. Over the past decades three major migrations have occurred in library academic services: from printed resources to online electronic databases; from online databases to bibliographic and full-text CD-ROM databases; and from CD-ROM databases to online Internet access to bibliographic and full-text/full-image databases.

CD-ROM DATABASES

CD-ROM is abbreviation for 'Compact Disc-Read-Only Memory' a type of optical disk capable of storing large amounts of data up to 1GB, although the most common size is 650 MB (megabytes). The term 'database' has been used in the literature in two different connotations. In Computer Science this is referred to as a database management system.

In this sense a database has a logically consistent structure in which records are actually linked. In library and Information science, these are referred to as bibliographic or inventory in nature and comprise a collection of related logical records here a database is defined as an organised and generally unlinked set of machine, or it can be said, these databases are the electronic version of published literature traditionally appearing in printed form in various field.

Databases are produced by different agencies in a computer readable form, the contents of which are accessible in various ways according to requirements with the help of suitable software. Various agencies (governmental and non-governmental) are involved in developing databases by collecting information from varieties of sources and packaging the information in the form of databases. Databases can be stored on CD-ROM, on the Internet, or on commercial sites that are accessible only if user's library has a subscription. CD-Rom in the library contains periodical indexes, abstracts, statistics, directories, and other complete texts. Some databases provide information that is primarily numeric, such as data from a recent government census and some contain information that is primarily textual. Database some time also called data bank.

USE CD-ROM DATABASES IN LIBRARIES

Access to Cd-Rom databases is fast, accurate and thorough. A clever search by a users may get them in seconds most of the information they need. In contrast, traditional print services may take months for same task, with still great deal of information left out. As a matter of fact, libraries can not possibly continue with the sluggish manual information service methods and hope to remain in business tomorrow.

Libraries can have economic access to information, space saving and users friendly Libraries and information centers used these databases in providing various library services as mentioned below

- Literature search services, current and retrospective literature searches
- Current awareness services in various forms including SDI

- Full text databases may be utilised for search services
- Document delivery services
- For producing digest trend reports, etc.
- Compilations of bibliographies
- Abstracting and Indexing Services

WHY WE DON'T WANT TO USE CD-ROM DATABASES

It is always beneficial to know about the pros and cons of any information so that one can proceed systematically.

- CD-ROM databases are not updated in time, some web journals or indexing services are available online even before their print editions roll out of the press. For example, Engineering Index on disc is updated quarterly, and Dissertation Abstracts on disc only once in a year.
- Retrieval from CD-ROM databases take seconds, as against online databases, which take only milliseconds, however complex the command search statement may be (of courses with higher bandwidth telecom pipes provided)
- If not acquired from a single producer, CD/DVD Rom databases require skills in using different search engines. Making menu-driven index searching or single keyword searching at command prompt may be easy to use in each system. But, users must make command, or Boolean searches, to get at exacter or less abstract hits. Sometimes users have been found key boarding DIALOG syntax instead of SPIRS one to search into MathSci Disc or PsycLIT from SilverPlatter, and vice versa. Both the search engines are so dissimilar in construct. Again, generally, users keyboard a collection of key words at the command prompt. They are flummoxed to discover that one access engine parses the search statement with "or" operator between words, and the other with 'and' operator. The former results come in too many hits and the latter in too few. Therefore, all new uses require basic education in the techniques of bibliographic database searching.
- If adequate jukeboxes are not provided for permanent mounting of optical databases, it is a great hassle for users to switch from one disc to another for either a different file or part of the same file. By comparison, on online services, like DIALOG's the process is just a click away.

Yet another disadvantage of CD-ROM, they are vulnerable to damage by dust, fingerprints and scratches, etc. Therefore they need very careful handing. Libraries will have to make backup copy of each CDS disc to be kept in safe custody, so fresh copies can be made.

SEARCHING CD-ROM DATABASE

Conducting effective searches requires knowledge of a number of techniques. Users should not only have been an understanding of the nature, content and structure of the database, but also be familiar with the various option available in the search screen, the tools and techniques for searching, and the techniques and formats for display of the search output. The search features commonly available are Keyword Search, Phrase Search, Boolean Search, Truncation, Index and/or Thesaurus Support, Proximity Search, Field-Specific Searches, Free-Text Search, Combing Search Sets and Search Refinement, Limiting or Range Search, Searching through the Retrieved Records and they may vary from one CD-ROM to another.

SELECTION OF DATABASES FOR COMPARISON

Four CD-ROM Databases have been selected for a discussion on the various search and retrieval features available, 'Ulrich's on disc', 'Books in Print' from the category of general or ready reference sources, 'Ei Compendex', 'LISA plus' are Bibliographic databases containing details of documents including abstracts and Emerald full-text database of journal articles.

Ulrich's on Disc

Ulrich's on Disc from R. R. Bowker provides the ability to search and browse the entire Ulrich's family of databases. They included nearly 250,000 titles from over 200 countries, Information on about 11,000 new titles per year, annotations for almost 90,000 titles, full text reviews from *Magazines for Libraries* and *Library Journal* for over 8,700 publications, indicators for over 21,000 refereed publications and complete names and addresses for 80,000 serials publishers and distributors. The main screen of Ulrich's is shown in figure.

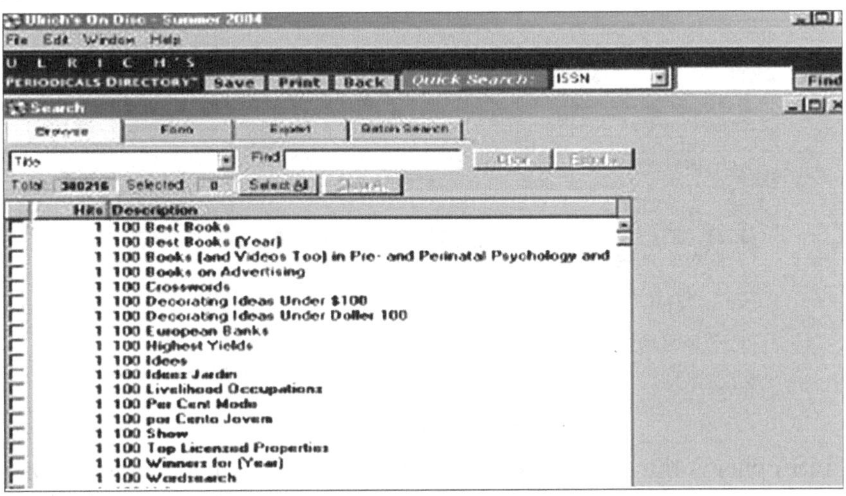

Fig. 'ULRICH'S on Disc' Main Screen.

EI COMPENDEX BIBLOGRAPHIC DATABASE

DIALOG OnDisc® Compendex, produced by (Ei) Engineering Information Inc., provides coverage of the world's significant engineering and technical literature. Subject coverage includes but is not limited to the various disciplines of engineering, applied physics, electronics and instrumentation, light and optical technologies, and other areas of significant technology. Compendex contains references to and abstracts from journals, technical reports, books, proceedings and conference papers, and more. Author-prepared abstracts are used when available. Publications from around the world are indexed, including approximately 4,500 journals and 2,000 conference proceedings per year. Approximately 10 percent of the documents indexed are in a language other than English.

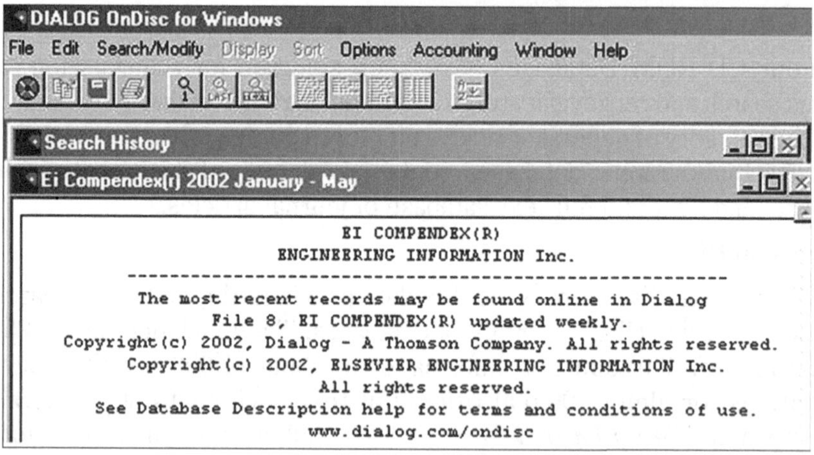

Fig. 'Ei Compendex' Main Screen.

LIBRARY AND INFORMATION SCIENCE ABSTRACTS (LISA PLUS)

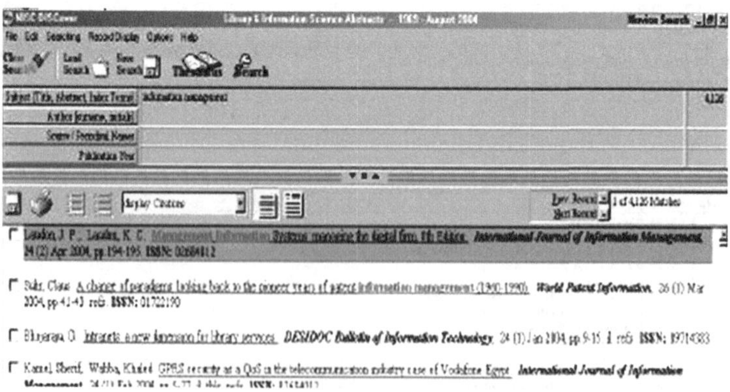

Fig. 'LISA Plus' Main Screen.

LISA plus is the world's best known resource for the coverage of ongoing research in all aspects of library and information studies. Over 245,000 abstracts keep user well informed about such topics as artificial intelligence, information and knowledge management, publishing and copyright, World Wide Web resources and much more since 1969. Lisa plus main screen is as figure

EMERALD FULL-TEXT DATABASE OF JOURNAL ARTICLES

Emerald is a full text database from MCB, covers more than 82 top journal across ten broad subject areas. It provides access to the full text of articles in PDF and HTML format published from 1994 to date. The subjects covered include Marketing, Human Resources, Quality Management, Information Management, Library and Information Services, Training and Education, General Management Property, Operations and Production Management, etc. Users can choose any subject and get a list of all the journals covered in that subject. First screen of Emerald is as figure

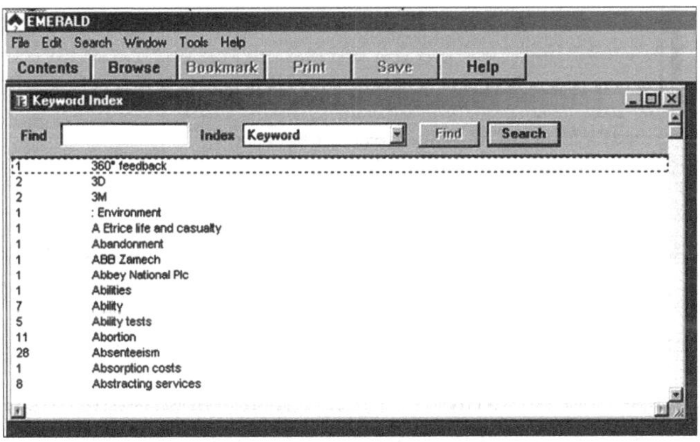

Fig. 'Emerald (Full-Text Database)' First Screen.

ACCESSING DIFFERENT DATABASES

Searching in Specific Field of Selected CD-ROM Databases

There are two forms of searching for information in CD-ROM databases – field-specific and free-text search. A user may know which field to search, or might like to restrict a given search to one or more fields. This is a field specific search. If the user are not sure of the field to be searched, they can conduct a free-text search, which means that the search is not restricted to any particular field.

While the free-text search is not universally available, field specific search is the simplest form of search, and CD-ROM databases offer various options to conduct searches on one or more specific fields. The simplest option is the form search, where the user can select a specific box for a particular field and can key in the search term/phrase. Which search field can be searched in a database depends on the content and structure of the database concerned, and there fore they differ from one database to another.

Ulrich's on Disc

Search fields are Abstracting and Indexing Service, Area Code, Circulation, CODEN Number, Country, Dewey Number, Document Availability, Electronic Vendor, ISSN, Keyword, Keyword In Title, LC Class, Media Type, Personnel Name, Price (US Dollar), Publication Code, Publisher, Special Features, Special Index, Status Code, Subjects, Title, US State/Zip, Year First Published. Search screen is shown by figure

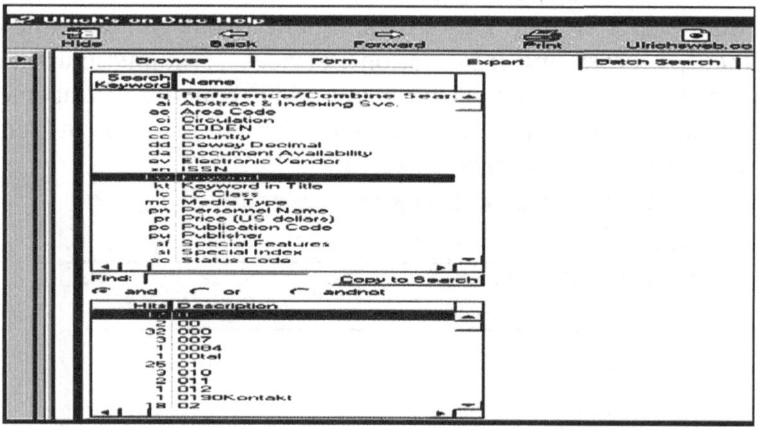

Fig. 'Ulrich's on Disc' Search Fields Screen.

Ei Compendex

Under option 'Search/Modify' search fields are Word/Phrase Index, EI Subject Headings, Author Name, Author Affiliation, Title Words, Journal Name, Conference Search Options (Conference Title, Conference Location, Conference Sponsor, Conference Year), Limit Options 'English...', Additional Search Options (Words/Phrases, EI Classification Codes, Major Subject Headings, Treatment Codes, Year of Publications, Language) different fields and Search results screen shown in figure

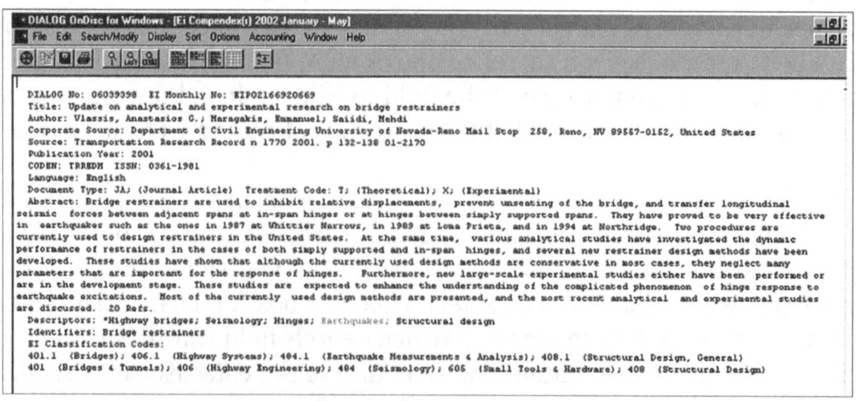

Fig. 'Ei Compendex' Different Fields and Search Results Screen.

LISA Plus

Subject, Title, Abstract, Index Term Or Keyword, Author, Source, Title Database Name,, Keyword, Language, Publication Date, Author Affiliation, Country Of Research, Record Number, CODEN, CATNI name, ISSN, Thesaurus term

Boolen Search

Combine terms to make the search broader or narrower. How broad or narrow the search is depends on the search logic used to combine search terms. Three logical connectors, or Boolean operators, are used to define the relationship between search terms: "and", "or ", and "not". The Boolean operators may be used to join search terms within search fields in all search modes and to join search criteria between search fields in the Advanced and Expert search modes only. (Novice mode always uses a Boolean AND between search fields). Boolean searches can not be conducted in the 'browse index' mode of CD-ROM.-

Ulrich's on Disc

Operators are AND, OR, NOT/AND NOT and Options are, In the Form Search mode user can combine terms/phrases with Boolean operators in a chosen field box, or can type one term/phrase in each box and click on a Boolean operator in the box next to the box next to the term on the right. In the search mode user have to type the Boolean operator to combine terms/phares from the same or different fields. Ei Compendex: Operators are AND, OR, NOT and Options are: use these operators to combine search terms in the 'Modify Search Option'

LISA Plus

Operators are AND, OR, ANDNOT (not can also be used in free-text search mode) Options: In the Easy Search mode, user can combine terms/phrases with Boolean operators in a chosen field box, or can type one term/phrase in each box and click on a Boolean operators in the box next to the term on the right. In the Expert Search Mode, user has to type the Boolean operator to combine terms/phases from the same or different fields. No nesting is possible. Emerald: Operators are And or, not and Options enter theses operators in the search in the search as well as Advanced Search Mode

Truncation Search

Truncation of the three kinds of truncation (left, right and middle truncation), left truncation is not commonly available in CD-ROM databases. The symbols for truncation and their syntax and effect vary, and the user has to learn these to conduct an effective search.

Ulrich's on disc

Ulrich's on disc: • or $ substitute for any number of characters and can be used for right truncation only. '?' Substitutes for one character, can be used anywhere in a word, or user can use multiple '?'Symbols. LISA: Truncation is the substitution of a wildcard symbol for any portion of a word to retrieve a group of words. Most often, truncation is used to abbreviate a word — to trim a term back to its stem, or root word.

Truncating lets user search for word variants thereby broadening the search. The asterisk • is a multicharacter wildcard and the question mark ? is a single character wildcard. Wildcards are typically used at the end of a word but may be embedded within a word as well. Right and middle or internal truncation is allowed. Both the symbols can be used for right as well as middle truncation. User can enter the symbol as appropriate in the Easy Search as well as the Expert Search mode. Multiple ? can be used. Wildcards are typically used at the end of a word but may be embedded within a word as well. Avoid truncating words to less than five characters or user may retrieve unwanted results.

Index Search and Thesaurus Search

The indexes allow users to select the search terms/phrases from the term index, and a thesaurus allows users to consult a map of available terms to widen or narrow down a given search, as required. CD-ROM retrieval software provides index search facilities, ie users can select an index to browse and select from the index for searching. There may be an index file or a separate index for each searchable field so that the user can choose a field and then browse the corresponding index file. Index search facilities are more commonly available than thesaurus facilities. Thesauri are hierarchically structured. This means that they go from broad terms to narrower, more specific, terms.

Ulrich's on disc

User can choose a field from either the search or the From Search mode. In each case user can display and browse the corresponding index and select a term/phrase from the index.

Ei Compendex

In order to conduct a search, user need to choose an index: author, subject heading, keywords, etc, and then the corresponding index will be open for user to browse and to select the search term

LISA plus

The thesaurus may be accessed via the Browse window by clicking on the Index drop-down list and selecting Thesaurus Term; highlight the required term and click View Titles. In the Expert Search mode enter the thesaurus term in the Search Query Box, click on ok or press Enter. Press the 'View Brief' button to display the results of the search ie the thesaurus block. A thesaurus term can be selected to conduct a search in the database as shown in figure

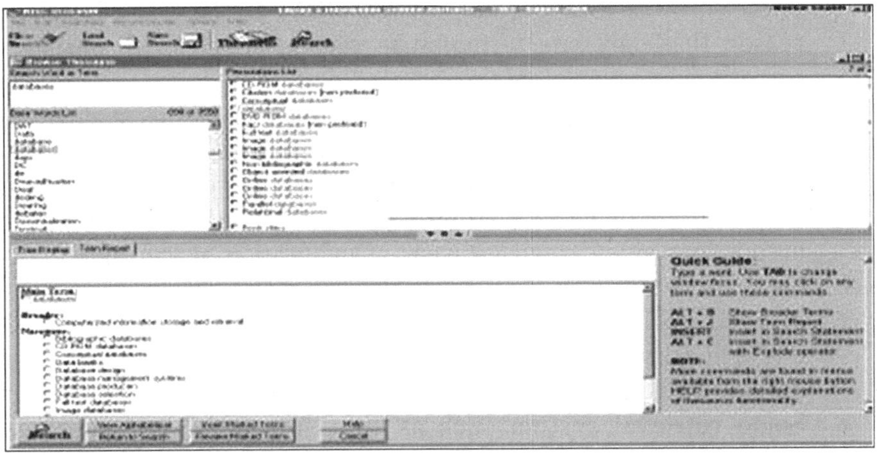

Fig. 'LISA plus' Thesaurus Search

Emerald

In the Advanced Search mode, user can choose one or more fields to search, and once users have entered a search term correspond to a field, they can click on the 'Thesaurus' button to get other words correspond to the search term.

Proximity Search

With a proximity search, user can specify the number of words allowed between the search terms. In a general sense, there is a correlation between the number of intervening words (the words creating the "distance" between search terms) and the topical relevance of users search results.

The closer the distance between users search words, *e.g.*, 5 words, the more relevant but fewer the results may be. Likewise, the wider the distance between the search words, *e.g.*, 20 words, the less relevant but larger the CD-ROM results may be. The type of proximity search operator to use depends upon whether user need search terms to be found in the same order as listed in the search statement (adjX) or found in the same or reverse order of what user originally specified (nearX).

RESULTS

After the comparison we come to know that all databases have almost same basic accessing techniques as keyword search, Phrase Search, Boolean Search, Truncation, Index and/or Thesaurus Support, Proximity Search, Field-Specific Searches, Free-Text Search, Combing Search Sets and Search Refinement, Limiting or Range Search, Searching through the Retrieved

Records and they may vary from one CD-ROM to another with a slight variation as given below

- Boolean searching is possible in all the CD-ROM database, through how it is carried out varies. Boolean searches cannot be conducted in the 'browse index' mode of a CD-ROM database for the obvious reason that only one term/phrase can be keyed in to display the corresponding portion of the index.
- None of the sample databases provides left-truncations facilities. The symbols for truncation vary from one database to another.
- Search refinement of a given search can be refined by adding or dropping one or more search terms or criteria, such as limiting the output to a given language, year of publication, price range, and so on.
- Some CD-ROM products have more than one search interface, for example, Ulrich's on disc, while others have on search interface giving options for both - simple, novice and other advanced/ expert search.
- Some retrieval system such as EI Compendex show the result instantly, while in others the user has to chose the view/display option, as in LISA plus
- Proximity search in CD-ROM databases allows users to conduct proximity searches in order to specify how closely the terms prescribed in a search expression.
- Two types of indexing practice are followed word index and phrase index.in the word index, each individual word in a field is indexed, while in the phrase index, a given phrase that may comprise several keyboard, is indexed. The user may need to check whether a field is a word- or phrase-indexed, by browsing through the index for the particular field, before entering a search term/phrase.
- CD-Rome databases do not usually provide facilities for ranking the search results according to relevance.

CONCLUSION

The Indian system of Higher education during the last 30 years or so has been expanding primarily for social and political reasons rather than on economic and manpower considerations. Nearly one-third of the total outlay on education in India is spent on higher education. Unfortunately, our colleges resemble the inherited imperial pattern of pre-independence India and suffer from the worst effect. Development of human resources lies at the core of the knowledge productive organizations, like libraries. The survival and success of organizations will increasingly depend on their ability to ensure that they are "smart" at all levels rather than only at the top. The standards for organising web-based resources are still in the early stages of development, and librarians are forced to utilise standards for print resources that were not designed for electronic resources. Additionally web-based information resources are volatile in the sense that may be moved from one site to another or may be removed altogether from web. Web-based library services will become more widespread and sophisticated as the web becomes common place throughout the world, and to be successful players in the E-world.

Libraries must continue to address the web design and implementation issues. As we actively transfer library services, our central purpose remain the same, to serve and teach users to find, evaluate, and use information effectively. The librarians should be expert to hold the hands of the users who are moving towards new communication paradigm a shift from face to face human contact to human machine interaction, from paper to electronic delivery, from text centered mode to multimedia and from physical presence to virtual presence. Despite these changes in communication technology, the reference interview will remain at the heart of the reference transaction. To meet these challenges the librarians may play a leadership role in providing better Web Based library Services facilities to their current techno savvy users.

In this fast changing environment the library and information workers are required to possess enhanced managerial, professional and technical skills, adequate knowledge and right kind of experience. So, training the existing manpower or recruiting new professionals will become essential. They must possess flexibility of attitude, imagination and scientific bend of mind. Further, the libraries need to be upgraded along with the changing environment from its traditional to a digital environment.

Even though the introduction and use of Information technology in the said libraries is in the initial stage in Manipur. Steps may be taken up to develop the libraries with IT rather than being just a custodian of documents. In the near future, if the conditions of the libraries doesn't change within 5-10 years than there is a chance that the libraries may be replaced by Internet café, knowledge kiosks etc. making way for other IT professionals. As a final word we would like to remind that immediate steps should be taken up for Human Resource Development keeping into view the changing digital environment.

7

Coordination

OVERVIEW

The term 'coordination' refers to syntactic constructions in which two or more units of the same type are combined into a larger unit and still have the same semantic relations with other surrounding elements.

The units may be words, phrases, subordinate clauses, or full sentences:

- My husband supports and adores Juventus Turin.
- My uncle or your in-laws or the neighbours will come to visit us.
- I realise that you were right and that I was mistaken.
- The pope dissolved the Jesuit order, and all the Indian missions were abandoned.

All languages appear to possess coordination constructions of some kind, but there is a lot of cross-linguistic variation. Individual languages may possess a wealth of different coordinate constructions that relate to each other in complex ways. It is the purpose of this chapter to introduce and discuss a wide range of conceptual distinctions that are useful for describing the cross-linguistic and language-internal variation.

This entails the use of a large number of technical terms, each of which is explained and illustrated as it is introduced. The particle or affix that serves to link the units of a coordinate construction is called coordinator. The coordinator is printed in boldface. By far the most frequently occurring coordinator is 'and' but coordinate constructions can also involve various other semantic types of linkers, such as 'or', 'but' and 'for'. 'And' - coordination is also called conjunctive coordination, 'or' - coordination is also called disjunctive coordination, 'but' - coordination is called adversative coordination, and 'for' - coordination is called causal coordination.

Examples of each of these four types are given in:

1. (conjunction) Snow-white ate and drank.
2. (disjunction) She was a countess or a princess.
3. (adversative coordination) The dwarfs were ugly but kind.
4. (causal coordination) She died, for the apple was poisoned.

The units combined in a conjunctive coordination are called conjuncts, and more generally, the units of any coordination will be called coordinands here. Adversative coordination is always binary, *i.e.*, it must consist of two coordinands. Ternary or other multiple coordinations are impossible here.

This is illustrated in:

- The queen tried to kill Snow-white but Snow-white escaped but she went through much hardship.
- The mountain climbers were tired but happy but bankrupt.

By contrast, conjunctions and disjunctions can consist of an indefinite number of coordinands.

The examples in show six coordinands each:

- You can vote for Baranov or Wagner or Lefèvre or McGarrigle or Ramírez or Abdurrasul.
- Cameroon, Nigeria, Niger, Libya, Sudan, and the Central African Republic have a common border with Chad.

Languages differ with respect to the number and the position of the coordinators used in coordinate constructions.

For instance, while English generally shows the pattern A co-B, Kannada shows the pattern A-co B-co:

- So:mas&e:kharan-u: pe:t5e-ge ho:-d-aru. Narahari-and Somashekhara-and market-DAT go-PAST-3PL 'Narahari and Somashekhara went to the market.'

The patterns of coordinator placement and the types of linkers are discussed here. Many languages have several alternative patterns for a given semantic type of coordination, as illustrated in the English examples. Coordination with the two-part coordinator both ... and describes the coordinands as contrasting in some way: is appropriate, for instance, if the hearer expects only one of them to make the trip.

These constructions will be called contrastive coordination in this chapter:

- Both Franz and Sisi will travel to Trieste.
- Franz and Sisi will travel to Trieste.

Moreover, many languages have special coordinators for negative contexts, as in the English example. This sentence is roughly equivalent semantically with, but again it has a more emphatic, contrastive Flavour.

The construction in will be called contrastive negative coordination:

- Neither Brahms nor Bruckner reached Beethoven's fame.
- Brahms and Bruckner did not reach Beethoven's fame.

Contrastive and negative coordinate constructions are discussed below: We saw in above that a coordinate construction can consist of different types of coordinands: words, phrases, clauses or sentences. But as the definition of coordination says, each coordinand must be of the same type within a coordinate construction.

Because the coordinands are syntactically different or at least semantically different:

- Guglielmo wrote to his bishop and to the pope.
- Guglielmo wrote a letter of protest and to the pope.
- Guglielmo spoke with the abbot and with the cardinal.
- Guglielmo spoke with eloquence and with the cardinal.

Different languages may require different coordinators depending on the syntactic type of the coordinands. Types of coordinands and their relevance for the structure of coordination are discussed below: In addition to the major semantic distinctions that we saw in, numerous more fine-grained distinctions can be made. For example, many languages distinguish between two types of disjunction: interrogative disjunction and standard disjunction. Mandarin Chinese uses two different coordinators for these two cases, haishi and huozhe:

1. You want I help you or want self do 'Do you want me to help you, or do you want to do it yourself?'
2. We at here eat or eat restaurant all OK 'We can either eat here or eat out.'

Next we discuss some special types of conjunction. Since, conjunction is the most frequent kind of coordination, it exhibits the greatest formal diversity.

The most prominent "special type" of conjunction involves the use of a comitative marker, as in Hausa, where da means both 'with':

- I went to the market with Audu.
- Go market 'Dauda and Audu went to the market.'

In addition to coordinations in which each coordinand is a regular syntactic constituent many languages allow non-constituent coordination. For the sake of clarity, the coordinands are enclosed in square brackets in these examples:

- [Robert cooked the first course] and [Maria the dessert].
- Ahmed [sent a letter to Zaynab] or [a postcard to Fatima].
- [Martin adores], but [Tom hates Hollywood movies].

The first coordinand is an ordinary constituent but the second coordinand is not. Only the second coordinand is an ordinary constituent. In order to assimilate non-constituent coordinations to patterns found elsewhere in the grammar, linguists have often described them in terms of ellipsis. That is, abstract underlying structures such as those in are posited which show ordinary constituent coordination.

In a second step, a rule of ellipsis of identical elements deletes the words underlined in resulting in the surface patterns:

- Robert cooked the first course and Maria cooked the dessert.
- Ahmed sent a letter to Zaynab or sent a postcard to Fatima.
- Martin adores Hollywood movies, but Tom hates Hollywood movies.

Finally, we discuss ways of delimiting coordination against less grammaticalised constructions and, perhaps most importantly, against subordination and dependency. The latter two notions will be discussed briefly here. The primary contrast is that between coordination and dependency. In a coordination structure of the type A(-link-)B, A and B are structurally symmetrical in some sense, whereas in a dependency structure of the type X(-link-)Y, X and Y are not symmetrical, but either X or Y is the head and the other element is a dependent.

When the dependent element is a clause, it is called subordinate clause. Although the distinction between coordination and dependency is of course fundamental, it is sometimes not evident whether a construction exhibits a coordination relation or a dependency relation.

The best-known distinctive property of coordinate structures is that they obey the coordinate structure constraint, which prohibits the application of certain rules such as extraction of interrogative words from coordinate structures.

This is illustrated, where the:

- Sentences show the basic structure, and the;
- Sentences show fronting of who.

As the examples make clear, only the dependency structures allow extraction:

- Dependency (subordination):
  - (basic sentence) You talked to someone before Joan arrived.
  - (who extraction) Who did you talk to _ before Joan arrived.
- Coordination:
  - (basic sentence) You talked to someone and then Joan arrived.
  - (who extraction) •Who did you talk to _ and then Joan arrived.
- Dependency:
  - (basic sentence) You saw Marvin with someone.
  - (who extraction) Who did you see Marvin with –.
- Coordination:
  - (basic sentence) You saw Marvin and someone.
  - (who extraction) •Who did you see Marvin and _.

Obeying the coordinate structure constraint is a formal property of constructions that is sometimes taken as the decisive criterion for coordinate status. As suggested, work with a primarily semantic definition of coordination, as given at the beginning of this section. The reason for this is that only semantically-based notions can be applied cross-linguistically – formal criteria are generally too language-particular.

DEVELOPMENT AND COORDINATION OF LIBRARY SERVICES TO STATE GOVERNMENT

In recent years the sise, complexity, pervasiveness and burgeoning growth of the federal government have made it a prime focus of the nation's news media, and it consequently has captured the attention of the general public. A similar expansion has occurred at the level of state government, but without as much commentary or analysis by the press. One author refers to the "surprising discovery that the largest growth sector in the 1960s and 1970s is not national Defence, automobile manufacturing, or even the federal government" but is instead state and local government. When the broadened scope of responsibilities, services and agency functions are considered, the changing nature and importance of state government is even more impressive. Like the federal government, state governments have responded to the needs of a population beset by accelerating technological, social, economic, cultural, and political change. Thus there are state agencies, com- missions, committees, bureaus, councils, and departments whose responsibilities and concerns range from atomic energy to drug addiction treatment, and from medical care to the aged to the development of the arts.

This expanding scope of interests has meant that the business of state government, in all its facets, requires an expanding variety of information sources and services. Like the rest of society in this postindustrial era, state government has become heavily information-dependent. How have state libraries responded to the burgeoning information needs of state government? Almost every state library gives some kind of information service to other agencies of state government and, indeed, many have been doing so Since, the early days of the Republic. The standards for Library functions at the state level makes clear the state library's responsibility to provide quality services to other agencies of state government.

The ways in which state libraries fulfil this responsibility, the variety of services offered, the intensity of effort, and the degree of coordination with other agencies varies widely among the fifty states. As early as 1966, Phillip Monypenny noted a variety of provisions to supply service to legislative, executive and judicial branches of state government, with varying degrees of coordination between law libraries, historical societies, archives, departmental libraries, and general state library agencies.

Some indication of the variety of such services offered by state library agencies may be gained from the 1977 Simpson survey, where state library agencies listed the following: library services to state government, consultant services to state agency libraries, research library for state agencies, special collection for state agencies, cooperation with agency and departmental libraries, reference services to state agencies and officials, centralised purchasing for agency libraries, centralised processing for agency libraries, audiovisual production and direction for state agencies, legislative reference library, reference services to legislature, special administrative and legislative library, legislative research, computerised on- line bill status, state law library as part of state library, current awareness services, depository for state publications, depository for historical records, distribution of state publications, index of state publications, published checklist of state documents, records management service for state government, consultant services to state institutions, and library services to state institutions.

State library collections range in sise from the large and comprehensive libraries of New York, Illinois and California, to the more typical 100,000-200,000 volume collections held by many states. A few state libraries, such as Maryland's, do not maintain collections, but provide reference service by other means. In addition to the services and collections of the state library itself, agency or departmental libraries exist in many states. Although reliable and up to date data on these are difficult to obtain, a US Office of Education (USOE) survey conducted in late 1977 of special libraries serving state government will provide such data when compiled and published.

It is known, however, that the number of such libraries varies from state to state (New York has nearly fifty, Texas twenty-three, New Jersey thirteen). Similarly, the collection sise, budget and number and level of staffing will vary widely from state to state, from major and sizable libraries (most typically court or law libraries) to office collections with part- time or no library staff. The literature on the activities of state library agencies during the past fifteen years has clearly dealt more with statewide library development and extension services than with other functions.

A similar bias was observed by Ralph Blasingame in a survey of library studies conducted between 1965 and 1969 based on an ERIC bibliography. He reported that only seven of the eighty-nine studies listed were concerned with services to state institutions (none specifically with services to state government), while two-thirds were studies of public libraries. A reading of the literature indicates that information services to state government have not been the leading edge of "state library" Programme development during this period.

This emphasis on statewide library Programmes is not surprising in view of the passage of the Library Services Act of 1956, and the attendant in- flux of federal funds to support this type of development. Forced to respond to pressure from the field and anxious to seise the opportunity to effectuate long-sought improvements in statewide planning and library system development, many state libraries clearly have not given the same attention to the development of information services to state government. Regulations of the federal Library Services and Construction Act specifically prohibited use of federal funds for service to state government.

Several states, however, have commissioned studies during this period designed to improve information service to state government. Studies in South Dakota, Ohio, Indiana and New York do indicate a growing concern and offer recommendations for implementation of Programmes in this area. Michael

Jackley, in a 1965 analysis of the functions of the South Dakota Library Commission, opted for greater centralisation. His recommendations take the form of central purchasing of library materials, with those appropriate to departmental libraries being placed on permanent loan with the departmental library as a branch of the central agency. Better access to materials held by archives, history and law would be promoted by close coordination with these agencies and the central library.

He suggested that those agencies of state government whose major function is research, such as the Legislative Research Council, should be housed with the state library on the Capitol grounds. Blasingame, in a 1968study for Ohio, advocated that the Information Resources and Services Division of the state library become a govern-mental service unit with three new staff positions. Each of these new staff members would work with a specific group of logically chosen state agencies in order to become knowledgeable about the concerns and problems of these groups. This would enable the state library to provide strong leadership in planning the development of information services in state agencies, and provide individual advice and assistance to those agencies with their own libraries.

Duplication of effort and materials would be avoided, and maximum exploitation of existing resources inspired. Recommendations by Genevieve Casey were made in 1970 in a study for the Indiana State Library.

Detailed recommendations for the coordination of services to the legislature and to state agencies include: consultant services to agencies desiring aid in cataloging and classifying materials; better circulation procedures; the provision of more sophisticated bibliographical services; centralised purchasing and processing; periodical print- outs and centralised records in the state library of the holdings of agencies; some form of current awareness service, with staff members working with administrators and librarians in the agencies assessing information needs and helping to establish acquisition policies; the use of existing TWX facilities by state employees; contracting for access to the collection and services of the Indiana University Medical Library for all state employees, especially those in the fields of health and environment; and the evaluation of the state library collection in terms of state government.

To provide guidance in establishing priorities for comprehensive information services, a council of persons responsible for department libraries and staff libraries in institutions would meet regularly with state library staff to discuss common problems and concerns. Work with large state agencies might be organised with small advisory councils within the agencies to work directly with the staff member from the state library responsible for that agency. Financial arrangements could take the form of either in- creased budget for the state library to support additional services to agencies, or an inter-accounting mechanism between the library agency and departments receiving special services. The state library would require additional funds in any case, primarily for new staff to implement these activities, but also for materials and equipment. In 1974, the New York State Library undertook a major review of information services to state government in other states. To obtain up- to-date information on existing patterns of service from the other forty- nine state library agencies, a brief but pointed questionnaire was developed and distributed in autumn 1974.

Follow up visits were made to Texas, North Carolina and Ohio in this study, and additional data were gathered from Washington State. These visits provided information on both innovative Programmes and the varying approaches to state agency services taken in each of the states. The Texas State Library, employing a former public library consultant, has emphasised cooperative activities with other state agency libraries in Austin, resulting in the development of a lively organisation called State Agency Libraries of Texas (SALT). SALT publishes a news-letter, holds regular meetings and workshops, and has developed a number of cooperative projects, including a union list of serials and a Texas state documents project.

Building on the recommendations of the Blasingame report summarised above, the Ohio State Library has expanded its services in recent years through an aggressive campaign to create awareness.

Acting Head, Information and Reference Division:

- Active marketing of the information provision capabilities of the State Library of Ohio is emphasised -through "sales calls," by presentations before department groups, through orientation and familiarisation classes and tours, with follow-through in the form of individualised current awareness services which provide an ordering tool to the recipient. In the last year, more than a third of the circulation to state government personnel can be traced to the stimulus provided by the direct mail current awareness Programme. An important positive aspect is the system for delivery to the requestor whether he is remotely sited or contiguous to the library.

Like Texas and Ohio, the North Carolina State Library created a special unit to provide service to state agencies, entitled the "Library Services to State Agencies Branch." The Programme differs from Texas's and Ohio's reference-centered operations in that a considerable portion of the unit's thrust is in the area of technical services.

In 1973-74, this unit provided cataloging, consultative and other support services to fourteen agency libraries, including the large Public Health Service library, the Department of Public Instruction, and newly organised libraries in the Labour and State Personnel departments. In the latter instance, the state library provided the necessary in-service training to assist the agency in starting the new library and the department provided staff, furnishings, shelving and a card catalogue. Central to an understanding of the Washington State arrangement is the fact that the state librarian is a cabinet officer reporting directly to the governor, and the state library is responsible for all library services for state government (except law), no matter where the facility served is located.

The former Washington State Librarian, described the Programme in refreshingly non-bureaucratic language:

- Some departments want us to operate fully and where they can generate federal funds for the service we enter into a "contract".... We pay no attention to the actual dollars so generated but render the service as needed. In some instances the department prefers to have the library staff on its payroll. . . . All materials are purchased and processed by us so that our catalog reflects the total information resource. The staffs are given orientation here so they realise we are back-up to their limited collection. The collections are weeded frequently and materials returned here for final decision as to retention. Some offices around the state have small collections but we encourage the employees to use their local public library and to call us directly. In addition to subscribing to key professional publications, we Xerox tables of contents and route them around. People write their names by the article desired and we send a Xerox copy which they can keep or throw away. It is a very wide ranging, flexible and effective programme.

Special consultative services are also available to state agencies by contract and have resulted in a comprehensive bibliography on disasters in Washington State for the Department of Emergency Services, and a combined subject index for environmental impact statements for the Department of Ecology. The New York State Library, building on an 86-year history of special services to the legislature, established a Legislative and Governmental Services unit in 1977, directed by a member of the top-level administration. This unit will promote library services to state agencies aggressively, pro- vide special research and bibliographic support, and conduct orientation and other Programmes for legislative and agency staff. Publications currently issued by the unit include Legislative trends (an annotated list of state library acquisitions on topics of interest to the legislature), Spotlight (guides to basic resources in selected subject fields), Topics on top (short bibliographies on topics of current interest), and comprehensive literature searches on requested subjects. Resources offered include free search services on twenty-six computerised data banks.

Despite the considerable variety of state library Programmes, certain general norms or patterns emerge which suggest the following elements as essential in developing an effective Programme of state library services to state agencies:

- *Attitude:* An aggressive, outreach approach is needed, based on a commitment to service and a wide-ranging, well-defined Programme to meet the needs of state agencies, officials and employees.
- *Organisation:* The state library should serve as the hub or center of library activity for state government, and should create a special office or unit which will provide leadership, coordination and the necessary monitoring of the programme. At the least, it should assign one or more staff members to carry out this outreach Programme on a continuing and preferably full-time basis. Staff should be carefully chosen for many of the same qualities which characterise successful field consultants, as well as for their perception of reference and bibliographic needs, and of the operation and structure of state government.
- *Agency Involvement:* As many agencies as possible should be involved, not only in the planning of service patterns, but in their refinement and evaluation as well. Even if the cooperating agency has no library *per se*, it should assign someone to work with the state library coordinator.
- *Shared Activities/Shared Financing:* Services which are beyond the capability of the individual cooperating agency should be explored care- fully and implemented as practicable, including centralised ordering and processing of library materials, union lists and other methods of bibliographic control, central computerised data banks with terminal access as required, cooperative storage and materials retirement plans, etc. Shared financing on some unit cost basis, by means of contractual or other arrangements, is desirable and tends to stimulate mutual involvement, respect and commitment, and provides a basis for evaluating cost-effectiveness.
- *Visibility, Direct Contact with Administration:* In order to gain the support of the administration and the legislature, the state library and its Programme of service to state government needs visibility, a voice and some degree of clout. This may be achieved organisationally, with cabinet rank for the state librarian or with strong advisory groups who can make their voices heard by the power structure. It may like- wise be achieved personally, through the visibility and personal dynamics of the chief state library officer and the programme specialists; and functionally, through the provision of services of demonstrable value and reliable quality. All these avenues may be necessary and should be bulwarked with an effective public relations Programme including publicity, orientation workshops and appropriate accountability through regular reports.

The data assembled in this chapter indicate that state library agencies generally accept information service to state government as a primary responsibility. Although this function does not appear to have been the "leading edge" of state library Programme development in recent years, there is evidence of increased interest and innovative activity in a number of states. As state government expands its interests, as legislative, judicial and executive agencies become increasingly information dependent, and as the relationship of information availability to cost-effectiveness and productivity becomes clearer, it may be expected that information service to state government will become an increasingly critical area of state library agency activity.

8

Staffing

CONCEPT AND IMPORTANCE OF STAFFING

CONCEPT

Staffing is one of the important management functions which is mainly concerned with proper arrangement and management of the required manpower for the organisation. After having prepared plans, as well as the structure of organisation for seeking the objectives, various positions are created. Effectiveness is not uni dimensional or one sided. To be effective in work setting people must do many things well and they as people must derive same value from their efforts. to have an effective staffing process, it requires as a first step the explicit specification of exactly what is that people must do well and what they will be offered in reward for doing it. - Benjamin Schneider Staff function of the management consists of the following features:

- To prepare manpower planning.
- To determine manpower requirements of organisation in terms of quantity and quality.
- To make all necessary arrangement for acquiring needed human force through proper and effective recruitment and selection.
- To maintain human force in organisation for a period of time.
- To formulating effective Labour policies for long period.
- To implementing the Labour policies in various projects.
- To develop manpower to its maximum by providing scientific training and conducting various development programmes.

IMPORTANCE OF STAFFING

- Staffing function is very closely related to other managerial areas of the business. It greatly influences the direction and control in the organisation. The effectiveness of other managerial functions depends on the effectiveness of the staffing function.
- Staffing function helps to build proper human relationships in the

organisation. Smooth human relations is the key to better communication and co-ordination of managerial efforts in an organisation.

- Skilled and experienced staff is the best asset of a business concern. The staffing function helps developing this asset for the business. It inculcates the corporate culture into the staff which in turn ensures smooth functioning of all the managerial aspects of the business.
- Staffing decisions have long term effect on the efficiency of an organisation. Qualified, efficient and well motivated staff is an asset of the organisation. Staffing function assumes special significance in the context of globalisation which demands high degree of efficiency in maintaining competitiveness.
- Staff selection should be based on the ability of the prospective employees to meet the future challenges that the organisation need to address. Therefore the potential contribution of the staff in their anticipated future roles should also be taken into account in staff selection.

STAFFING AS PART OF HUMAN RESOURCE MANAGEMENT

It is a function which all managers need to perform. It is a separate and specialised function and there are many aspects of human relations to be considered. It is the job of managers to fill positions in their organisation and to make sure that they remain occupied with qualified people. Staffing is closely linked to organising Since, after the structure and positions have been decided, people are required to work in these positions.

Subsequently, they need to be trained and motivated to work in harmony with the goals of the organisation. Thus, staffing is seen as a generic function of management. The staffing function deals with the human element of management. Managing the human component of an organisation is the most important task because the performance of an organisation depends upon how well this function is performed. The success of an organisation in achieving its goals is determined to a great extent on the competence, motivation and performance of its human resources.

It is the responsibility of all managers to directly deal with and select people to work for the organisation. When the manager performs the staffing function his role is slightly limited. Some of these responsibilities will include placing the right person on the right job, introducing new employees to the organisation, training employees improving their performance, developing their abilities, maintaining their morale and protecting their health and physical conditions. In small organisations, managers may perform all duties related to employees salaries, welfare and working conditions. But as organisations grow and number of persons employed increases, a separate department called the human resource department is formed which has specialists in managing people. The management of human resources is a specialised area which requires the expertise of many people. The number of human resource specialists and sise of this department gives an indication of the sise of the business as well. For a very large company, the Human Resources Department itself will contain specialists for each function of this department. Human Resource Management includes many specialised activities and duties which the human resource personnel must perform.

These duties are:

- Analysing jobs, collecting information about jobs to prepare job descriptions.
- Defending the company in law suits and avoiding legal complications.
- Developing compensation and incentive plans.
- Handling grievances and complaints.
- Maintaining labour relations and union management relations.
- Providing for social security and welfare of employees.
- Recruitment, *i.e.*, search for qualified people
- Training and development of employees for efficient performance and career growth.

STAFFING PROCESS

- The very first step in staffing is to plan the manpower inventory required by a concern in order to match them with the job requirements and demands. Therefore, it involves forecasting and determining the future manpower needs of the concern.
- Once the requirements are notified, the concern invites and solicits applications according to the invitations made to the desirable candidates.
- This is the screening step of staffing in which the solicited applications are screened out and suitable candidates are appointed as per the requirements.
- Once screening takes place, the appointed candidates are made familiar to the work units and work environment through the orientation programmes. placement takes place by putting right man on the right job.
- Training is a part of incentives given to the workers in order to develop and grow them within the concern. Training is generally given according to the nature of activities and scope of expansion in it. Along with it, the workers are developed by providing them extra benefits of indepth knowledge of their functional areas. Development also includes giving them key and important jobs as a test or examination in order to analyse their performances.

- It is a kind of compensation provided monetarily to the employees for their work performances. This is given according to the nature of job-skilled or unskilled, physical or mental, etc. Remuneration forms an important monetary incentive for the employees.
- In order to keep a track or record of the behaviour, attitudes as well as opinions of the workers towards their jobs. For this regular assessment is done to evaluate and supervise different work units in a concern. It is basically concerning to know the development cycle and growth patterns of the employeesin a concern.
- Promotion is said to be a non-monetary incentive in which the worker is shifted from a higher job demanding bigger responsibilities as well as shifting the workers and transferring them to different work units and branches of the same organisation.

RECRUITMENT: MEANING AND SOURCES

Acquiring and retaining high-quality talent is critical to an organisation's success. As the job market becomes increasingly competitive and the available skills grow more diverse, recruiters need to be more selective in their choices, Since, poor recruiting decisions can produce long-term negative effects, among them high training and development costs to minimise the incidence of poor performance and high turnover which, in turn, impact staff morale, the production of high quality goods and services and the retention of organisational memory.

At worst, the organisation can fail to achieve its objectives thereby losing its competitive edge and its share of the market. Traditionally, Public Service organisations have had little need to worry about market share and increasing competition Since, they operate in a monopolistic environment. But in recent time, the emphasis on New Public Management/ Public Sector Management approaches has forced public organisations to pay closer attention to their service delivery as consumers have begun to expect and demand more for their tax dollars.

No longer are citisens content to grumble about poorly-produced goods and services and the under-qualified, untrained employees who provide them. As societies become more critical and litigious, public service organisations must seek all possible avenues for improving their output and providing the satisfaction their clients require and deserve.

The provision of high-quality goods and services begins with the recruitment process. Recruitment is described as "the set of activities and processes used to legally obtain a sufficient number of qualified people at the right place and time so that the people and the organisation can select each other in their own best short and long term interests". In other words, the recruitment process provides the organisation with a pool of potentially qualified job candidates from which judicious selection can be made to fill vacancies. Successful recruitment begins with proper employment planning and forecasting.

In this phase of the staffing process, an organisation formulates plans to fill or eliminate future job openings based on an analysis of future needs, the talent available within and outside of the organisation, and the current and anticipated resources that can be expended to attract and retain such talent. Also related to the success of a recruitment process are the strategies an organisation is prepared to employ in order to identify and select the best candidates for its developing pool of human resources.

Organisations seeking recruits for base-level entry positions often require minimum qualifications and experience. These applicants are usually recent high school or university/ technical college graduates many of whom have not yet made clear decisions about future careers or are contemplating engaging in advanced academic activity. At the middle levels, senior administrative, technical and junior executive positions are often filled internally. The push for scarce, high-quality talent, often recruited from external sources, has usually been at the senior executive levels. Most organisations utilise both mechanisms to effect recruitment to all levels.

THE RECRUITMENT PROCESS

Successful recruitment involves the several processes of:

- Development of a policy on recruitment and retention and the systems that give life to the policy;
- Needs assessment to determine the current and future human resource requirements of the organisation. If the activity is to be effective, the human resource requirements for each job category and functional division/unit of the organisation must be assessed and a priority assigned;
- Identification, within and outside the organisation, of the potential human resource pool and the likely competition for the knowledge and skills resident within it;
- Job analysis and job evaluation to identify the individual aspects of each job and calculate its relative worth;
- Assessment of qualifications profiles, drawn from job descriptions that identify responsibilities and required skills, abilities, knowledge and experience;
- Determination of the organisation's ability to pay salaries and benefits within a defined period;
- Identification and documentation of the actual process of recruitment and selection to ensure equity and adherence to equal opportunity and other laws.

Documenting the organisation's policy on recruitment, the criteria to be utilised, and all the steps in the recruiting process is as necessary in the seemingly informal setting of in house selection as it is when selection is made from external sources. Documentation satisfies the requirement of procedural transparency and leaves a trail that can easily be followed for audit and other purposes.

Of special importance is documentation that is in conformity with Freedom of Information legislation, such as:

- Criteria and procedures for the initial screening of applicants;
- Criteria for generating long and short lists;
- Criteria and procedures for the selection of interview panels;
- Interview questions;
- Interview scores and panellists' comments;
- Results of tests;
- Results of reference checks.

Recruitment Strategies and Processes

Recruitment may be conducted internally through the promotion and transfer of existing personnel or through referrals, by current staff members, of friends and family members. Where internal recruitment is the chosen method of filling vacancies, job openings can be advertised by job posting, that is, a strategy of placing notices on manual and electronic bulletin boards, in company newsletters and through office memoranda. Referrals are usually word-of-mouth advertisements that are a low-cost-per-hire way of recruiting. Internal recruitment does not always produce the number or quality of personnel needed; in such an instance, the organisation needs to recruit from external sources, either by encouraging walk-in applicants; advertising vacancies in newspapers, magazines and journals, and the visual and/or audio media; using employment agencies to "head hunt"; advertising on-line via the Internet; or through job fairs and the use of college recruitment.

Public service agencies enjoy greater exposure to scrutiny than most private sector organisations; therefore, openness and transparency in recruitment and selection practices are crucial.

The discussion that follows will identify some of the options available for attracting applicants to the public service job market and discuss strategies for managing the process.

POSTING VACANCIES

As indicated earlier, job posting refers to the practice of publicising an open job to employees and listing its attributes, such as criteria of knowledge, qualification, skill and experience. The purpose of posting vacancies is to bring to the attention of all interested persons the jobs that are to be filled.

Before posting a vacancy, management needs to decide whether:

- It intends to retain the job in its present form and with its present title, remuneration and status;
- Selected attributes of the job, for example, skill or experience, will change;
- There are sufficient qualified, potential applicants serving in other positions within the organisation who may be potential candidates for that job;
- The organisations stands to benefit more, in the long-term, from recruiting applicants from external sources.

Also necessary is the availability of a functional human resource information system that supports recruitment.

An effective, computerised system would:

- Flag imminent vacancies throughout the organisation to ensure that the recruitment process is timely;
- Ensure that no candidates are lost but, instead, move through the process and are kept informed of their status;
- Ensure that good candidates whose applications are pending are kept in touch to maintain their interest in the organisation;
- Assist in analysing hiring, transfer and exit trends and provide other data that are helpful in planning, evaluating and auditing the recruitment process;
- Identify any adverse impacts of the recruitment process on vulnerable groups;
- For internal recruiting, control the internal job posting process, generate the notices, and then match internal applicant qualifications with job specifications;
- Where jobs are not being posted, generate a list of qualified internal candidates.

An organisation needs to analyse the benefits and disadvantages of recruiting its personnel through internal or external sources and, where the latter is selected, whether formal or informal systems should be used.

Recruiting from Internal Sources

There are sound reasons for recruiting from sources within the organisation:

- The ability of the recruit is known so it is easy to assess potential for the next level. By contrast, assessments of external recruits are based on less reliable sources, such as references, and relatively brief encounters, such as interviews.
- "Insiders" know the organisation, its strengths and weaknesses, its culture and, most of all, its people.

- Promotions from within build motivation and a sense of commitment to the organisation. Skilled and ambitious employees are more likely to become involved in developmental activities if they believe that these activities will lead to promotion.
- Internal recruitment is cheaper and quicker than advertising in various media and interviewing "outsiders". Time spent in training and socialisation is also reduced.

At the same time, several disadvantages exist:

- Sometimes it is difficult to find the "right" candidate within and the organisation may settle for an employee who possesses a less than ideal mix of competencies.
- If the vacancies are being caused by rapid expansion of the organisation there may be an insufficient supply of qualified individuals above the entry level. This may result in people being promoted before they are ready, or not being allowed to stay in a position long enough to learn how to do the job well.
- Infighting, inbreeding, and a shortage of varied perspectives and interests may reduce organisational flexibility and growth, and resistance to change by those who have an interest in maintaining the *status quo* may present long term problems.
- In times of rapid growth and during transitions, the organisation may promote from within into managerial positions, regardless of the qualifications of incumbents. Transition activities and rapid organisational growth often mask managerial deficiencies; it is not until the growth rate slows that the deficiencies become apparent and, then, the organisation finds it difficult, if not impossible, to undo the damage. The resulting cost of remedial training can prove prohibitive.

Recruiting from External Sources

External recruiting methods can be grouped into two classes: informal and formal. Informal recruiting methods tap a smaller market than formal methods. These methods may include rehiring former employees and choosing from among those "walk-in" applicants whose unsolicited résumés had been retained on file. The use of referrals also constitutes an informal hiring method. Because they are relatively inexpensive to use and can be implemented quickly, informal recruiting methods are commonly used for hiring clerical and other base-level recruits who are more likely than other groups to have submitted unsolicited applications.

Former students who participated in internship programmes may also be easily and cheaply accessed. Formal methods of external recruiting entail searching the labour market more widely for candidates with no previous connection to the organisation. These methods have traditionally included newspaper/magazine/journal advertising, the use of employment agencies and executive search firms, and college recruitment.

More often, now, job/career fairs and e-Recruiting are reaching the job seeker market. Posting vacancies externally through the various arms of the media or via employment agencies reaches a wider audience and may turn up a greater number of potential candidates from which the organisation can choose.

At the same time, this method is relatively expensive and time-consuming as the organisation works through initial advertisements, short-listing, interviewing and the other processes that precede selection. Even then, there is no guarantee that the results will be satisfactory to the organisation, Since, the cost of advertising often limits the frequency and duration of the job posting, as well as the amount of information made available, thus making it difficult for a job seeker to accurately judge the worth of the position being offered.

In addition, the organisation may hire a candidate who fails to live up to the high potential displayed during the selection process. Recruiting firms/ employment agencies are gaining in popularity, especially in the search for management level/executive talent. Recruiting via this medium is expensive, whether the organisation uses a contingency firm or has one on retainer. Executive search firms tend to match candidates to jobs faster that most organisations can, on their own, primarily because the recruiting firms/ employment agencies possess larger databases of, and wider access to, persons and have a greater awarene of the location of competencies needed by the client agencies.

Of course, it is possible to for an organisation to reduce the risks and high costs of recruitment by maintaining a small cadre of full-time, permanent employees and meeting an unexpected and temporary need for staff through the use of *ad hoc* and short-term contract workers who come to the position already trained. It is frequently said that the best jobs are not advertised; their availability is communicated by word of mouth. Networking, therefore, continues to be a viable mechanism for recruiting, especially at the senior management level in certain industries. In many instances, networking is a strategy used by the recruitment firms/employment agencies.

ON-LINE APPLICATIONS/RECRUITING ON THE INTERNET

Using the Internet is faster and cheaper than many traditional methods of recruiting. Jobs can be posted on Internet sites for a modest amount, remain there for periods of thirty or sixty days or more - at no additional cost - and are available twenty-four hours a day. Candidates can view detailed information about the job and the organisation and then respond electronically. Most homes and workplaces are now using computerised equipment for communication; the Internet is rapidly becoming the method of choice for accessing and sharing information. First-time job seekers are now more likely to search web sites for job postings than to peruse newspapers, magazines and journals. The prevalence of eadvertising has made it easier.

The Internet speeds up the hiring process in three basis stages:

- Faster posting of jobs.
  - The submission of information to the media house and its appearance in print disappears. On the internet, the advertisement appears immediately and can be kept alive for as long as the recruiter requires it.
- Faster applicant response.
  - Jobs posted on the Internet and requiring responses via the same medium receive responses on the same day.
- Faster processing of résumés.
  - An applicant sending a résumé electronically can immediately have the application processed, receive an acknowledgement, be screened electronically, and have details of the application and résumé despatched to several managers at the same time.

On-line recruiting also provides access to passive job seekers, that is, individuals who already have a job but would apply for what appears a better one that is advertised on the Internet. These job seekers may be of a better quality Since, they are not desperate for a job change as are the active job seekers who may be frustrated, disgruntled workers looking for a new position. Companies that are likely to advertise on-line usually have a Web site that allows potential candidates to learn about the company before deciding whether to apply, thus lowering the incidence time-wasting through the submission of unsuitable applications.

The Web site can be used as a tool to encourage potential job seekers to build an interest in joining the organisation. Job web sites offer unlimited space which can be used, by management, to sell the organisation. The site can then be used, not only to post vacancies, but also to publicise the organisation. That will allow candidates to become more familiar with the company, know what skills the company is looking for and get to know about its culture. Most importantly, the system will provide a proper path to securing quick responses to job openings. On-line recruiting facilitates the decentralisation of the hiring function by making it possible for other groups in the organisation to take responsibility for part of the function.

- Some applicants still place great value on face-to-face interactions in the hiring process. Such applicants are likely to ignore jobs posted, impersonally, on-line.
- Companies are overwhelmed by the volume of résumés posted on the Internet. This can, in fact, lengthen the short-listing process. If the screening process is not well done, the quantity of applications/

résumés logged-on may be more of a hindrance to the process that an aid to selection.

Job seekers who demand confidentiality in the recruitment process may be reluctant to use the Internet as a job search mechanism.

For effectiveness in the use of the strategy of e-Recruiting, companies are advised to:

- Use specialised Job Sites that cater to specific industries; interested in joining the company;
- Take advantage of the fact that Internet job advertisements have no space limitations so recruiters can use longer job descriptions to fully describe the company, job requirements and working conditions offered;
- Use valid Search Engines that will sort candidates effectively, but will not discriminate against any persons or groups;
- Create attention-grabbing newspaper advertisements that prompt people to visit the company's Web site. They will then see all vacancies that are advertised;
- Encourage employees to e-mail job advertisements to friends;
- Design and implement a successful e-Recruitment strategy.

COLLEGE RECRUITMENT

College recruiting – sending an employer's representatives to college campuses to prescreen applicants and create an applicant pool from that college's graduating class – is an important source of management trainees, promotable candidates, and professional and technical employees. To get the best out of this hiring strategy, the organisation and its career opportunities must be made to stand out.

Human resource professionals are aware that few college students and potential graduates know where their careers will take them over the next fifteen to twenty years. Therefore many of the an opportunity for recruiters to select the potential employees with the personal, technical and professional competencies they require in their organisation. The personal competencies identified may include, *inter alia*, a positive work ethic, strong interpersonal skills, leadership capacity and an ability to function well in a work team. The opportunity to discuss a student's current strengths and potential future value to an organisation cannot be replicated in any other setting. Two major advantages of this strategy are the cost (which is higher than word-of-mouth recruiting but lower than advertising in the media or using an employment agency), and the convenience (Since, many candidates can be interviewed in a short time in the same location with space and administrative support provided by the college itself). Unfortunately, suitable candidates become available only at certain times of the year, which may not always suit the needs of the hiring organisation. Another major disadvantage of college recruiting is the lack of experience and the inflated expectations of new graduates and the cost of hiring graduates for entry-level positions that may not require a college degree. To make college recruiting effective, the recruiting organisation must first determine how many and which schools should be targeted. It may prove cost-effective to do intensive recruiting in a few, carefully-selected institutions, establishing a presence and building the organisation's reputation among students and faculty.

Timely and frequent dissemination of literature, the offer of internships and the award of prises for academic and/or social prowess help to advertise the organisation as a preferred place of employment. Subsequent invitations to the organisation's offices, made to students identified as potential employees, may serve to solidify the firm's image. Public Service organisations are usually unable to compete financially with their Private Sector counterparts and are therefore less likely to pay competitive salaries.

However, most public service agencies provide their employees with a wealth and range of experiences that are available nowhere else. It is for that reason that many college graduates use the Public Service as an employer of first resort to gain the experiences that will make them marketable in the short term. The strategies may not work as smoothly for public service recruiters, Since, the laws that govern their organisations' recruitment practices may be more stringent than those that apply in private sector companies. There may also be questions about the legality of the on-line application form. If this strategy were to be employed, public service recruiters must first decide on the criteria that should guide the process. The Public Service is seldom immediately seen as an attractive employer, mainly because salaries are uncompetitive.

Except for those students who have a commitment to public service, the top ten percent of college graduates will select the Private Sector as the employer of choice, partly because of the prestige value but primarily because of the remuneration package and because the recruiters may have been more successful in marketing their company. Therefore, it is understood that many of the graduates who enter the Public Service will stay for a short time and either return to school or proceed to another sector once they have acquired the requisite skills and experience that make them marketable. Recruitment and retention strategies in the Public Service must, therefore, reflect this reality and efforts made to get the most out of college graduates before they move on; conversely, the organisation may need to plan to recruit those students whose academic records suggest that they will remain in an organisation that pays less.

Retention strategies will focus on ensuring opportunities for intense training and development for skill enhancement and personal satisfaction.

College recruitment also offers opportunities for internships. These programmes may provide the organisations with quality employees at low cost per hire. Some interns are hired at low cost (perhaps minimum wage) and are offered work experience.

Interns are able to have business skills, check out potential employers, and learn more about employers' likes and dislikes before making final career choices. Some of the better interns are recruited after graduation. College recruitment is relatively expensive and time consuming for the recruiting company. The process involves screening the candidate, that is, determining whether he/she is worthy of further consideration and marketing the company as a preferred place of employment. An alternate strategy for college recruitment is the career planning workshop.

These activities are usually (but not exclusively) associated with adolescent school leavers. They do not immediately produce ready candidates for the job market but provide the opportunity for an organisation to present itself as an employer worthy of consideration. Co-ordinators of career planning workshops co-opt professionals and organisations to present career options to potential school leavers in a controlled setting so as to lay out the range of possibilities to young job seekers. Career planning workshops are used mainly as information-giving tools which the school leaver can use to make informed career choices. Some organisations use the workshops as a base for internships.

Job Fairs

The concept of a job fair is to bring those interested in finding a job into those companies who are searching for applicants. Job fairs are open fora at which employers can exhibit the best their companies have to offer so that job seekers can make informed choices. They are considered one of the most effective ways for job seekers to land jobs. At the job fair, employers have a large pool of candidates on which to draw, while job seekers have the opportunity to shop around for dozens – sometimes hundreds – of employers, all in one place.

Notwithstanding the fact that the atmosphere at the fair is more relaxed than at an interview, employers are still on the look out for qualified, potential employees who have interest, dedication and initiative.

Maintaining Fairness/Equity in the Recruitment Process

It is often difficult to ensure and maintain fairness/equity in the recruitment process although, in every jurisdiction, there are laws that protect individuals and vulnerable groups from the negative impact of discriminatory practices. Where necessary, systems, detailed procedures and processes exist or must be established to minimise discrimination. Each country designates/identifies a group or groups for special notice; women, visible minorities and the disabled are usual targets. The Government of Canada, in articulating its "Employment Equity Act and Regulations", identified four designated groups as employment equity targets: women, Aboriginal people, members of visible minority groups, persons with disabilities.

In the legislation, managers' responsibilities for employment equity are stated as:

- Ensuring effective overall performance and continuous progress of the employment equity goals within the operation;
- Achieving, fostering and maintaining a representative workforce;
- Showing leadership in employment equity and demonstrating commitment to it by ensuring that discrimination and stereotyping are not tolerated; and
- Informing and educating employees in the organisation about employment equity and diversity.

The Australian Public Service Commission, in ensuring that there were no infringements against individuals rights, issued general guidelines on workplace diversity, some of which related to recruitment:

- Integrate workplace diversity with the agency's goals and business.
- Reflect agency workplace diversity objectives in workplace agreements and certified agreements.
- Integrate workplace diversity principles into human resources policies and practices.
- Include implementation of workplace diversity objectives in the corporate plan, business plan and client service charters.
- Ensure information about employment opportunities is available in accessible formats.
- Review recruitment and selection processes to ensure that current and potential employees are not discriminated against.

Gather information on demographics. It is the goal of every jurisdiction to minimise or eliminate any instance of obvious discrimination against individuals or groups. In discussing policies on employment equity, scholor explains: "Employment equity policies and Programmes are about fairness in the workplace, not about reverse discrimination. Fairness is achieved when no one is denied employment opportunity and no one benefits for reasons unrelated to ability. Employment equity Programmes attempt to change the composition of the Workforce so that employees better reflect the community. The facts (both historical and current) show that members of the four designated groups face discrimination, enjoy less access to educational Programmes and training, and are often denied employment and promotions even when they have the necessary skills and experience."

The University's policies give special attention, *inter alia*, to the existence of systemic barriers and instances of intentional discrimination in the process of recruitment. Service Commissions were enshrined in the Independence Constitutions of the territories of the Commonwealth Caribbean and given *inter alia*, the power to recruit/appoint persons into the Public Service and, in so doing, reduce the influence of politicians on the staffing process.

In order to discharge their authority for making appointments, the Commissions have influenced the development of legislation and regulations that circumscribe the practice of recruitment, primarily to ensure that no discrimination attends the exercise.

To this end, entry into the Public Service follows the procedures of:

- Application on prescribed forms;
- Selection on the basis of seniority of application; application of age limits for entry into certain defined grades/classes; the use of written examinations and/or competitive interviews as the basis for permanent appointment to certain grades/classes.

The rules established by the Commissions enforce compliance in an attempt to minimise or eliminate the possibility of bias in staffing on the basis of race/ethnicity, creed, age, social status or physical disability.

SELECTION—PROCESS

In the context of evolution, certain traits or alleles of genes segregating within a population may be subject to selection. Under selection, individuals with advantageous or "adaptive" traits tend to be more successful than their peers reproductively—meaning they contribute more offspring to the succeeding generation than others do. When these traits have a genetic basis, selection can increase the prevalence of those traits, because offspring will inherit those traits from their parents. When selection is intense and persistent, adaptive traits become universal to the population or species, which may then be said to have evolved. Scientists who do experimental genetics employ artificial selection experiments that permit the survival of organisms with user-defined phenotypes.

Artificial selection is widely used in the field of microbial genetics, especially molecular cloning. Whether or not selection takes place depends on the conditions in which the individuals of a species find themselves. Adults, juveniles, embryos, and even eggs and sperm may undergo selection. Factors fostering selection include limits on resources (nourishment, habitat space, mates) and the existence of threats (predators, disease, adverse weather). Biologists often refer to such factors as selective pressures. Natural selection is the most familiar type of selection by name. The breeding of dogs, cows and horses, however, represents "artificial selection". Sub-categories of natural selection are also sometimes distinguished. These include sexual selection, ecological selection, stabilising selection, disruptive selection and directional selection. Selection occurs only when the individuals of a population are diverse in their characteristics—or more specifically when the traits of individuals differ with respect to how well they equip them to survive or exploit a particular pressure. In the absence of individual variation, or when variations are selectively neutral, selection does not occur.

Meanwhile, selection does not guarantee that advantageous traits or alleles will become prevalent within a population. Through genetic drift, such traits may become less common or disappear. In the face of selection even a so-called deleterious allele may become universal to the members of a species. This is a risk primarily in the case of "weak" selection (*e.g.*, an infectious disease with only a low mortality rate) or small populations. Though deleterious alleles may sometimes become established, selection may act "negatively" as well as "positively." Negative selection decreases the prevalence of traits that diminish individuals' capacity to succeed reproductively (*i.e.*, their fitness), while positive selection increases the prevalence of adaptive traits. In biological discussions, traits subject to negative selection are sometimes said to be "selected against," while those under positive selection are said to be "selected for," as in the sentence Desert conditions select for drought tolerance in plants and select against shallow root architectures.

TYPES AND SUBTYPES OF SELECTION

Patterns of Selection

Aspects of selection may be divided into effects on a phenotype and their causes. The effects are called patterns of selection, and do not necessarily result from particular causes (mechanisms); in fact each pattern can arise from a number of different mechanisms. Stabilising selection favours individuals with intermediate characteristics while its opposite, disruptive selection, favours those with extreme characteristics; directional selection occurs when characteristics lie along a phenotypic spectrum and the individuals at one end are more successful; and balancing selection is a pattern in which multiple characteristics may be favoured.

Mechanisms of Selection

Distinct from patterns of selection are mechanisms of selection; for example, disruptive selection often is the result of disassortative sexual selection, and balancing selection may result from frequency-dependent selection and overdominance.

EMPLOYEE SELECTION PROCESS

Employee Selection is the process of putting right men on right job. It is a procedure of matching organisational requirements with the skills and qualifications of people. Effective selection can be done only when there is effective matching.

By selecting best candidate for the required job, the organisation will get quality performance of employees. Moreover, organisation will face less of absenteeism and employee turnover problems. By selecting right candidate for the required job, organisation will also save time and money. Proper screening of candidates takes place during selection procedure.

All the potential candidates who apply for the given job are tested. But selection must be differentiated from recruitment, though these are two phases of employment process. Recruitment is considered to be a positive process as it motivates more of candidates to apply for the job. It creates a pool of applicants.

It is just sourcing of data. While selection is a negative process as the inappropriate candidates are rejected here. Recruitment precedes selection in staffing process. Selection involves choosing the best candidate with best abilities, skills and knowledge for the required job.

The Employee selection process takes place in following order:

- It is used to eliminate those candidates who do not meet the minimum eligiblity criteria laid down by the organisation. The skills, academic and family background, competencies and interests of the candidate are examined during preliminary interview. Preliminary interviews are less formalised and planned than the final interviews. The candidates are given a brief up about the company and the job profile; and it is also examined how much the candidate knows about the company. Preliminary interviews are also called screening interviews.
- The candidates who clear the preliminary interview are required to fill application blank. It contains data record of the candidates such as details about age, qualifications, reason for leaving previous job, experience, etc.,
- Various written tests conducted during selection procedure are aptitude test, intelligence test, reasoning test, personality test, etc. These tests are used to objectively assess the potential candidate. They should not be biased.
- It is a one to one interaction between the interviewer and the potential candidate. It is used to find whether the candidate is best suited for the required job or not. But such interviews consume time and money both. Moreover the competencies of the candidate cannot be judged. Such interviews may be biased at times. Such interviews should be conducted properly. No distractions should be there in room. There should be an honest communication between candidate and interviewer.
- Medical tests are conducted to ensure physical fitness of the potential employee. It will decrease chances of employee absenteeism.
- A reference check is made about the candidate selected and then finally he is appointed by giving a formal appointment letter.

TRAINING AND DEVELOPMENT: CONCEPT, IMPORTANCE AND METHODS OF TRAINING

Changes in technology, especially information technology, generate knowledge spreading up at tremendous speed, as well as its quick obsolence. In the period between 1900 and 1950, the amount of human knowledge doubled, and Since, then it has doubled every 5 to 8 years. Knowledge is becoming obsolete so quickly that all of us need do double our knowledge every 2 to 3 years in order to keep up with the changes. On the other hand, the increasing complexity, turbulency and uncertainty of the environment requires different and greater knowledge. Modern business requires more and more knowledge and skills that are still inadequatly present in the formal school education, *i.e.*, the gap between business reqiurements and the knowledge acquired at school is growing.

The period of mass producing is over and the customers are very selective. Increased consumer demands require new solutions and knowledge. Due to increasing competition, the organisation is required to constantly revise its product and service mix, managerial methods, and to increase productivity. Modern conditions of dynamic competition, sophisticated information technology, knowledge economy, market globalisation, has changed the relation to importance of human resources in organisation. These conditions actualise the human capital as the strategic resource of every organisation. Differences between the organisations exist exactly due to the differences between human capital, *i.e.*, the organisations human resources, ways of their management and development.

In a more and more global, complex and turbulent environment, knowledge is the only reliable source of competitive advantage. Traditional factors of manufacturing as the soil, Labour and capital did not disappear, but their significance is not primary anymore. Knowledge is viewed as the key of realisation of a competitive advantage. And therefore the question of where the corporative knowledge is located, how to release it and develop to achieve organisational goals has become very important.

Since, the organisational knowledge is largely located inside the human mind, *i.e.*, the head of employees, as carriers of knowledge and activities, human resources are becoming the key factor of business success. Organisational development is always conditioned by human knowledge and skills. That is why, contemporary organisations pay more and more attention to the development of their emplozees. Thus, employee education and training are becoming an optimal answer to complex business challenges, and the management of human resources is taking central role in modern management.

Through the process of employee training and development, the management of human resources provides constant knowledge innovation, creates conditions for mutual knowledge and experience exchange and proactive behaviour, in this way contributing to competitive advantage and satisfaction of all participants in business procedures. As a consequence of these procedures a learning organisation has formed. The aim of this chapter is to point to the fact that education and development of human potential are the basic factor for creation of basis for transformation from traditional to a learning company. Learning organisation is organisation that promotes learning of all of its members and it transforms permanently. Individuals and societies that do not have enough knowledge are in inferior position, compared to societies and organisations that have it and even permanently acquire new knowledge. That is the reason why we say that success is not among the educated but among those that are learning permanently, and everything changes except knowledge acquirement, which is constant.

EMPLOYEE TRAINING AND DEVELOPMENT

Understanding the phenomenon of employee training and development requires understanding of all the changes that take place as a result of learning. As the generator of new knowledge, employee training and development is placed within a broader strategic context of human resources management, *i.e.*, global organisational management, as a planned staff education and development, both individual and group, with the goal to benefit both the organisation and employees. To preserve its obtained positions and increase competitive advantage, the organisation needs to be able to create new knowledge, and not only to rely solely on utilisation of the existing. Thus, the continous employee training and delopment has a singnificant role in the development of individual and organisational performance.

The strategic procedure of employee training and development needs to encourage creativity, ensure inventiveness and shape the entire organisational knowledge that provides the organisation with uniqueness and differentiates it from the others. Education is no longer the duty and privilege of those in higher positions and skilled labour, but it is becoming the duty and need of everyone. The larger the organisations, the more funds they spend on education and provide their employees with greater and diverse possibilities of education and development.

Understanding the tremendous significance of education for the modern organisation and confident that it represents a good and remunirative investment, present day organisations set aside more and more resources for this activity. Most of the organisations invest 3 to 5 per cent of their revenue into adult education. It is estimated that the organisations that desire to keep the pace with changes need to provide their employees with 2 per cent of total annual fund of working hours for training and education. Thus, it is necessary to accept the model of permanent, continuous learning.

That truth has been known for more than two centuries. Denis Diderot, a French philosopher and literate of the Age of Enlightment, wrote the following:

"Education shouldn't be finished when an individual leaves school, it should encompass all the ages of life . . . to provide people in every moment of their life with a possibility to maintain their knowledge or to obtain new knowledge". The only way for present day organisations to survive is the imperative to innovate or perish.

Since, this depends on the knowledge the organisation possesses, this imperative could be read as: learn faster than competition. The logical sequence is: knowledge creation – innovation – competitive advantage. If knowledge is good, is it not true that the more knowlegde we have, the better we are? Many organisations which consider knowledge as a good thing are trapped into the pitfall of gathering as much knowledge as possible. Knowledge that is not necessary is exatly what it is: unnecessary. And the efforts to obtain it are wasted efforts.

The only important knowldege is the knowledge with strategic importance to the company, knowledge that helps to increase the value of the company, knowledge with significance to the strategy of the company. It is not about knowledge for the sake of knowledge, but rather knowledge according to the needs, applicable knowledge, knowledge to create innovation and competitive advantage. Obtaining knowledge, learning, education, all could have a real effect on the quality of labour only if they are harmonised with the needs of a particular organisation, its goals and the goals of its employees.

The further choice of educational contents and educational methods, and the efficiency of educational effectiveness control depend on clearly defined educational goals and needs, answers to the questions of which knowldege is necessary to realise the strategy and the survival of the organisation in general, which employees need to possess this knowledge and will this knowledge solve certain problems. Employee training and development does not imply only obtaining new knowledge, abilities and skills, but also the possibility to promote entrepreneurship, introduce employees to changes, encourage the changes of their attitude, introduce the employees to important business decisions and involve them actively in the process of decision making.

To precisely define expectations and attract skilled workforce, more and more employment advertisings offer a certain number of annual hours or days for education. The most wanted resources are the people with particular knowledge, skills and abilities. Managers must learn to manage them, and the organisations to employ and retain them. Knowledge based organisations must preserve their competitive advantage by retaining skilled workforce, workers of knowledge, strengthening their motivation and improving the reward and compensation systems according to the workers' performances.

Within the context of learning organisation, it is not sufficient for the worker only to add value to the organisation based on his knowledge, but he also has to receive knowledge. He gives as much knowledge as he receives. For the present day employees the wage by itself is not a sufficient incentive, but they also need investment into themselves in a sense of investing in their knowledge. Empolyees no longer work for money alone, nor can they be influenced by traditional attractive financial packages.

CONCEPT OF A LEARNING ORGANISATION

Every individual should appreciate lifelong learning, and every successful organisation has to become a permanently learning organisation. Many successful organisations describe themselves as learning organisation or one of their strategic goals is to become such an organisation. Companies such as Coca-Cola, Motorola, General Electrics and Cisco have assigned vice presidents for knowledge, learning or intellectual capital whose task is to create knowledge management systems that enable them to quickly adopt development tendencies, influencing in that way the customers, competitors, distributors and suppliers.

The organisation is not only the user of knowledge, but also its creator. Peter Senge described in the book named "The Fifth Discipline", the learning organisation implies free flow of knowledge, *i.e.*, lifting of all barriers on developing knowledge and new ideas at the very beginning. In the future it will not be possible to "unthread things from above" and for all the others to follow the "big brother's" instructions anymore. The top organisations of the future will be distinguished by their knowledge about how to encourage engagement and develop the learning potential on each organisational level. Peter Senge's model of a learning organisation is very interesting Since, it recognises the organisation as a whole, *i.e.*, in his organisation, through their functions and sectors within the organisation, all the employees influence the course of business procedures, and the knowledge creation, consequently the creation of new values both for the organisation and its customers. With this definition, Senge has made significant qualitative progress compared to the classical organisation, Since, he emphasised the necessity of ability development through the process of learning.

Besides Senge, Chris Argyris was a great populariser of a learning organisation as well. In his book "Teaching smart people how to learn", he says: "Any company that aspires to succeed in the tougher business environment must first resolve a basic dilemma: success in the marketplace increasingly depends on learning, yet most people don't know how to learn.

What's more, those members of the organisation that many assume to be the best at learning are, in fact, not very good at it. I am talking about the well-educated, highpowered, highly committed professionals who take up key leadership positions in the modern corporation." Organisations learn only through the learning individuals. Individual learning does not guarantee organisational learning. But without it there is no organisational learning as well. The ablity to learn faster than the competitors may be the only sustainable competitive advantage.

Thus, the learning organisation is the organisation that learns and encourages people to learn in the organisation. It motivates information exchange between employees and creates staff with different knowledge. Chris Argiris explains this: "On the other hand, there is a problem of existence of individuals within the organisation who know how to learn, but that doesn't create automatically conditions for the organisation to learn as well. This is due to the indisputable view that knowledge is still the only private property the man owns. This means that individual learning, and even learning of all the employees, doesn't imply the existence of a learning organisation. To have a learning organisation, it is necessary to know how to transfer individual into organisational knowledge, *i.e.*, into organisational learning." The starting point of knowledge management concept is in the fact that power does not come from knowledge, but from the exchange of knowledge.

It starts from the synergic effect. By exchanging knowledge, combining individual knowledge, we get much more qualitative knowledge than the individual knowledge. Obtaining and sharing knowledge is the core of the learning organisation. The reasons to become a learning organisation are the following: people are developing (greater motivation, flexibility of employees, people are more creative, improved social interaction), better working teams and groups (knowledge sharing, mutual dependence), benefiting organisations (greater work productivity, more qualitative products/services/ procedures, competitive advantage, profit).

APPROACH TO TRAINING AND DEVELOPMENT WITHIN OUR ORGANISATIONS AND NEED FOR TRANSFORMATION

Unfortunately, the procedures of employee training and development within our organisations are undeveloped. They are mainly performed occasionally, and not connected with organisational strategy, nor do they have some strategic significance. They are mostly enforced when such business problems occur or are perceived that are considered relievable or solvable by organising a training, course or seminar for some of the employees. Employees view the training as an imposed obligation, rather than a way to maximise their potential and they do not realise that by improving their performances and innovation of their knowledge they may contribute to better business results of the organisation they belong to. Unfortunately, top managers do not realise this as well. From their relationship with the employees it is plain to see that the employees are still treated as an expense, rather than an investment worthy of investing. In our organisations there is no culture of obtaining and sharing of knowledge. Many of our managers are under the influence of prejudices such as: training is expensive, training is an expense burdening the current business, it is not rewarding, training is for the young, etc., Knowledge is expensive, but ignorance is even more expensive.

Human possibilites to learn are unlimited, unless idviduals do not limit their abilities within their minds. Many studies have shown that investing in employee training and development has larger business effects than investing in equipment and other material resources. Our organisations must harmonise their approach to employee development with the changes. Employee training and development has to be connected with the organisational goals and strategy, they need to fulfil the new reqiurements of the environment.

Employee training and development needs to become a managerial function. It is a managerial challenge to consider the employees of the organisation from a strategic perspective (future orientedness) and constantly monitor and encourage the development of new skills and knowledge as the foundation of organisational development. This is not about assigning the employees to appropriate jobs, but rather about the constant dynamic of encouraging and discovering new possibilities. This is a new type of leadership, significantly different from the classical model of organisational management.

The leaders are no longer expected to be all-knowing bosses and supervisors, but rather moderators and inspirators. Since, people do not share the information which is the source of their power instictively, the leaders need to recognise, attract and release knowledge in the organisation. One of the main challegnes of modern organisations therefore is how to manage the process of knowledge transfer.

"The answer is that wisdom, just because it is the most important, doesn't need to be located inside a tall building where the chief executive and his main assistants hang their hats (and soon their heads as well – unless they join the revolution of the mind). This pictoresque answer of Tom Peters refers to decentralisation and substantivity of employees (turning every workplace into business), which implies a high degree of employee competence and orientation Towards the participative style of management.

The process of democratisations, transitions, opening towards the EU, privatisations and arrival of foreign companies and praxis contributed considerably to transformation of approach to employee training and development within our organisations, from the *ad hoc* processes that originate from the goals and strategies, to a modern approach where human resources and their knowledge are gaining more and more significance.

IMPORTANCE OF TRAINING AND DEVELOPMENT

- Training and Development helps in optimising the utilisation of human resource that further helps the employee to achieve the organisational goals as well as their individual goals.

- Training and Development helps to provide an opportunity and broad structure for the development of human resources' technical and Behavioural skills in an organisation. It also helps the employees in attaining personal growth.
- Training and Development helps in increasing the job knowledge and skills of employees at each level. It helps to expand the horizons of human intellect and an overall personality of the employees.
- Training and Development helps in increasing the productivity of the employees that helps the organisation further to achieve its long-term goal.
- Training and Development helps in inculcating the sense of team work, team spirit, and inter-team collaborations. It helps in inculcating the zeal to learn within the employees.
- Training and Development helps to develop and improve the organisational health culture and effectiveness. It helps in creating the learning culture within the organisation.
- Training and Development helps building the positive perception and feeling about the organisation. The employees get these feelings from leaders, subordinates, and peers.
- Training and Development helps in improving upon the quality of work and work-life.
- Training and Development helps in creating the healthy working environment. It helps to build good employee, relationship so that individual goals aligns with organisational goal.
- Training and Development helps in improving the health and safety of the organisation thus preventing obsolescence.
- Training and Development helps in improving the morale of the Workforce.
- Training and Development helps in creating a better corporate image.
- Training and Development leads to improved profitability and more positive attitudes towards profit orientation.
- Training and Development aids in organisational development, *i.e.*, Organisation gets more effective decision making and problem solving. It helps in understanding and carrying out organisational policies
- Training and Development helps in developing leadership skills, motivation, loyalty, better attitudes, and other aspects that successful workers and managers usually display.

IMPORTANCE OF TRAINING OBJECTIVES

Training objectives are one of the most important parts of training Programme. While some people think of training objective as a waste of valuable time. The counterargument here is that resources are always limited and the training objectives actually lead the design of training. It provides the clear guidelines and develops the training Programme in less time because objectives focus specifically on needs. It helps in adhering to a plan. Training objective tell the trainee that what is expected out of him at the end of the training Programme.

Training objectives are of great significance from a number of stakeholder perspectives:

- Trainer.
- Trainee.
- Designer.
- Evaluator.

Trainer

The training objective is also beneficial to trainer because it helps the trainer to measure the progress of trainees and make the required adjustments. Also, trainer comes in a position to establish a relationship between objectives and particular segments of training.

Trainee

The training objective is beneficial to the trainee because it helps in reducing the anxiety of the trainee up to some extent. Not knowing anything or going to a place which is unknown creates anxiety that can negatively affect learning.

Therefore, it is important to keep the participants aware of the happenings, rather than keeping it surprise. Secondly, it helps in increase in concentration, which is the crucial factor to make the training successful. The objectives create an image of the training Programme in trainee's mind that actually helps in gaining attention. Thirdly, if the goal is set to be challenging and motivating, then the likelihood of achieving those goals is much higher than the situation in which no goal is set. Therefore, training objectives helps in increasing the probability that the participants will be successful in training.

Designer

The training objective is beneficial to the training designer because if the designer is aware what is to be achieved in the end then he'll buy the training package according to that only. The training designer would then look for the training methods, training equipments, and training content accordingly to achieve those objectives. Furthermore, planning always helps in dealing effectively in an unexpected situation. Consider an example; the objective of one training Programme is to deal effectively with customers to increase the sales. Since, the objective is known, the designer will design a training Programme that will include ways to improve the interpersonal skills, such as verbal and non- verbal language, dealing in unexpected situation, *i.e.*, when there is a defect in a product or when a customer is angry. Therefore, without any guidance, the training may not be designed appropriately.

Evaluator

It becomes easy for the training evaluator to measure the progress of the trainees because the objectives define the expected performance of trainees. Training objective is an important to tool to judge the performance of participants.

TRAINING AS CONSULTANCY

Training consultancy provides industry professional to work with an organisation in achieving its training and development objectives.

Estimation of Training Outsourcing

It has been estimated that 58 per cent of the emerging market in training outsourcing is in customer education, while only 42 percent of the market is in employee education. The training consultancies offer various benefits such as:

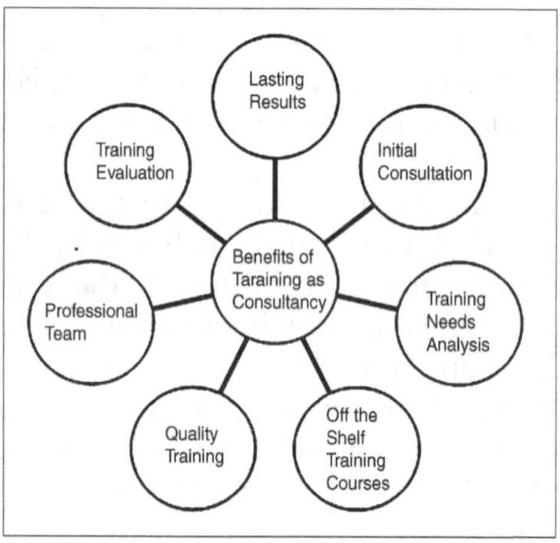

Training Courses that Consultancies Offer

- Business Training Courses:
  - Management Development:
    a. Conflict Management;
    b. Managing Diversity;
    c. Project Management;
    d. Stress Management;
    e. Time Management; and
    f. Senior Management Workshops.
  - Sales:

    a. Negotiation Skills; and
    b. Sales Technique.
- Customer Care:
    a. Customer Care Training; and
    b. Managing Customers.
- Human Resource :
    a. HR Administration;
    b. Induction Training;
    c. Recruitment and Selection; and
    d. Successful Appraising.
- Personal Development Courses.
- Workshops on:
    a. Assertive Skills;
    b. Building Confidence;
    c. Coping with Change;
    d. Interview Techniques; and
    e. Maximise Potential.
- One to One Coaching:
    a. Focused entirely on personal objectives;
    b. Move forward at individual pace;
    c. Material used in tailor made to specific development Need; and
    d. A strict code of confidentiality.

Importance of Training Consultancies:

- It helps in enhancing company's image.
- It helps in strengthening the team spirit.
- It helps in applying knowledge, developing core competencies, and reducing work load.
- It helps in improving the work relations.
- It helps in developing focused and inspired staff.
- It leads to greater chances of success.

Consultants can provide help on following areas:

- Management Development.
- Team Building Leadership.
- Health and Safety Training.
- Interpersonal Skills.
- Sales Training.

TRAINING AND HUMAN RESOURCE MANAGEMENT

The HR functioning is changing with time and with this change, the relationship between the training function and other management activity is also changing. The training and development activities are now equally important with that of other HR functions. Gone are the days, when training was considered to be futile, waste of time, resources, and money. Now a days, training is an investment because the departments such as, marketing and sales, HR, production, finance, etc. depends on training for its survival. If training is not considered as a priority or not seen as a vital part in the organisation, then it is difficult to accept that such a company has effectively carried out HRM. Training actually provides the opportunity to raise the profile development activities in the organisation.

To increase the commitment level of employees and growth in quality movement (concepts of HRM), senior management team is now increasing the role of training. Such concepts of HRM require careful planning as well as greater emphasis on employee development and long term education. Training is now the important tool of Human Resource Management to control the attrition rate because it helps in motivating employees, achieving their professional and personal goals, increasing the level of job satisfaction, etc., As a result training is given on a variety of skill development and covers a multitude of courses.

Role of HRD Professionals in Training

This is the era of cut-throat competition and with this changing scenario of business; the role of HR professionals in training has been widened. HR role now is:

- Active involvement in employee education
- Rewards for improvement in performance
- Rewards to be associated with self esteem and self worth.
- Providing pre-employment market oriented skill development education and post employment support for advanced education and training.
- Flexible access, *i.e.*, anytime, anywhere training.

MODELS OF TRAINING

Training is a sub-system of the organisation because the departments such as, marketing and sales, HR, production, finance, etc depends on training for its survival. Training is a transforming process that requires some input and in turn it produces output in the form of knowledge, skills, and attitudes (KSAs).

THE TRAINING SYSTEM

A System is a combination of things or parts that must work together to perform a particular function. An organisation is a system and training is a sub system of the organisation.

The System Approach views training as a sub system of an organisation. System Approach can be used to examine broad issues like objectives, functions, and aim. It establishes a logical relationship between the sequential stages in the process of training need analysis (TNA), formulating, delivering, and evaluating. There are four necessary inputs, *i.e.*, technology, man, material, time required in every system to produce products or services. And every system must have some output from these inputs in order to survive.

The output can be tangible or intangible depending upon the organisation's requirement. A system approach to training is planned creation of training Programme.

This approach uses step-by-step procedures to solve the problems. Under systematic approach, training is undertaken on planned basis.

Out of this planned effort, one such basic model of five steps is system model that is explained below. Organisation are working in open environment, *i.e.*, there are some internal and external forces, that poses threats and opportunities, therefore, trainers need to be aware of these forces which may impact on the content, form, and conduct of the training efforts.

The internal forces are the various demands of the organisation for a better learning environment; need to be up to date with the latest technologies.

The three model of training are:

- System Model.
- Instructional System Development Model.
- Transitional model.

SYSTEMATIC MODEL TRAINING

The system model consists of five phases and should be repeated on a regular basis to make further improvements. The training should achieve the purpose of helping employee to perform their work to required standards.

- *Analyse and identify the training needs*, *i.e.*, to analyse the department, job, employees requirement, who needs training, what do they need to learn, estimating training cost, etc The next step is to develop a performance measure on the basis of which actual performance would be evaluated.
- *Design and provide training to meet identified needs*. This step requires developing objectives of training, identifying the learning steps, sequencing and structuring the contents.
- *Develop* - This phase requires listing the activities in the training Programme that will assist the participants to learn, selecting delivery method, examining the training material, validating information to be imparted to make sure it accomplishes all the goals and objectives
- *Implementing* is the hardest part of the system because one wrong step can lead to the failure of whole training Programme.
- *Evaluating* each phase so as to make sure it has achieved its aim in terms of subsequent work performance. Making necessary amendments to any of the previous stage in order to remedy or improve failure practices.

TRANSITIONAL MODEL

Transitional model focuses on the organisation as a whole. The outer loop describes the vision, mission and values of the organisation on the basis of which training model, *i.e.*, inner loop is executed.

- *Vision*—focuses on the milestones that the organisation would like to achieve after the defined point of time. A vision statement tells that where the organisation sees itself few years down the line. A vision may include setting a role mode, or bringing some internal transformation, or may be promising to meet some other deadlines.
- *Mission*—explain the reason of organisational existence. It identifies the position in the community. The reason of developing a mission statement is to motivate, inspire, and inform the employees regarding the organisation. The mission statement tells about the identity that how the organisation would like to be viewed by the customers, employees, and all other stakeholders.
- *Values*—is the translation of vision and mission into communicable ideals. It reflects the deeply held values of the organisation and is independent of current industry environment. For example, values may include social responsibility, excellent customer service, etc.

Bibliography

A. Gopikuttan and K.P. Vijayakumar: *Research @ Library and Information Science*, Ess Ess Publication, 2011.

Ajay Kumar Srivastav and Rajesh Kumar Singh: *Glossary of Library Information Communication and Technological Terms and Acronyms*, Shree Pub, 2007.

Ajit Singh Siwatch: *Encyclopedic Dictionary of Library and Information Science, Vols. I to III* , Shree Publishers, 2010.

Amjad Ali: *Ane's Encyclopedic Dictionary of Library and Information Science*, Ane Books India, 2006.

B S Aggarwal: *An Introduction to Library and Information Science*, ABD, 2005.

B. Chattopadyay, D.N. Singh, Jaipal and G.S. Rana: *Manual on Core Library Information System (CORIS)*, Oil and Natural Gas Corporation, 1995.

Bhupendra Narayan Singh: *Encyclopaedia of Library and Information Science in the Digital Age Vols. I to III*, Anmol Pub, 2011.

Bikika Laloo Tariang: *Essays on Library and Information Science Education*, Ess Ess Publications, 2012.

C K Sharma; Rakesh Kumar and Akhil Kumar Singh: *Library and Information Science (3 Vols-Set)*, Atlantic, 2008.

C.R. Karisiddappa: *Current Studies in Library and Information Science*, Manak, 1994.

Cherian Mathew: *Dynamics of Library and Information Science*, Cyber Tech Publicaitons, 2011.

D.B. Patil and M.M. Kooganuramath: *Library and Information Science*, APH, 2011.

D.C. Ojha and D.V. Kothari: *Advances in Library and Information Science: Vol. 5. Digital Libraries*, Scientific, 2005.

G. Devarajan: *Applied Research in Library and Information Science*, Ess Ess Pub, 2005.

G. Devarajan: *Research in Library and Information Science*, Ess Ess Pub, 2002.

H.K. Srivastava, Mohit: *Foundation of Library and Information Science*, 2011.

I.M. Goswami: *Encyclopaedia of Library and Information Science*, Commonwealth, 1997.

Jogender Singh Burman: *Encyclopaedic Survey of Library and Information Science : Principles and Practices (5 Vols-Set)*, Rajat Publication, 2006.

K.A. Isaac: *Glimpses of Library and Information Science* , Ess Ess, 2001.

Khalid K. Faruqi and Mehtab Alam: Net Studies in Library and Information Science, Aakar Books, 2005.

Krishan Kumar And Jaideep Sharma: *Library And Information Science Education In India*, Har-anand Publications, 2009.

Kundan Godia: *Electronic Services in Library and Information Science*, Adhyayan, 2007.

L.B. Rakesh: *Library and Information Science in Digital Age*, Alfa Pub, 2006.

L.S. Ramaiah: *Images and Perceptions in Library and Information Science*, Ess Ess, 1998.

M.A. Khan: *Personnel Management in Library and Information Science*, Cosmo, 2002.

Mahendra Kumar Seth: *A Guide to Library and Information Science Jobs*, Abhijeet Publications, 2006.

Mahendra Singh Sodhi: *Advancement in Library and Information Science*, Adhyayan Pub, 2006.

Manisha Dawra: *Encyclopaedia of Modern Library and Information Science (5 Vols-Set)*, Rajat Pub, 2003.

P K Singh: *Current Trends and Techniques in Library and Information Science*, Shree Pub, 2007.

P. Balasubramanian: *Advanced Computer Application in Library and Information Science*, Deep and Deep, 2011.

P. Balasubramanian: *Library Information and Communication Technology*, Deep and Deep, 2011.

Pawan K. Gupta and Tirth Das: *Modern Trends in Library and Information Science*, Scientific Publishers, 2010.

Poonam: *HRD in Library and Information Science* , ACE Books, 2010.

Poonam: *Modern Handbook of Library and Information Science* , Akansha Pub, 2010.

R P Bajpai: *Current Trends in Library and Information Science* , Shree Pub, 2007.

R.G. Prasher: *Library and Information Science: Parameters and Perspectives : Essays in Honour of P.B. Mangla (2 Vols - set)*, Concept, 1997.

Raghunath Pandey and M.N. Velayudhan Pillai: *History of Library and Information Science*, Jnanada Prakashan, 2011.

Sambhu Nath Halder and Sibsankar Jana: *Library and Information Science in Changing Paradigm*, Ess Ess Publications, 2013.

Index